Football Re
in Scotl

A History of its Organisation and Development
1873 -2023

Drew Herbertson

Contents

List of Tables

Acknowledgements

A number of people are due my sincere thanks for their assistance in writing this book: the staff at the Scottish Football Museum, in particular Richard McBrearty (Curator), the now retired Colin Lobban (Administrator) and Callum Livingston (Visitor Services Officer), all of whom enabled me to access the SFA minutes books and other material; my successor at the SFA, Steven Harris, for providing me with information at various points following my retiral; my former colleague Donald McVicar who read the initial draft and gave me the comfort and reassurance I was looking for and made me think I had achieved what I had set out to do; and Douglas Gorman, a keen football historian and author who provided excellent advice and suggestions to enable me to get the draft into its final form.

I am indebted to the following friends from the refereeing world who were able to provide me with the first names of five Referee Supervisors from the early period of the supervisory system: Graeme Alison, Alan Cunningham, John Dearie and Stuart Macaulay. Initials ruled the waves in SFA Handbooks for many years so it was fantastic to complete a long quest to establish the first names of all the Referee Supervisors.

Lastly, my great thanks to my son Craig for his artistic skills in designing the book cover to such superb effect.

Glossary

There are a number of terms used throughout the book which readers may not be entirely familiar with. In this respect, I hope that this Glossary will help to explain things.

Affiliated Association	An association which is in full membership of the SFA (other than an Affiliated National Association)
Affiliated National Association	The group of National Associations such as the Scottish Junior FA, the Scottish Amateur FA and Scottish Schools' FA which govern the playing of football under their jurisdiction
Council	The SFA's "parliament" which comprised elected representatives of the game and from which committees were appointed
District Association	An equivalent term for an Affiliated Association
FIFA	The world's governing body for football
Grassroots referees	The referees who officiate in football organised by the Affiliated National Associations (other than the Scottish Junior FA)
IFAB	The International Football Association Board, the body responsible for the Laws of the Game. Its members are the four British National Football Associations and FIFA
Judicial Panel	The body formed by the SFA in 2012 to exercise disciplinary control in the game in Scotland

Judicial Panel Protocol	The Protocol which enables the operation of the Judicial Panel
Junior clubs	Clubs in membership of the Scottish Junior FA
Junior football	Football played under the jurisdiction of the Scottish Junior FA. It is the level below senior football and the highest tier of the Affiliated National Associations
Laws of the Game	The rules by which football is played and which are overseen by IFAB
List of Referees*	The List of Referees compiled each season by the SFA for use in senior football.
Listed Officials	The Referees included in the List of Referees
Minor associations	Member associations of the Affiliated National Associations (other than the Scottish Junior FA)
Minor football	Football organised by the Affiliated National Associations (other than the Scottish Junior FA)
National Association	A country's National Football Association
Non-Listed/Unlisted officials	Those referees not included in the List of Referees prior to the introduction of the Registration Scheme for Referees
Points of Play	Incidents arising in football matches which generate discussion, debate and decisions on how they should be dealt with in terms of the Laws of the Game
RA	Referees' Association
RA Manager	Referees' Association Manager
Recognised football body	An Affiliated Association, an Affiliated National Association (and constituent members)and Leagues
Senior football	The level of the game in which the SFA

	member clubs participate
SFA	Scottish Football Association
SFL	Scottish Football League
SPL	Scottish Premier League
SPFL	Scottish Professional Football League
Supplementary List	A List compiled by the SFA to supplement the List of Referees where the referees included were designated to referee in certain competitions
The Football Association	The national association of England
UEFA	The member confederation of FIFA which is responsible for governing football in Europe

* List of Referees

I have used this term throughout the book and shortened it further to "The List" for expediency. Until season 1993-94, it was known as the "Official List of Referees" and was commonly referred to as the "Official List". Since 1994-95, the List has gone through a number of name changes as follows:

List of Senior Referees: 1994-95 to 2001-02

Register of Senior Referees: 2002-03 to 2004-05

Referee Categories for Senior Football: 2005-06 to 2008-09

List of Referees: 2009-10 to present

Preface

My whole 38-year working career was spent with the Scottish Football Association (SFA). Other than the initial 18 months, I worked in referee administration, combining it with the disciplinary function for 25 years. In that time I was the Secretary to the Referee Supervisors' Committee, the Disciplinary & Referee Committee and the Referee Committee.

It was an extremely fascinating job for someone who grew up in thrall to football. Discipline and refereeing are core functions in football and I was very fortunate in having such a central role in that side of the game's administration. Both elements of the job were hugely absorbing. I found the refereeing part very interesting, particularly as I was "working" with major figures in refereeing such as Jack Mowat and Tom Wharton. That interest was increased with the occasional foray I had to make through the old Referee Supervisors' Committee minutes which were held in two standard A4 folders going back to 1945, the year that the SFA directly took control over the organisation of refereeing in Scotland by putting the supervisory and referees' association structure in place. I have always had an appreciation of football history and history was certainly contained in these minutes. There was a story to be told, I figured, and one worth telling. The germ of an idea to do something about that took hold inside me and grew stronger over time. I resolved that once I retired, I would have the time to devote myself to the task.

There have been countless books on football – club histories, player autobiographies and such like. There has been very little, if anything, on refereeing. There was a gap to be filled, I thought, and I reckoned I was in an ideal position to try to fill it. And, as I had never written a book before, I was naive enough to attempt it too. By doing so, I would hopefully widen the knowledge and understanding of refereeing in Scotland.

I retired at the end of season 2018-19. My initial intention was to write a history of refereeing through the Referee Supervisors' and Referee Committee minutes from 1945. Having served for 36 years in referee administration, it was unnerving to realise that I had been around for almost half of the time since introduction of the refereeing structure. Curiosity got hold of me. I then thought it would be worthwhile delving into how things were in refereeing before the Second World War to provide some form of foundation and context. That thought quickly expanded and I decided that my task should become bigger. I would attempt to write the history of refereeing in Scotland from when the SFA was formed in 1873.

I started my research in the autumn of 2019.   I paid regular visits to the Scottish Football Museum at Hampden Park to go through all the SFA Committee minutes which are held there. It was a fascinating exercise going through the minute books, and difficult not to become sidetracked as I came across so much other interesting areas of football business. The Covid pandemic interrupted the research for a good period. The SFA minutes, the Referee Supervisors' Committee minutes and other related SFA publications provide the source material for the book.

Introduction

Carrying out the research for the book gave me time and space to work out how best to approach the task of writing this history of Scottish refereeing. I came to the view that I would best be served by dividing the time period from 1873 to the present day into several parts and to address various subject headings within each part in chronological order. As refereeing had developed, it became clear to me that there were natural dividing lines over 150 years to enable this approach to be taken. It seemed to me that it would be better to do it this way rather than attempt to record the entire subject in true chronological order. There is a tremendous complexity in how refereeing has developed and I think and hope that my approach has served the overall topic well. If there is any downside to this approach, it is that there is the occasional necessary repetition in some sections for the purposes of putting the subject into context. It is a small price to pay to enable the story to be told.

Parts One and Two cover the period to 1945 when the SFA put the refereeing structure in place and which provided the solid platform for all that followed. Part Three deals with the operation of the new structure in that first momentous season of 1945-46. Part Four addresses how things developed over the next 40 years. The huge progress in refereeing since the late 1980's is the subject of Part Five.

The book does not seek to go into the historic disciplinary function which the Referee Committee exercised over players and clubs until 1994. That would be a book in its own right. Reference is made, though, to cases where referees found themselves in trouble with the SFA. In this respect, it is not a completely sanitised version of refereeing history. It has only been since 1994 when the Referee Committee's business has focussed solely on refereeing. Further, the book does not look at the many refereeing controversies in matches which clubs and supporters have held to have happened down the years and which have been given so much oxygen by the media to keep

1

the wheels of argument and debate turning on an almost constant basis. That also would be a book on its own and I am happy to leave such a task to someone else. What the book does seek to do is to record the organisation and development of refereeing in Scotland over 150 years through the formal SFA structures which have existed and which are reflected through committee minutes. The breadth of activity involved in refereeing is quite astonishing, even to someone like me who worked in referee administration for almost 40 years. I certainly bore witness to huge changes and developments in refereeing during my career. Refereeing touches every part of the game in some way.

Referees are *a part of* the game of football, but at the same time, they are *apart from* it. For good reason too, in many ways, in order that a separation of roles can exist. Few people in football will have any proper appreciation of the refereeing world and what has gone on, and goes on, within it. Football supporters will have even less knowledge. To them, the referee is essentially the fall guy to criticise at each match and generally be held responsible for spoiling the game. The referee is just as much a part of a game of football as the players. There is a great amount that goes on to get a referee, and his assistants, to a match. There is a huge network of volunteers in the refereeing movement giving support and guidance to referees at all levels of the game. It is all done because they love football and the connection they have to it. They are unseen heroes who enable, in their own way, football to be played.

For any readers who are, or who have been, referees, I hope that they will find it to be of particular interest, regardless of the level they officiate, or officiated, at. Referees are actually in much the same position as club officials and supporters in that they would have no real appreciation or understanding of how things really operate at the top of the refereeing structure. I hope that the book shines some light into the unknown world of Scottish refereeing, not just for referees but for all readers.

2

Part One

1873-1914

The Origins of the Referee Committee

The Referee Committee has its genesis in the SFA's desire in the mid-1880's to rid football of the growing problem of rough play. Prior to then, the General Committee handled all business following the SFA's formation in 1873 with the Business Committee overseeing refereeing matters from 1879.

A Sub-Committee on Rough Play was formed in season 1886-87 with Bye-Laws being introduced to address the problem. In the Bye-Laws, rough play, as specified in Rule 10 of the then Laws of the Game, was defined as tripping, ducking, hacking, jumping at a player, pushing, and charging from behind. Referees were empowered, without consulting the umpires, to deal with players guilty of violent charging, or using threatening and abusive language. (In football's early years, two umpires, one per team, were used and to whom each side could appeal. If the two umpires could not agree, the point was referred to the referee, who stood on the touchline keeping time, for a decision.)

Referees had to submit a report on a player infringing the Bye-laws to the SFA Secretary within three days of the match. Players found guilty of violating the Bye-laws were suspended from taking part in cup ties and friendly matches for such time as the Committee deemed expedient. Home clubs were required to secure the services of a neutral referee and to take all precautionary measures for the safety of officials and the visiting team.

As a consequence of the introduction of the Bye-Laws, the Sub-Committee was next required to compile an official list of referees *"whose duty it would be to see that nothing of a questionable nature would pass unnoticed"*, the first hint of expectations being placed on referees. Approximately 100 were placed on the List, which was approved unanimously by the Business Committee in January 1887.

These developments merited comment in the SFA's Annual Report for season 1886-87. Hope was expressed that the Bye-Laws *"if effectively put into force, cannot fail to crush this disreputable feature [rough play] for ever from our midst"*. Of the referees, it was *"earnestly hoped that they will not fail on any occasion to prove themselves worthy of the trust reposed in them".*

The Sub-Committee gave the SFA Secretary responsibility for the appointment of referees. A fee of one shilling was charged to a club when applying for a referee to be appointed – this was due to the trouble and expense very frequently caused in procuring referees. Applications for the appointment of a referee were to be made no later than the Wednesday prior to the game on a Saturday.

In 1887, the General Committee approved instructions for referees which had been drawn up by the Business Committee. The principles established in these instructions hold to the modern day and will be easily recognised by those with knowledge of the Laws of the Game. Inherent in them was the understandable need for referees to be thoroughly conversant with the Laws. Referees were given responsibility to determine the playability of a pitch (and have the power to prohibit a cup tie from being played in the event of the pitch being unplayable). They had to inspect players' boots, make sure that corner flags were in place, act as timekeeper for the match (making allowance for time lost) and submit the result and the team lines to the SFA Secretary. Referees were required to rigidly enforce the Bye-Laws on rough play and had to remember that they had *"great powers entrusted to them"* and that these should be used *"fearlessly"*, especially in respect of a claim. Referees were to decide in favour of the team appealed against. Direction was also given to umpires. They were not to give advice to either team nor make any claim on behalf of either side unless appealed to and were also to always support the referee, *"knowing his decisions are final"*.

The approach taken to deal with rough play highlights the need for a National Association to adopt measures to control the playing of the game. Creating a list of referees to do that initiated a basic premise within Scottish football (and indeed the wider football world) – that the referees were the association's instrument to allow matches to be controlled and played in a sporting fashion. This position has been a running thread throughout football in Scotland. The basic requirement placed on referees to apply the Laws of the Game has been constant.

5

After operating as a Sub-Committee on Referees for a number of years, the Referee Committee was finally instituted as a full Standing committee of the SFA for season 1895-96, due to the growing need to deal with disciplinary reports submitted by referees. It brought with it responsibility for overseeing referees and refereeing.

Organisational Developments
As football developed, reference to referees had to be introduced into the SFA's Articles of Association. A new "rule" was incorporated into the Articles in 1887 when two classes of referees were defined – professional and amateur. Professional referees were to satisfy a sub-committee of the Business Committee of their qualifications for the post and were to be remunerated according to the SFA's tariff. The Tariff contained no mention of match fees. Amateur referees received travelling expenses only. The Article also stated that a member of the General Committee could not be a professional referee, thereby marking a clear separation of roles from what had previously operated when committee members acted as referees. From the formation of the SFA, officials such as Presidents, Secretaries and members of the SFA Committee had regularly been appointed as referees for major matches. For standard club matches, the referees came from the competing clubs.

1891 was a momentous year as the International FA Board (IFAB), the body responsible for the Laws of the Game, formalised the role of referee into the Laws of the Game. Authority was given to the referee to send players off and award penalty kicks and free kicks without listening to appeals. The two umpires became linesmen. This development led to a swift adjustment in the appointing of officials to matches. Individuals who were recognised as "proper" referees came into their own. The role of referee had become specialised.

For season 1909-10, a major step was taken in formalising matters on referees when a change was made to the SFA's Articles. All games between clubs under the SFA's jurisdiction had now to be controlled by a referee on the List, a principle which still applies.

In 1912, the SFA Council approved a recommendation from the Referee Committee that professional referees should not be eligible to be committee members of affiliated bodies.

The List of Referees

Once the Referee Committee was formed, a pattern quickly became established in regard to its business. It met frequently, with the List being regularly revised. It was confirmed and approved in the early part of each season with referees added at various points thereafter as and when it was considered appropriate (even as late in March one season). Often, applicants not selected were placed on a provisional list and others were held over for further consideration. As referees were periodically removed from the List during a season, operating on this basis was a sensible and pragmatic approach to take. The number of referees on the List had to be maintained to service the game.

Whilst evidently a national List of referees had been in existence for over 20 years, the committee decided to revamp things in season 1908-09. The President and Secretary were instructed to write to all recognised football bodies, outlining a scheme for an Official National List of Referees and requesting the submission of their own Referee Lists. If no such Lists existed, they were to *"submit the names of gentlemen recognised to be competent referees in their district"*. A National List was duly drawn up from the lists received.

Tight control was exercised over the List. Referees were removed from it on a fairly regular basis. From time to time, referees who had either been deleted from the List or had their applications refused, appealed the committee's decision. In the vast majority of cases, such appeals were refused. Only on a very rare occasion was a referee reinstated. The committee decided in season 1913-14 not to entertain applications from referees who had previously been deleted.

On occasions referees were added to the List with the stipulation that they be only used in the local competitions of the bodies submitting their names. This happened with the Scottish Amateur FA in 1910 and the Aberdeenshire FA in

7

1911, with 10 and 6 referees from these bodies being included in the List, respectively.

An application form for the List was introduced during season 1909-10. Applicants had to undergo a written and oral examination, although there is no reference as to how these processes operated. From season 1913-14, applicants for the List had to submit references in support of their application. An instruction to this effect was printed on the application form.

The number of referees on the List was never recorded in the committee minutes. The first List in 1886-87 had approximately 100. By 1894-95, 20 professional referees (from 50 applications) were selected for the List with others placed on it through the season. In the committee's first season, the number of referees on the List increased to 41. For seasons 1912-13 and 1913-14, 80 and 74 applications were received, respectively.

Oversight of Other Lists
When the national List was formed in 1909-10, the recognised bodies were advised that they should not add referees to their Lists without the committee's approval. All the referees concerned were registered with the SFA once the Lists were submitted and approved. As with the national List, these Lists were tightly controlled. Perthshire FA was censured in 1910 for appointing two referees for its cup ties who were not on its List. During season 1912-13, the Referee Committee decided that referees not on the SFA List could only officiate in the competitions of the particular body registering them, or in friendly matches. That same season requests from various District FA's to add referees to their Lists were refused. Requests from the Border Amateur League, the Scottish Central League and the Eastern League to have their referees recognised, were refused.

The committee had to occasionally remind the recognised bodies that referees who had been struck off the national List should not be included on any List. Season 1913-14 was a busy one in this respect, with the committee having to deal with several leagues for using referees who had been deleted from the List. The Scottish Reserve League had to provide additional names of referees as the majority of those it had submitted had been deleted. The League also had to be told that a referee it had used was deemed to be incompetent and could not be appointed. The Scottish Football League (SFL) appointed a referee who had been deleted from the List, something which had come to notice simply because the referee had submitted a report to the SFA.

Scrutiny of Referees
An important decision was taken by the Sub-Committee on Referees during season 1894-95, namely that *"cognisance would be taken of all derelictions of duty on the part of referees"*. Referees came under scrutiny for the best of reasons – ensuring that standards of performances would be high for the good of football. Such expectations have always been placed on referees down the years and carrying this burden has been a constant companion.

Whilst scrutinising referees has always had an important place in the committee's business, there has always been a strong element of protectiveness employed towards them. An important marker was set by the committee in 1901 when it determined that a member's report on the referee of a Dundee v. St. Mirren match was strictly private to the committee. This approach has been maintained continuously by the SFA. Many a club down the years has had its request to receive a copy of the Supervisor's/Observer's report declined.

From the early days of the Referee Committee, a system was in place whereby the members reported on referees. Reports were regularly submitted and discussed with plans made to inspect referees. Letters from clubs and the members' own discussions had a significant bearing on which referees came under the microscope. During season 1906-07 the committee decided that members should write to the Secretary when considered necessary on a referee they had seen and that a record would be retained for future reference.

Complaints from Clubs
Dealing with letters from clubs complaining about referees' performances quickly became a regular feature of the committee's business. Consideration of these complaints

formed an important basis for scrutinising referees. It was common for referees to be called to attend meetings as a consequence of clubs' complaints or to assist the committee in its investigations into disciplinary cases.

A meeting in 1896 gives a flavour of the way business was conducted when several letters were dealt with concerning referees' performances. In regard to one complaint, the committee determined that the game in question had been a very difficult one to referee and, under the circumstances, the referee had *"come out of the ordeal fairly satisfactorily, allowing perhaps one mistake regarding an offside goal"*. The matter was dropped. The committee felt in another case that a club's view on the referee's handling of the match had been exaggerated and that the other clubs had to substantiate their views.

A decade later, Kilmarnock went to the length of submitting diagrams showing how several of the referee's decisions were wrong in a match against Beith. The referee was given the chance to put his side of the story. He denied all the allegations and *"was at pains to prove it was only the complaints of a beaten club"*. The committee, on the basis of the referee's steady performances throughout the season, came out in support of him.

Following complaints having been received during season 1911-12, certain referees were written to and reminded of the terms of the Laws of the Game in regard to operating with neutral linesmen. A referee had to be informed that, when he had no doubt about a point of play, he must not consult with a neutral linesman.

Deletion and Suspension of Referees

The reporting system played its part in the deletion and suspension of referees. The traffic was quite regular over the seasons. 1907-08 was a particularly busy one as 18 referees were dealt with during the season. 12 were suspended in one fell swoop from 1st January 1908. The committee recommended to the General Committee that a referee *"struck off the List for incompetency be not allowed to referee in Scotland."* One of the suspended referees had been replaced by another referee by the two clubs, St. Johnstone and Lochgelly United at half-time. The committee did not disapprove of the action of the two clubs and the referee was suspended *sine die*. Several referees were called to meetings to be interviewed in regard to the performances and the relevant clubs invited to provide their comments. On making enquiries, the Scottish Football Referees' Association (SFRA) was advised that "*general incompetency*" or "*having been officially inspected on the field*" were reasons for referees being deleted from the List. In 1912, a referee enquired as to the reason for his deletion from the List. He was bluntly told by the committee: incompetence.

There was a notable suspension of a referee during season 1907-08 which arose from the consideration of a disciplinary case. Celtic was fined £15 for missile throwing by spectators at a home match against Airdrieonians. The committee determined that the referee, John Stark, "*had not shown a proper conception of his duties in suppressing rough play*" in the match and suspended him for a month. This was a hugely significant decision as Stark was a top referee at that time. He refereed the Celtic v. Rangers Scottish Cup Final in season 1908-09 (when the Cup was withheld due to crowd disorder) and a number of internationals in that era.

The issue of suspending referees during 1907-08 brought forth a response from the Scottish Football League (SFL). It argued that the suspension of a referee should not take effect until after the "*expiry of league engagements*". The committee did not agree with this view as it held that its stance would be in the "*interests of football generally*". Rather intriguingly, the SFL had been suspending referees itself as the SFRA wrote to the committee protesting at the SFL's actions. Dialogue between the SFA and the SFL on referees' suspensions took place and an agreement (siding with view of the SFL) came into operation.

Another noteworthy suspension happened in season 1909-10. Following a Celtic v. Rangers match, the referee, J. Faichney, and officials of both clubs were interviewed by the committee. Faichney was suspended from mid-April to mid-September 1909.

A referee found himself suspended for two months during season 1909-10 for failing to carry out his duties at a Qualifying

Cup tie at Bo'ness United. He had allowed the match to start and be played without goal lines being marked. The situation was made worse as his attention had been drawn to the absence of markings before the match.

Guidance and Direction to Referees

A key element of the committee's business has always been providing regular guidance to referees on what is expected of them. One early example came in season 1895-96, when referees were reminded of the requirements of the Law relating to the taking of a throw-in – namely that the player taking the throw-in must stand with both feet on the touch line facing the field of play.

In 1903, the committee was moved to point out *"that when a referee has blown his whistle, he cannot avoid putting into operation the penalty which he had in mind when he blew his whistle"*. Something had obviously happened to provoke this statement but no mention of it is carried in the minutes.

The committee felt it necessary in 1905 to *"impress upon referees the necessity of not allowing players to discuss points of play with them on the field."*

The following season, referees' attention had to be drawn to the need to look in the direction of the player taking free kicks and to insist on opponents standing back six yards from the player taking the free kick. The latter guidance had to be emphasised again a few seasons later when the Laws were changed to require opposing players to be 10 yards from a free kick.

During season 1912-13 referees were recommended to arrive at grounds *"not less than fifteen minutes before time fixed for kick-off to enable them to see that the ground is properly marked off, and that the appurtenances of the game are in order."* Later that season, the committee was obliged to state that referees had to carry out these inspections themselves and not delegate the duty to their linesmen, a practice which had obviously quickly emerged.

The Scottish Football Referees' Association

Reference to the wider organisational structure of referees in Scotland is first mentioned in the Referee Committee minutes of September 1899 when it was stated that the representative body of referees, the Scottish Football Referees' Association (SFRA), had requested a meeting with the Referee Committee. The request was declined. The date of the formation of the SFRA is not known but it is no surprise that such an association had come to be formed, as it would have been a natural consequential development in football. It is likely that local Referees' Associations were formed also during this period in areas of the country where football had rapidly developed.

In 1906, the SFRA submitted for consideration a Referees' Chart, prepared by The Football Association, offering guidance on refereeing and the application of the Laws of the Game, and asked if it could be adopted in Scotland. With a degree of insularity, the committee decided that The Football Association had drawn up the guidance to meet the conditions in England and that these did not apply in Scotland.

Dialogue with the SFRA developed. A deputation from the SFRA met the committee in 1912 and various points were put forward for consideration. The dialogue became drawn out and it took two years for it to be brought to a conclusion. The committee agreed that it would keep in mind the points raised by the SFRA when compiling the List. The minutes do not reveal what these were but it is likely that the committee had been persuaded of the validity of some of the SFRA's points.

There is no reference at all in the minutes in these early years of the game as to how referees were recruited or trained. It would seem that such things were left in the hands of the SFRA and its member associations.

Rough Play and Player Indiscipline
Issues concerning the indiscipline of players were a continuing and dominant thread through the committee's business. During season 1904-05 referees were given more direction in the application of the Laws of the Game. They were requested "*to ensure they were not negligent in dealing with rough play*", a matter which had been discussed by the SFA's General Committee. That such matters were being discussed at that level indicates that an idealistic approach to the playing of football still held sway within the SFA.

Celtic submitted a letter in season 1905-06 complaining that they had *"suffered severely through referees neglecting to observe that charging was allowable and that a goalkeeper may be charged whilst holding the ball"*. The club suggested that the SFA should emphasise the *"existence of the above"*. The committee responded by agreeing to *"formally draw to the referees' attention that charging is permissible but it must not be violent or dangerous"*.

In a further attempt to control the game, circulars were issued to clubs and referees during season 1907-08. Referees were notified, in simple terms and in the language of the day, by the SFA Secretary, John McDowall: *"My Committee desire to direct your attention to the regrettable prevalence of Rough Play and Misconduct, and wish to impress on Referees that the powers given to them by Law 13 and the Rough Play Bye Laws should be fully exercised."* McDowall's letter to clubs stated: *"My Committee noting the increasing tendency to Rough Play and Misconduct appeal to the Executive of clubs to assist them by impressing on their players the necessity of abstaining from all foul methods. The Committee is convinced that the hearty co-operation of clubs in rigidly discountenancing Rough Play will tend to bring about the desired improvement."* The circulars did not achieve their aims as players continued their indiscipline. Things were to worsen over time, not improve.

Committee Decisions

Throughout its existence, the committee has had to come to a view on a range of football issues and give its verdict to the game's participants.

That passions run high in the game is a well established truism in football and, in this respect, a mention of this is recorded in 1906. The committee *"strongly expressed its disapproval"* of the reported actions of some club officials who were in the *"habit of shouting and hooting"* at decisions of referees. This view fell on stony ground very quickly and has been well ignored by many ever since.

The committee also agreed at the meeting that an official statement to the Press should be made at the close of each meeting, an indication of the great interest taken in football. It was also agreed that fines imposed would be given to charity.

There were two noteworthy developments in the early part of 1910. Firstly, the committee decided to recommend to the SFA Council that a proposal be put before IFAB that *"referees' reports must be received within 2 days (Sunday not included.)"* This was duly adopted by IFAB. Secondly, a motion to present a badge to the referee of the Scottish Cup Final was defeated.

Referees travelling to and from match appointments in these early days of football would have faced a few problems, being heavily reliant on public transport. This is highlighted by the following minute from 1910: *"Southern Counties FA informed that a reasonable allowance as hotel expenses must be made to referees sent by this Association to matches in the district west of Castle Douglas and Kirkcudbright and east of Stranraer during such period as the only suitable train is the 5.10am from Glasgow."* For any referee who chose to take the train at that time, that was surely a demonstration of commitment on his part.

Part Two

1919-1945

The Inter-War period was one of developing maturity in the running of the game, with the SFA reaching its 50th anniversary in 1923. The work of the Referee Committee developed on a steady basis. Influence began to be exerted by the SFL and the SFRA sought to establish a regular dialogue with the committee to advance the cause of refereeing. A picture emerges of these two bodies pushing the SFA to make changes and improvements to refereeing, each coming at things from its own standpoint.

The List of Referees
In the years after the First World War, the List was compiled each season along previously established lines. It was generally confirmed in September each season, with new applicants being considered at certain points thereafter during the season.

The Referee Lists of the recognised bodies were submitted for registration in the early part of the season. Occasionally, a recognised body was censured for using non-registered referees. These bodies regularly submitted fresh names of referees for registration. Control continued to be exercised over these Lists, as demonstrated by the Highland League, Aberdeenshire FA and the North of Scotland FA being advised in October 1925 to delete a referee from their Lists.

Appeals from referees to be reinstated to the List continued from time to time, as did the occasional deletion. In 1929 a referee was informed that any referee considered unsuitable by the SFA cannot officiate in any match under its jurisdiction.

An issue regarding eligibility for inclusion on the List arose in September 1929, when Aberdeenshire FA was informed by the committee that, insofar as the SFA was aware, the SFL Referee List was not confined solely to members of the SFRA. The SFL was operating its own List of Referees, separate from the SFA's List.

During the period 1929-31, the reinstatement of referees to the List was a recurring theme as the SFA dealt with major governance issues relating to the breakaway Scottish Intermediate League formed by some Junior clubs. These were resolved in the summer of 1931 and as part of the agreements reached, all referees who had officiated in the League were reinstated under SFA jurisdiction and eligible to apply to any body under whose auspices they wished to officiate.

Season 1932-33 saw a failed attempt to introduce some significant changes to the conditions to be met for admission to the List. The committee put forward a detailed proposal to update the relevant Article of Association at the SFA's AGM. It proposed that all candidates for the List should be *"examined"* by the committee or by an Affiliated Association on behalf of the committee; that an examination fee of five shillings should apply; that a referee being included on the List should pay an annual registration fee of one shilling to the SFA; a referee was not to be removed from the List during a season *"unless for a misdemeanour"* and that the List was to be compiled on the basis of the geographical areas used for Council Divisions.

The proposal was withdrawn at the AGM. No reason was given, but the politics of the game no doubt lay behind it. However, a change in the process of the compilation of the List did happen in any case. A new way of working came into play.

Following the AGM, the committee appointed the Office Bearers to confer with the SFL before the List was revised. Procedures for revising the List and the consideration of new applicants were approved. Sub-committees were formed to interview referees. The List was compiled in August with a Supplementary List issued later. The following season, when the List was being revised and confirmed, new applicants were dealt with on reports from a Sub-Committee and Affiliated Associations. Appeals from referees who had not been admitted to the List were still received and refused. In June 1936, the committee interviewed new applicants and received reports from Affiliated Associations. It then conferred with representatives of the SFL Management Committee and thereafter revised the List.

The SFL initiated a lengthy dialogue with the committee during season 1937-38, which culminated in significant changes to the way things were dealt with (This dialogue is referred to in the SFL section which follows). The List was revised in June 1938 in accordance with the procedures which had been agreed. Referees were classified into three groups:

Class 1 - Considered efficient for any match

Class 2 - Recommended for engagement as linesmen as referee in minor matches only

Class 3 - Considered likely to qualify for Class 1 after gaining experience

Referees in Class 1 were recommended to be employed in both Divisions of the SFL; referees in Class 3 could be engaged by the SFL and the Scottish Alliance (a reserve league for SFL First Division clubs) on suitable occasions so that they could gain necessary experience; referees in Class 2 were to be used as linesmen until Class 1 was sufficiently enlarged to provide a sufficient number of referees to enable the SFL and the Alliance to make all their appointments from that category irrespective of the nature of that appointment.

The List continued to be kept open for potential applicants after it had been approved. Arrangements were made for dealing with new applicants and in July, a Sub-committee met to interview applicants from several of the SFRA's Associations for the List. The existence of a maximum age of 30 years for new applicants emerged from a meeting between the SFA and the Highland League, Aberdeenshire FA and North of Scotland FA in 1938. The examination of referees was raised by the Highland League. It was confirmed that the Referee Committee had decided to keep the List open during the season, so that referees could be added to it any time and that it would not strictly adhere to the maximum age of 30 years for new applicants from the North, provided that they were recommended as being suitable otherwise. The intimation of a maximum age for new applicants is the first reference to age limits regarding the List, and the view expressed demonstrated a touch of pragmatic flexibility. In an area where referee numbers might be comparatively low, there was little point in denying football the services of someone who was a year or so over the maximum age.

By the late 1930's, the issuing of a Supplementary List had become a regular feature. The number and quality of referees was improving to enable this to happen. The SFRA was informed that the committee graded referees on the List in accordance with reports received from Affiliated Associations and other recognised bodies.

Scottish Football League

The SFL put forward during season 1923-24 that the SFA List should be the only List in Scotland, that referees should be graded and that an adequate number of inspectors should be appointed, with their expenses to be borne by the SFA or jointly with the SFL.

There was a very mild outcome from the committee's deliberations. The SFL's generous suggestion that there should only be the SFA's List in operation was turned down. The SFL continued to operate its own List for a number of years, with the SFA seemingly content to allow such a situation to exist.

In regard to the inspection of referees, the committee's view was that this topic *"has always had, and will continue to have careful attention"*. The SFL was evidently wishing for the existing system of inspection to be expanded but the committee was content with the *status quo*, whatever that was at the time. There was some success for the SFL in one regard: the committee agreed to confer with the SFL when compiling the List.

In 1934 the SFL and the SFA met to discuss a variety of issues. On refereeing, the SFRA was a major topic of discussion. The SFL was informed that *"this was a matter entirely for the Referee Committee who had already this season given full and careful consideration to the position of the SFRA"*. (This, however, is not discernable from the committee minutes of that season). To progress matters, a meeting of the SFA, the SFL and representatives from all known referees' associations, was held in April 1934.

The SFRA attended together with the following member Associations: - Glasgow and the West of Scotland RA, Eastern RA, Aberdeen and District RA, Lothian RA and Dumfries and District RA. Arising from the meeting, the various referees' associations were to confer and reach agreement. On what, there is no mention and there was no reference to continuing consideration of this particular item of business in the following season's minutes.

The SFL returned to the subject of a system of inspection of referees in season 1937-38. A dialogue ensued, with the committee making the following suggestions: that the appointment of officials to inspect referees in SFL matches was, and must remain, essentially a matter for the SFL; that the Affiliated National Associations and their member bodies be used in compiling the List; that neutral linesmen be appointed for all Second Division matches; that the practice of having a separate list for each League Division be discontinued.

The SFL responded with their own suggestions: that an "Inspection Committee" be appointed and that no referee be admitted to the List unless favourably reported upon by two members of that Committee; referees complained against would be inspected. Appointing neutral linesmen was held to be a matter for the Second Division clubs. The SFL also proposed that an applicant favourably reported on should be admitted to the List at any time, so that he could be tried in League or Alliance matches.

Concluding the dialogue, the committee decided on the basis for the future compilation of the List. The assistance of the Scottish Junior FA was sought, an indication of its place in the game with Junior football being the stepping stone for referees progressing to the List. Application forms were to be sent through the Scottish Junior FA to its member associations with a request for a report on the known capabilities of the applicants; these associations were to be asked to recommend referees for inclusion in the List who had been seen officiating in two or more matches by two or more officials of their Association; the List would remain open so that applicants recommended for trial in SFL or Alliance matches could be added at any time provided that the foregoing conditions are met.

The committee considered that this procedure would *"ensure that only referees who are efficient and have gained the necessary experience will be included in the List"*. The committee was open to returning back to a system of having only one List serving senior football and hoped that this would be considered by the SFL. It also hoped that the SFL would again consider making neutral linesmen compulsory for the Second Division.

21

Scottish Football Referees' Association

The SFRA had regular dialogue with the SFA throughout the inter-war period. Its letters were always considered by the SFA Council in the first instance and then passed to the Referee Committee rather than being directly submitted to it. This was an indication of the SFA's working practices and the power and standing of Council in the game, and also reflected the political delicacy of dealing with the SFRA. Exchanges of correspondence dragged out unnecessarily on many occasions before meetings were held. There was probably an element of "keeping them in place" used by the SFA in its dealings with the SFRA. The SFRA fulfilled its role well on behalf of the referees over this period.

In 1920, the SFRA sought discussions on recognition of its association, the appointment of neutral linesmen in Scottish Cup ties and on the interpretation of the Laws of the Game. The committee advised that the Articles of Association did not allow for the SFRA to be officially recognised and that the only form of recognition which existed was that which applied to accepting individual referees on the List who had passed the SFRA examination. A later meeting achieved an increase in the fees for the Scottish Cup and the Qualifying Cups. A request to increase travel expenses failed.

In season 1923-24, spectator misbehaviour at matches had been rearing its head and causing difficulties for match officials. The SFRA sought a response from the committee on these incidents. The committee professed that it was satisfied with measures which had recently been taken by the police and courts in dealing with football cases brought before them.

The level and status of appointment has always been an important factor in refereeing and, in 1924, the Office Bearers, in response to an enquiry from the SFRA, conveyed that a recent alteration to a Cup Competition Rule regarding appointment of referees and linesmen, referred only to Scottish Cup ties, which appointments took precedence over other previous engagements, irrespective of when they were made.

Despite the SFA's refusal to give it recognition, the SFRA began to press for more involvement in the affairs of the committee. In February 1927, the committee informed the

SFRA that "*its request to have representation when matters pertaining to referees or refereeing are being discussed, cannot be granted, and that a deputation on that question would serve no purpose.*" The SFRA did not give up. It submitted the following request during season 1927-28: - "*a delegate be allowed to be present at all meetings of Referee Committee or when matters pertaining to referees and refereeing are to be discussed, such delegate to have no voice or vote in any part of the business, but merely to hold a watching brief and only if requested by your Association to carry back here any suggestions, reports or decision.*" The request was declined.

The SFRA was unsuccessful with another attempt for recognition during season 1928-29. The committee had been delegated by Council to meet the SFRA to discuss this and other matters, including issues relating to the suspension of referees arising from their involvement in the Scottish Intermediate League and the apparent existence of two referees' associations operating within the area of Aberdeenshire FA. This latter element resulted in Aberdeenshire FA being advised that inclusion on its list of referees should not be contingent on being in membership of any particular referees' association or branch.

During season 1929-30, the SFRA achieved an increase in the referee's fee to four guineas (£4.20) for the Scottish Cup Final but was unsuccessful in requesting that the referee be given a medal. The committee's view was awarding a medal "*cannot be entertained*". A request for financial assistance was declined by the Emergency & Finance Committee.

In 1931, the SFRA sought a meeting to address a "*decision stated to have been made by a minor body restricting their appointments to referees who are in membership of a new referees' association formed under the title of the Glasgow and West of Scotland Referees'Association*". The outcome was that the matter was "*left in abeyance*", which can be taken as meaning that the Referee Committee had no issue with the formation of a new referees' association or indeed the alleged decision of the minor body.

23

The SFRA met the committee during season 1935-36 to discuss *"several matters which call for decision and action"*. This resulted in some important decisions being taken. The List was to be compiled not later than 30th June each year, and that prior to deciding the List either the committee or a sub-committee was to co-operate with the SFL, having examined the renewal applications and interviewed new applicants. All applications had to be lodged on or before 15th June each year. The Affiliated National Associations were advised that it had been decided that all referees on the List must have passed the SFRA examination. It was suggested to the Affiliated National Associations that they should consider requiring referees to report all players cautioned in matches.

Given these outcomes, there can be little doubt that the SFRA's approaches had been successful and helped steer the progress of refereeing in an appropriate direction. This was a prime example of the influence that referees, operating as a group, could achieve to benefit the game. There was one strand of the SFRA's proposals, however, which was not successful. The Committee declined to accede to request that members of the SFRA's National Council be admitted to matches on presentation of their membership cards.

Issues relating to non-membership of the SFRA came to the fore in season 1938-39. The SFRA requested a meeting with all Affiliated National Associations to discuss its concerns at the employment of non-members and those who had been suspended from its membership. The committee declined the request. From the SFA's perspective, such a position was understandable – its scope and concern was just for football at SFA member level and it had little interest in delving into the world below, as long as that level produced referees to service the SFA's List. In raising these issues, the SFRA seemingly had a wider and more rounded view of the overall position of referees and was aware of the benefits of referees being in membership of an association to help them progress in their careers.

General Committee Business
In the latter part of season 1923-24, a member put forward the following motion: *"That the question of referees be considered and scheme devised for their improvement"*. Its progress was slow. It was deferred at the following meeting and at the next it was remitted to the following season's committee. And there it died a death, because there is no reference to the motion at any point thereafter.

In October 1930, the committee informed Celtic that it regarded as *"highly irregular and improper that they should have sent to the Press, for publication, a letter addressed by them to the Association, particularly as the letter went outwith a complaint about a referee in a particular match"*. The letter was a very strong complaint from the club regarding the performance of the referee in the Glasgow Cup Final against Rangers and recounted various match incidents, including repeated alleged fouling of its players, which were held to be disadvantageous to the club. The committee *"enjoined referees to entirely disregard the communication of Celtic to the Press"*. The SFRA consequently submitted a letter to the committee expressing its *"very keen appreciation of the action taken"* in the matter. The committee was in high dudgeon at its September 1931 meeting when it made a vigorous protest regarding articles which had appeared in the Daily Express earlier that month which, in its opinion, were harmful and detrimental to the game. A letter was sent to the newspaper. The modern-day criticism of referees is nothing new, given these two examples.

Controlling the Game
The need to convey instruction and guidance to referees has been an ever present requirement of football administration.
Concern about player behaviour was never far from the surface and this came to the fore early in season 1929-30. The following circular was issued to clubs and to referees: - *"I am instructed to draw the attention of your club to the increasing prevalence of the practice of questioning referees' decisions by players. A player is entitled to enquire from a referee as to his decision, but he is not entitled by word or action to show dissent from any such decision. Clubs and players are warned that this*

undesirable practice of players surrounding the referee and making frantic appeals must cease forthwith, and referees are instructed to strictly administer the Law dealing with this matter. This notice must be prominently displayed in the players' dressing room."

The committee issued much the same guidance in 1934 to clubs and referees, taking the view that players appealing against referees' decisions continued to be too prevalent. Referees were exhorted not to tolerate appeals or remarks by players. The committee also took the opportunity to instruct referees that *"Henceforth, any player cautioned by a referee for any offence will be reported to this Association and a record of such reports will be made. The caution should be given in definite terms and the player informed that a report will be made. A record of such reports will be compiled by this Association for reference if necessary."*

Dissent was obviously a constant concern in the game. The terms of the first circular, for example, remain entirely applicable today in the modern game, perhaps even more so. Nothing has ever changed despite repeated attempts down the years to curb dissent. The second circular gives clear direction as to what referees were required to do in terms with dealing with players and reporting offences. A standardised process was beginning to emerge.

During season 1934-35 a circular containing instructions on the control of matches and drawing attention to certain points of the Laws of the Game, was issued to referees. These instructions were held to be so important that they were printed in the SFA handbook for future guidance.

Dealing with the application of the Laws of the Game and disciplinary matters has not always been the sole reason for guidance having to be issued. Maintaining clear lines of demarcation between referees and clubs has been a historic feature of the game. By the start of season 1933-34, the committee addressed some issues which had come to notice. All clubs and referees were advised that it strongly disapproved of the practice of referees being entertained in club boardrooms after matches and that it should be discontinued at once; that a referee travelling to or from a match in the company of either team was undesirable and that a referee would be immediately removed from the List and banned from the game if found to be acting as an agent for any club.

Laws of the Game Queries
During the 1920's and 1930's there was a steady stream of enquiries on the Laws of the Game submitted to the SFA. These were regularly dealt with by Council, which again reflects the power it held at that time. It can be imagined that Council would have been guided by the Secretary in terms of providing a definitive response, rather than there being a convoluted and risky debate on each enquiry. Providing the answer at Council would also have served as a good means of disseminating it to the SFA's members. In the world of Scottish refereeing, getting an answer from the SFA to an enquiry was always held to be the authoritative "gold standard".

The SFA had some significant standing and authority in the football world during this era. It can be the only plausible explanation for the Ohio State Referees' Association to write to the SFA, rather to its own National Association, with two Laws of the Game enquiries in 1925. The Office Bearers duly determined firstly that, despite an intentional infringement, a goal cannot be awarded unless the ball has actually passed between the goal posts, under the bar; and secondly, a goal cannot be disallowed on account of ball striking upright or crossbar before passing between the posts, at taking of a penalty kick after the expiry of time. These may be fairly obvious responses but the difficulties caused in games where these sorts of incidents occurred (as surely they did), can be imagined particularly if the incidents were not governed by the Laws of the Game at the time. Such types of incidents are indicative of how responding to them contributes to the evolution of the Laws of the Game.

The SFRA raised enquiries with the SFA for clarification from time to time. One such enquiry was determined by Council in season 1925-26: a referee could request, or order, a player *"to bring back a ball he has wilfully kicked away"*. The committee (not Council in this instance) in 1936 dealt with another SFRA enquiry: *"While play is in progress, the referee observes the full back striking his own goalkeeper, the incident taking place in the goal area. What action should the referee take and under which Law? How should the game be resumed?"* The committee decided that such an occurrence should be dealt with under Laws 9, 13 and 17.

During season 1926-27, Council determined three enquiries from Aberdeenshire and District Referees' Association. Firstly, that a player leaving the playing enclosure during a match without consent of the referee may be deemed guilty of ungentlemanly conduct and should be dealt with accordingly under Law 13. Secondly, a player, striking a team mate, commits a breach of Law 9 and thirdly, a referee must exercise judgement in the case of a player standing in the back of the net who rushes out and kicks the ball out of the goalkeeper's hands into the net. The same association submitted another enquiry two seasons later. This time, the Emergency and Finance Committee provided clarification: treating a referee's decision with contempt is ungentlemanly conduct and should be dealt with accordingly.

There were occasions when the SFA, rather than deciding upon an enquiry, felt it more appropriate to refer such matters to IFAB. One example arose in 1930 when Council remitted a query from the SFRA regarding Law 12 to IFAB. The SFA requested a decision in the case of a player committing an offence within the penalty area before reporting to the referee, as required by Law 12, on his return to the field of play after leaving for boot repairs. IFAB determined that the player should be cautioned for this offence and that if he committed another, separate offence, he should be penalised according to the Law. Given the SFA's membership of IFAB, the route to that forum with Laws of the Game queries has always been highly valued within Scottish refereeing.

War Time 1939-45

Following the outbreak of the Second World War in September 1939, the SFA disbanded all the standing committees and replaced them with two, the Finance and Insurance Committee and the Emergency Committee. Football continued throughout the Second World War although in a reduced and altered form –

regional professional leagues operated rather than the national SFL. There was still a need for referees. The Emergency Committee handled the business of the Referee Committee which continued along established lines with the List being revised and confirmed each season.

Whilst the deprivations of war impacted on everyday civilian life, it also provided an opportunity to the SFA to take stock of football and to look ahead to life after the war. During season 1942-43, the SFA set up a Committee on Reconstruction. Its purpose was to formulate a *"scheme which will place the government of the game in Scotland on a m*ore *satisfactory basis, particularly having in mind reconstruction which will be essential after the war"*. The SFA had been in existence for 70 years by this time and such an exercise was no doubt long overdue. The SFL was invited to participate in the committee's work.

Sub-committees were created to look at various elements of the game. Proposals emerged to remodel the formation and composition of Council and to create six Standing Committees, one of which was "Referee and Refereeing". Its *"Duties and Powers" were to deal with all reports made by referees on misconduct and with all matters affecting the Official List of Referees"*.

As an adjunct to the Committee on Reconstruction, a Committee on Coaching Etc. was formed in December 1944 to *"consider methods calculated to secure an advance in the quality of football, to formulate schemes a) for the training of coaches and referees; and b) for the most beneficial use of approved coaches, and to make suggestions or recommendations to Council on any other matters arising from their deliberations on this remit."*

On 18th July 1945 the committee approved a scheme for *"reorganising training and control of referees and referees' associations"*. The Secretary, George Graham, was instructed to confer with selected "approved" referees and former referees and to report their views to the next meeting. That meeting with referees was held on 31st July and unanimous approval was given to the scheme. The committee consequently agreed on

8thAugust to recommend the scheme to Council so that immediate effect could be given to it.

A new refereeing structure in Scotland was about to emerge.

Part Three

1945-1946

The New Structure
Although appointed by Council in December 1944, the Committee on Coaching etc. did not meet until July 1945. Yet, at that meeting, the committee approved the scheme for implementation and agreed, at its next meeting in August, to recommend its adoption to Council. The prime architect in the preparation of the proposals was the SFA Secretary, George Graham, the ideal person to fulfill this task. Appointed Secretary in 1928, he would have been entirely in tune with the progression of football's development and keenly aware as to what required to be done. He would have been conscious of the growing pressure being exerted by the SFL during the 1930's to improve refereeing (the SFL had made a proposal in this respect in 1943 as part of the early stages of the overall reconstruction project) and would have been aware too of the needs of refereeing to better serve the game.

The recommendations which were approved by Council are hugely significant in the context of Scottish refereeing and fully merit being set out in their entirety:-

"That local referees' associations should be set up in 8 districts in Scotland as follows:
1. *Aberdeenshire and North of Scotland*
2. *Angus and Perthshire*
3. *Fifeshire*
4. *East of Scotland*
5. *Stirlingshire*
6. *Glasgow,   Lanarkshire,   Dunbartonshire   and Renfrewshire*
7. *Ayrshire*
8. *South of Scotland*

The organisation in each of these areas will formulate their own Constitution and appoint their own Office-Bearers, but both Constitutions and Office-Bearers must be submitted to the SFA for approval.

Each Referees' Association shall have power –
   a)   to conduct classes of instruction
   b)   to examine candidates

c) *to issue diplomas after practical experience and experience and examination on the field of play and approval by SFA supervisor*

The SFA will appoint one or more supervisors in each district. These supervisors will be the liaison between the SFA and the Referees' Associations. Their duties will be –

a) *to ensure that proper facilities are available for classes of instruction;*
b) *to provide uniformity of examinations;*
c) *to approve referees for admission to the SFA list of referees, after report by referees' associations;*
d) *to make arrangements for physical training of referees on the SFA official list and to see that referees attend. Attendance registers must be kept and examined by Supervisors;*
e) *to arrange "refresher" examinations when considered desirable;*
f) *to notify SFA of any referee who fails to attend his training or otherwise fails to keep himself fit.*

It will be the duty of supervisors to see that training facilities are adequate. If it is necessary to incur expense for obtaining facilities, they will seek approval from this Association who will defray all approved expenditure.

Supervisors will have the right to attend any instruction class in their own areas.

Supervisors will have a quarterly conference at a suitable centre. Expenses attending these Conferences will be met by the SFA.

There will be a Summer school at a suitable centre open to all referees where lectures and discussions and interchange of ideas can take place under the supervisors and other officials. The SFA will make arrangements for the Course and the supervisors will arrange the programme of lectures and discussions. The SFA will meet the expenses of their Supervisors.

The services of Supervisors will be voluntary. Only men of known enthusiasm and integrity will be appointed. They should not be members of a Referees' Association but must have long practical experience in refereeing."

George Graham's meeting with referees and former referees on 31st July was with those who had been identified as prospective Supervisors. Gaining their agreement to be part of the proposed scheme, Graham submitted their names to the Committee on Coaching etc. meeting on 8th August to have their appointments confirmed.

The Supervisors appointed were:-

1. Aberdeen and North of Scotland – Peter Craigmyle
2. Angus and Perthshire – Tom Small
3. Fifeshire – Charles Brodie
4. East of Scotland (2) –Neil Kilgour and Andrew Watt
5. Stirlingshire –David Turner
6. Glasgow, Lanarkshire, Dunbartonshire and Renfrewshire (4) – Bobby Calder, James Craig, Willie Livingstone, and Willie Webb
7. Ayrshire – Bert Benzie
8. South of Scotland – Andrew Young

The minutes record the benefits which were expected from the new structure:-

1. *The SFA for the first time will take a share in the work of Referees' Associations.*
2. *Local bodies will have self-government in all domestic matters. They will also have easy yet direct access to the SFA through the Supervisors and their quarterly conferences.*
3. *Physical training for referees has been non-existent unless those who cared to make their own arrangements, which may or may not have met the desired end.*
4. *It will not matter whether or not an approved referee attends meetings, so long as he attends to his training. Referees will not feel as they are being over-governed.*
5. *The Supervisors will be advisers in all practical questions and there will be uniformity of control. If they do their work properly, the Supervisors will be a great power for good in the control of matches.*
6. *The Summer School will provide an opportunity for the leaders of the game and others to meet referees and have open discussions."*

Given that there was a gap of eight months between the Committee on Coaching's formation and its first meeting, it would have been an enormous task to carry out all the discussions needed to get people on board with what was being proposed and to reach the stage of presenting the scheme to the Committee. The minutes of the meeting are entirely silent as to the background work which was undertaken.

Most significantly, there is a complete absence of any reference to the SFRA in the proposals. It can only be speculated as to the possible scenarios which may have unfolded – was the SFRA approached on the proposals?; if so, did any dialogue take place with the SFRA about the possibility of it being recognised by the SFA as part of the new scheme?; if negotiations were held, did they break down due to the positions adopted by either party?; at which point did the SFA declare that it was going to set up its own Referees' Associations?; did the SFA seek to bypass the SFRA at any stage of any negotiations to go directly to the SFRA membership? There is also no reference in the minutes to the transfer of referees from the SFRA to the new Referees' Associations being set up under the SFA, a movement which had to happen to enable the List to be populated by experienced referees. After all, at this time, the SFA did not have any referees of its "own". It seems likely that a very strong and persuasive setting out of what was expected to happen must have been presented to the SFRA membership – that transferring to the new SFA Referees' Associations was a prerequisite of maintaining a place on, and being admitted to, the SFA List. There can be no doubt that the SFA's plan and intention was to supplant the SFRA entirely and for it to control refereeing in Scotland.

Of the twelve Supervisors appointed at the start of the season, ten were active referees. Six were Class 1 – Peter Craigmyle, Bert Benzie, Bobby Calder, Willie Livingstone and Willie Webb. Four were at Class 2 – Nicol Kilgour, Andrew Watt, Charles Brodie, Andrew Young and David Turner. The former referees were Tom Small and James Craig. Small had to resign in January 1946 due to work commitments and was replaced by Andrew Donaldson, another former referee. Over the following few seasons, the active referees quickly retired with Turner being the last Supervisor to operate as an active referee in season 1949-50 when he was at Class 3B.

The First Season of Operation
With the new structure now in place, busy times lay ahead for the Supervisors' Committee and it quickly set to work. The first meeting was held on Friday 19th October 1945 at 11.00am in the then SFA Offices in Carlton Place, Glasgow. It was agreed that the Chair would be occupied on an alphabetical rotation. Brodie chaired the meeting. George Graham was in attendance to provide an expert guiding hand. Numerous areas of refereeing business were addressed.

Reports were made on the inauguration of all of the Referees' Associations with the exception of South of Scotland RA (later confirmed in December). Constitutions and lists of Office Bearers were to be submitted to the SFA within 14 days of the meeting.

Reports were made in regard to arrangements made for instruction classes for trainee referees. Press announcements to advertise these classes were to be made once arrangements were confirmed to the SFA. Authority was given for the purchase of magnetic boards, with a diagram of the field of play, for use at the training classes.

The Supervisors reported on arrangements made for physical training. Permission was given for training to be held at SFL football grounds on nights when players were not there. The SFA confirmed that any necessary expenses incurred would be covered.

Given the scale of the new system, it was not surprising that some adjustments required to be made fairly quickly. It was soon realised that the association covering Glasgow, Lanarkshire, Dunbartonshire and Renfrewshire was too large. As a consequence, by December, Lanarkshire had been formed as an association in its own right. On the recommendation of the Supervisors, the Referee Committee appointed Bob Carruthers, a Class 1 referee, as Supervisor to Lanarkshire RA.

The Referee Committee readily agreed to delegate authority to the Supervisors to re-grade the List. This was another huge milestone in the history of refereeing in Scotland. This put in place the last building block of the new structure – that the compilation of the List was to be the responsibility of former referees and that their recommendations would be submitted to the Referee Committee. With the Referee Committee being composed of representatives of clubs, leagues and associations, a clear separation of duties was created. The Supervisors were to operate below the Referee Committee and report to it.

An Examination Sub-Committee was appointed to compile an Examination Paper, the Key Answer Paper and a Guide for Marking for use by all associations. The Examination Paper was approved in December and a Refresher Examination paper approved in January.

It was agreed that successful candidates of the examination should be given a Certificate of Acceptance and that referees who become Class 1 should receive a National Diploma. Later in the season a basic but important principle was established – that to sit the examination, a candidate had to attend the training class. Another important decision was agreed in January – that referees who passed the examination would not automatically be admitted to the List but were to apply to the SFA for potential inclusion.

A suggestion from Craigmyle that the services, free of charge, of young trainee referees could be offered to minor associations to give them experience, was approved by the committee.

In similar vein, the Scottish Reserve League accepted a proposal that trainee referees be used as linesmen in matches. The Supervisors were asked to make such appointments to matches in their areas. The Scottish Central Junior League was approached with the same offer, which led to a meeting of a number of Supervisors with various Junior bodies to explain the scheme.

A textbook of Instructions was prepared for referees for distribution for the following season. The Football Association's Referees' Chart formed the basis of the book with the Scottish version being developed in "*simple terms*". The SFA still thought it appropriate to obtain a further supply of The Football Association's Referees' Chart for distribution.

A regular Bulletin for referees on matters of interest was introduced.

The Referee Committee gave permission for the Supervisors to be provided with a card to enable them to attend matches of all grades. All the Affiliated National Associations were requested to recognise these cards.

The committee addressed with the Scottish Reserve League reports of referees being appointed to its matches who were not included in the List.

It was decided in February that passing the examination was crucial to being accepted into membership of one of the Referees' Associations, no matter how *"proficient the candidate might be at practical work"*.

Plans to hold a "Summer School" unfortunately came to naught, despite Craigmyle's best efforts to find an appropriate venue. The intention had been to have a maximum attendance of 60 (including Supervisors), with small quotas from each Referees' Association attending.

In May, the Supervisors requested the Secretary to write to the Highland League suggesting that, once the League resumed, the minimum fee payable should be one guinea (£1.10) (plus usual expenses) as the fee hitherto was regarded as being inadequate. The same issue subsequently arose with other leagues. Over the next few years, the Supervisors initiated correspondence with a number of football bodies in regard to fees and expenses, fighting the corner for referees.

Part Four

1946-1988

Referee Supervisors

Establishing the System

The minutes of the Committee on Coaching etc. record that *"only men of known enthusiasm and integrity"* and who *"have long practical experience in refereeing"* would be appointed as Supervisors. George Graham carried out a sterling job in identifying those for appointment. His task was not easy, particularly as the pool of potential candidates would have been restricted in the aftermath of the war. This was reflected in the fact that 10 of the 12 selected were still active referees at the time. His knowledge of the individuals was key to their selection and he would have been persuasive in selling the role to be performed. The longer term vision of the worth of the new structure outweighed the fact that the majority of the Supervisors were still active. It was anticipated that their refereeing careers would end within a few seasons and that would then enable them to focus fully on their supervisory roles. And so it proved, with the last active referee retiring at the end of season 1949-50. An exception was Willie Livingstone, who resigned as a Supervisor in November 1949 to continue for a couple more seasons as a Class 1 referee. He was re-appointed a Supervisor in 1959.

It was established at the outset that Supervisors should not be members of a Referees' Association. This was to ensure independence from an association, to enable the Supervisor to act as the "SFA's man" and to provide a guiding hand as and when required. Referees who came to be appointed as a Supervisor for their "own" association would undoubtedly have had great loyalty to it but none the less would have fully understood the role they were required to perform. They provided wise counsel to their associations on countless occasions.

The attributes of a good Supervisor were loyalty and commitment to the refereeing movement, to the association to which they were appointed and, most importantly, to the SFA. The Supervisors routinely deferred to the SFA Secretary when it came to matters of business given that he was instrumental to their appointment. They also commanded great respect within their associations although, on occasions, there would be exceptions to this.

Doing it for the Good of the Game
The services of Supervisors were on a voluntary basis, although it was confirmed at the start of the system that they would receive expenses in line with the SFA's Referee Tariff for carrying out their duties.

In 1952 the Referee Committee, appreciating their contributions, approved a suggestion from the Supervisors that some form of honorarium might be paid to them. It recommended to the Finance Committee that £50 be granted to each Supervisor. However, before it could be considered by the Finance Committee, the Supervisors, remarkably, withdrew their suggestion. The background to this change of heart is not known but it did not affect their service for the "good of the game".

Terms of Appointment
A system in regard to the duration of Supervisors' appointments emerged in October 1948 when the Referee Committee accepted proposals from the Supervisors. From the commencement of season 1948-49 one third of the Supervisors were appointed for a period of one year only, a further third for a period of two years and the remainder for a period of three years. When these periods, and any subsequent periods of re-appointment expired, the question of re-appointment for a further period of three years was to be considered and decided by the SFA. The system was put into operation and at the May 1949 meeting those Supervisors who had been on one year appointments were appointed for a further three years.

Probationary appointments were introduced in 1969 when Frank Scott was appointed to Renfrewshire RA on a two-year probationary basis. This style of appointment came into regular use for some years. It was a way to ensure that the SFA was content with the way the Supervisor was discharging his duties before confirming the appointment on a permanent basis. It was also to show that appointments were not guaranteed to be permanent.

A Turnover of Supervisors

The first few seasons of the new structure saw a turnover in Supervisors due to a variety of circumstances. The commitment required to be given to the role was certainly a factor for some, with Small's resignation as the Angus & Perthshire RA Supervisor being an early example in January 1946.

Nicol Kilgour, a Supervisor for the East of Scotland RA, was one of four resignations during 1948. A linesman in the 1938 Scottish Cup Semi-Final, Kilmarnock v. Rangers, he went on to become Chairman of Heart of Midlothian FC and a member of the SFA Council in 1960. At the time of his death in October 1964, he was the SFA's 2nd Vice President, Chairman of the International and Selection Committee and was serving on UEFA's Non Amateur and Professional Committee. He is certainly one individual who made a significant contribution to football in the various roles he held.

Changes to appointments happened fairly frequently over the years, due to resignations (for a variety of reasons, mostly business), deaths (sadly) and a number of appointments being terminated.

Identifying Supervisors

Finding suitable candidates to appoint as a Supervisor was not always a straightforward task. The pool to pick from was never large.

In the early years of the system, the Supervisors were tasked with recommending candidates when replacements were needed. There was a gradual change over time as the SFA Secretary took greater control in conjunction with Jack Mowat. Unless the circumstances were particularly difficult at the time, the SFA was always aware of potential candidates and also those who were deemed not suitable for appointment. Being appointed a Supervisor was coveted by many referees, although many others had no interest due to the demands of the role. Candidates were indentified with care, although there was always a risk with an appointment.

In some instances, a candidate would stand out quite easily although the timing of a vacancy was crucial. A suitable person might not always be available at the right time. Generally, those

42

appointed as a Supervisor had served on the List. It was certainly an advantage to have been a Class 1 referee as that brought a degree of credibility in assessing referees. There was not always going to be a suitable former Class 1 referee available for a supervisory appointment in many of the associations, particularly in those areas away from Scotland's conurbations. Often, referees who had served as a Class 3B, or who had reached Class 2, were identified for the role. There were times when the choice had to be made from referees serving on the List.

Some associations experienced a relatively fast turnover in Supervisors which caused issues in identifying suitable replacements as the pool had been diminished by the previous appointments. Having a long-serving Supervisor in place was a great benefit for the SFA and indeed the association in question. The worth of having continuity in football can never be underestimated and the same applies in the world of refereeing. Having a safe pair of hands on the tiller at an association has been a blessing for the SFA in many respects over the years.

On rare occasions, someone who had never served on the List was appointed as a Supervisor. One such appointment occurred when Ian Barbour was appointed in 1976 to Glasgow RA. He had taken up refereeing after playing amateur football, officiating at that level before being appointed as Secretary of the Scottish Amateur FA in 1974. Barbour was a person of integrity and very diligent in his approach. He served refereeing well in his 16 seasons in the role.

Termination of Appointments

Appointing a Supervisor was not always guaranteed to be a success. The SFA had to resolve problems when they arose. There was an early example in 1953 when the Referee Committee decided that it would be in the best interests of Edinburgh & District RA for James Calder to be replaced by a Supervisor acceptable to them, which suggests that a serious rift had emerged. Calder's appointment was terminated.

The Supervisors were informed in 1970 that the Referee Committee had decided to terminate the appointments of Willie Livingstone at Glasgow RA and Tom Shirley at Ayrshire RA.

There is no record, however, of such a decision in the committee's minutes. The tactic of "smoke and mirrors" to disguise who was controlling business was put to good effect on a regular basis on a variety of issues. Channels of communication operated behind the scenes away from committee meetings and there can be little doubt that there would have been good grounds to have come to a decision to replace a Supervisor.

In August 1971, the appointment of Bill Morrice at Aberdeen & District RA was terminated after just three years in the post. This was followed two months later by the removal of Joe Oates at Fife RA. He had been identified as the culprit for a leakage of information in connection with that season's List.

A sad affair in Moray & Banff RA in season 1986-87 relating to examinations led to the dismissal of its Supervisor, Campbell MacIntosh. He had been complicit in passing a key answer paper over to the class coach.

Requests for an Additional Supervisor

Referees' Associations were, from time to time, wont to make a request to the Referee Committee for an additional Supervisor to be appointed. Edinburgh & District RA did so unsuccessfully in 1954 and 1960. Such an appointment was declined as *"not being necessary"* in the first instance and, in the second, it was held that two Supervisors were *"adequate to cover the needs of the membership"*.

Aberdeen & District RA succeeded in its request for an additional Supervisor in 1957. It was a very logical request given the association's huge geographical area. Jim MacKay was appointed to cover the *"North of Scotland area"*, a massive territory in its own right. Two years later, North of Scotland RA was formed.

Angus & Perthshire RA requested, to no avail, an additional Supervisor during season 1976-77. That same season, Jim McMillan asked that he be given an assistant to help him in North of Scotland RA, but this was declined. Another request from Aberdeen & District RA was refused on the standard basis that there was already adequate coverage of the area.

Unattached Supervisors

An exception to the standard convention of appointing a Supervisor to an association was made in November 1962 when George Mitchell and Donald Kyle were appointed on an "unattached" basis. Mitchell had retired as a Class 1 referee at the end of the previous season and Kyle resigned as a Class 3B official to take up the position. Their appointments were rare evidence of the SFA, at that time, wishing to capitalise on their expertise and knowledge for the benefit of referees. With Jack Mowat having just become the Chairman, he would have had an influential role in their appointments. In their "unattached" capacity, it is fair to say that Mitchell and Kyle were the first "Referee Observers" as their duties effectively related only to assessing referees given that he did not have a role with an association.

Kyle was appointed as a Supervisor for Glasgow in 1965 and Mitchell took over as the Stirlingshire RA Supervisor on the retirement of David Turner in 1967. After 22 seasons, Turner was the last of the original Supervisors to step down from the role.

Appointments

During season 1958-59, the Supervisors were advised that the Referee Committee had decided that there should be changes to personnel. Peter Craigmyle had resigned as a Supervisor at the end of the previous season and his departure presented the opportunity to freshen things up. During the year, four new Supervisors were appointed. Two appointments were replacement appointments with two others being removed from their positions.

Jack Mowat was appointed as a Supervisor for Glasgow RA in 1960 after retiring as a referee. To mark his refereeing career, a presentation was made to him at an SFA Council meeting by the President, Bob Kelly. Kelly expressed the SFA's pleasure that Mowat had accepted an appointment as a Supervisor "*in which capacity he would undoubtedly make a valuable contribution to the game*". Never a truer word was spoken as Mowat became the dominant figure in Scottish refereeing for the next 30 years.

It took a year to replace Willie Livingstone at Glasgow RA, the SFA being content to wait for Tom Wharton to retire as a referee in 1971 before appointing him to the vacancy.

The retiral of Jimmy Stewart after 26 years service at the end of season 1974-75 led to the appointment of Drew Fleming, who resigned as a Class 3B official to take up the position at Glasgow RA. At 35 years of age, he was the youngest man to be appointed as a Supervisor and went on to serve the SFA and the referee movement with great distinction for many years.

The power of the SFA Secretary was demonstrated in 1978 when Ernie Walker told the Supervisors that he was making new appointments for Renfrewshire RA and Edinburgh & District RA. Barbour was switched from Glasgow RA to cover Renfrewshire RA and Bill Mullan was appointed to Edinburgh & District RA.

Commitment to the cause

The SFA has been well served by its Supervisors and many of them gave unstinting service over many years.

Jack Mowat stepped in temporarily as a Supervisor at Ayrshire RA in 1970 until a replacement for Tom Shirley was appointed. That situation lasted for 12 seasons, all the more remarkable for the fact that Mowat continued to operate as a Supervisor for Glasgow RA. This circumstance shows that either there were no ideal candidates in Ayrshire RA over that period or Mowat liked carrying out the role, in which case it is a real demonstration of his commitment to refereeing.

When Joe Oates' time as a Supervisor for Fife RA was ended in 1971, the four Supervisors of the neighbouring associations operated on a rota basis to provide cover at the association until his successor was appointed. They did this for four years until Archie Webster was appointed. He provided excellent service to the SFA for the next 25 years.

On top of his role at Glasgow RA, Tom Wharton acted as Renfrewshire RA's Supervisor for two seasons from 1976-77 following the termination of Willie Elliott's appointment.

George Mitchell was given a presentation by his colleagues in December 1987 to mark his 25th year as a Supervisor and his 50th in the refereeing movement. Bill Quinn, a Dumfries man and a long-serving Class 3B official, had moved to Stewarton in Ayrshire in the early 1960's. Appointed as the South of Scotland RA Supervisor in 1977, he faithfully undertook a 122 mile round trip at least once a week to carry out his duties. He was succeeded by Louis Thow of Ayr – he had a journey of 120 miles.

Robbie Harrold resigned from the List as a Class 3B referee to become the Supervisor for Moray & Banff RA when it was formed in 1981. After serving the association for two seasons, he was switched to cover North of Scotland RA following the death of Jim McMillan. He was there for two seasons until a job move from Elgin took him to Aberdeen. He was a Supervisor for Aberdeen & District RA for 22 seasons until acting as a Referee Observer for four seasons.

Every Supervisor gave an inordinate amount of time to performing the role. There was a constant demand on their time, juggling full-time jobs with the role, attending their association's meetings and training, attending matches to assess referees and attending meetings at national level. Their commitment was undoubted.

Referee Supervisors' Committees

The Chairman

For the Supervisors' meetings in season 1945-46, the Chairman was elected on a rota basis in alphabetical order, with Charles Brodie acting as the first Chairman. This system operated for the first season and a half of the committee's existence, with 12 Supervisors taking it in turns to act as Chairman. Such a method, however, could not be sustained for practical purposes and the need for a permanent Chairman was eventually realised. Peter Craigmyle was appointed in February 1947 to act as the Chairman through to the end of the season. He was re-elected as the Chairman for the next two seasons.

Andrew Donaldson served as Chairman for season 1949-50 and was succeeded by Bob Carruthers for season 1950-51. Craigmyle returned as Chairman for season 1951-52 and held the position until he resigned in April 1959 when he was *"warmly thanked for the service and attention given to refereeing over many years".*

Craigmyle's successor as Chairman was John Smillie, a former Class 1 referee who was a Supervisor for Glasgow RA and Lanarkshire RA during the 1950's.

A year after being appointed Vice-Chairman, Jack Mowat became the Chairman following Smillie's death in 1962. A very close bond developed between Mowat and SFA Secretary Willie Allan and with his successor Ernie Walker. There were regular instances of Mowat controlling items of business and exercising the referral of business, particularly points regarding policy, to the Secretary. Equally, tight control was exercised by Allan and Walker over the Supervisors. The importance of refereeing within SFA structures was reflected in the regular attendance at meetings by Allan and Walker throughout their terms of office.

The Chairman also acted as the Chairman of the Sub-Committee/Executive Committee.

Committee Business

The Supervisors' meeting of December 1946 was attended by the Referee Committee Chairman, R. Williamson. This stemmed from the Referee Committee deciding that there should be a closer liaison between the two committees. Williamson was present at a further three meetings during the remainder of the season which brought this liaison to an end. The Referee Committee had wished to keep an eye on proceedings for a period to observe how business was being handled and satisfied itself as to how things were being done.

There was much interest in the new structure and the workings of the Supervisors. Following the February 1947 meeting of the full committee, George Graham wrote to the Supervisors setting out that *"the information relative to the transaction of business at any Sub-Committee or Committee meeting of the Supervisors shall not be conveyed to the press by any member of the Committee but shall be made known to the press through the medium of a minute of each meeting to be conveyed to the press by the Secretary."* It is not known how long such press releases continued. This clear openness of approach was countered somewhat in December 1947 when the committee declined a request from the East of Scotland RA to be issued with a copy of the minutes of the meetings.

Supervisors were expected to report back to their associations on the business of the Supervisors' Committees. This was done in a generalised way with specific details not being conveyed.

Meeting Schedule

The Supervisors met on seven occasions during season 1945-46, with a Monday being the day of choice after the first meeting, the starting time of 3.00pm maintaining a fine football tradition. The best day to hold meetings was debated over the season. Saturday mornings were contemplated briefly but it was ultimately decided that a Friday evening would be the most suitable. With the odd exception down the years, Fridays remained the favoured day. Given the scheduling of meetings, the willingness to take time away from jobs to serve and contribute to refereeing was clearly demonstrated from the outset.

The meeting schedule evolved over the years. Meetings were held on a monthly basis over the early seasons, given the amount of business being dealt with. The frequency of the Sub-Committee meetings declined, however, from eight in season 1947-48 to one in seasons 1950-51 and 1951-52. Over the seasons from 1952-53, there is actually little record of Sub-Committee meetings being held other than the Grading meeting where the List was compiled for the following season.

There was largely a relative balance in the number of full committee and sub-committee meetings during the 1960's – generally there were four full meetings and four Executive Committee meetings each season. In the early to mid-1970's the Executive Committee met only once a season – for the Grading meeting.

By the late 1970's and 1980's a settled pattern emerged to the schedule. The full committee met four times a year – September/October, December, April/May and June. The first meeting was always followed by the Annual Dinner, the meeting in April/May was always held on the eve of the Scottish Cup Final, and the Executive Committee's recommendations on the List were presented at the June meeting. It was not until 1970 that the June meeting was scheduled for the weekend of the Referees' Conference, with it always being held on the Friday afternoon.

The Executive Committee met only twice per year - in February and in late May or early June. Occasionally, another meeting would be arranged depending on business to be dealt with. An important element of the February meeting was that it was always a "stock taking" exercise in regard to the List - discussing those referees who were to come under scrutiny through to the end of the season, either those near the lower end of the assessment markings or those Class 2 referees in the frame for potential promotion. The May-June meeting was the all important Grading meeting when the List was compiled for the following season.

Sub-Committee – Executive Committee: Appointments and Structure

A small Sub-Committee was formed to deal with compiling the List for season 1946-47. The importance of being on the committee was quickly recognised as it did not take long for a fairly predictable point to emerge. A motion that each Referees' Association should be represented on the Sub-Committee was not supported in August 1948 and that was quickly followed at the next meeting with a request that the classification of referees should be done by the full committee rather than the Sub-Committee. That request was refused. These moves were motivated by the thought that it was to the advantage of a Supervisor to be on the Sub-Committee so that he would be well placed to speak up for his "own referees" to the detriment of referees from other associations. Such a belief existed for many years.

The Sub-Committee was appointed each season. By the end of season 1948-49, it was decided that it should consist entirely of non-active referees.

The composition of the Sub-Committee altered gradually over the period to 1954. When it was confirmed for season 1954-55, it was decided that the appointments, other than the Chairman and Vice-Chairman, should be of a defined duration, ranging from one to three seasons, thus mimicking the system then in use for the appointment of each Supervisor. Future appointments to the Sub-Committee would be for a period of three years.

This system operated until season 1958-59 when the committee members, now termed the Office Bearers, were to be appointed each year with no member being permitted to serve more than two consecutive years on the Sub-Committee. The Chairman's appointment was to be for a maximum period of three years.

The system reverted back in 1960 to the earlier tiered duration of appointments. It was also decided that no Office Bearer should hold position for more than three consecutive seasons.

Change was in the air again during season 1961-62 when the Referee Committee suggested to the Supervisors that a Sub-Committee might be given powers to meet at regular intervals during the season to transact the business, and that the full committee would then meet at less regular intervals. However, the Supervisors took the view that the system in place should be maintained. One minor change was agreed, with it being decided that in future the Chairman, Vice Chairman and the Sub-Committee should be appointed at the first meeting each season rather than at a meeting at the end of a season as had been the practice.

By September 1963, the Supervisors came round to the Referee Committee's view of two seasons earlier. The Sub-Committee was replaced by the Executive Committee. The SFA was requested to appoint five members, with two reserves. All decisions taken by this committee were to be recorded and circulated to members of the full committee. It was agreed that the existing Office Bearers should continue to serve on the Executive Committee. At the full meeting the following month, Jack Mowat announced the appointment by the SFA of the Executive Committee. The appointments to the Executive Committee were to be on a seasonal basis, with appointees being eligible for re-selection.

The Executive Committee was given full powers with exception of grading and Points of Play. In the case of the latter, a decision of the Executive Committee would be referred to the full committee for a final decision within seven days. This reflected the importance that decisions on Points of Play had with the refereeing movement.

In regard to the grading of referees and the compilation of the List, the full committee retained power. The recommendations of the both the previous Sub-Committee and the new Executive Committee had to be presented to the full committee before being submitted to the Referee Committee. These were always open to be changed. The full committee meetings when the List recommendations were presented were always fraught with danger for the Sub-Committee or Executive Committee. There were few years when alterations to the recommendations did not materialise. The full committee could out vote the Sub-Committee or Executive Committee and with some collaboration amongst the ordinary members changes could be forced. The dynamics of these scenarios were an ever-present concern and there were many heated debates when the recommendations regarding the List were considered.

The annual confirmation of the Executive Committee became standard practice from the mid-1960's onwards. Once the SFA announced the composition of the Executive Committee, the elections of the Chairman and Vice-Chairman were made by the Executive Committee members, with the election of the Chairman never up for discussion during the Jack Mowat years. His re-appointment remained a given until he retired in 1990. The position of Vice-Chairman during the 1960's and through to the mid-1970's was held by George Mitchell (2 seasons), Jimmy Stewart (1 season) and Frank Crossley (9 seasons). Following Tom Wharton's appointment to the Executive Committee in June 1975, Crossley did the very honourable thing of expressing his wish to relinquish the position of Vice-Chairman saying he thought it was time for a change. This paved the way for Tom Wharton to take his place as the Vice-Chairman. The two "big beasts" of Scottish refereeing at that time became the main players of the Supervisors. Tensions and politics were never far away from the surface between the two, with regular strong arguments being had from time to time at meetings, but always for the benefit of refereeing and with normal relationships being resumed post-discussion.

Grading Meeting

Right from the start of the supervisory system, this was the key meeting of each season. By the late1960's, the meeting was held in hotels over two days, with the Scores Hotel, St. Andrews being the first such venue in 1968. Providing a pleasant environment for the Grading meetings became a staple part of the process with the SFA recognising that the importance of the work being carried out by the Executive Committee deserved more than a little something back in return. The Executive members appreciated the way the SFA looked after them, by providing a venue which combined some relaxation with the business they conducted. The Queen's Hotel in Largs was the 1969 venue and, with the exception of 1970, the Grading Meeting was held there every year until 1984 when it transferred to the Seamill Hydro. From the mid-1970's the meeting ran from the Friday evening through to Sunday lunchtime, with a focus being given to the preparations of the Referees' Conference once the List had been dealt with.

Many heated discussions took place at the Grading meeting, as the members argued the case for the referees to be promoted, downgraded or deleted. Alliances were formed between members to give support to each other to achieve their purposes. Some decisions would be relatively straightforward whilst others would be strongly debated and argued over. Tension filled the air at the crucial moments leading up to a vote or decision on a referee. The means of eliminating a candidate from consideration was brutal at times – a poor mark or comment in a Supervisor's report from the season before would sometimes be used to rule someone out. The casting vote of the Chairman was called upon to decide an issue on more than one occasion.

Reflecting the way business was conducted, there was a period in the 1970's when the recording of dissent (not being in agreement with the decision taken) by a member came into vogue. The Grading meeting of 1976 was particularly fractious. 13 instances of dissent were recorded in total at the meeting. Mitchell and Wharton recorded dissent against a decision not to downgrade a Class 1 referee, Mowat recorded dissent against the promotion of a Class 2 referee, and nine dissents in total were recorded against four Class 2 referees who were not promoted, Mowat being one of the dissenters in regard to one of the referees. The arguments continued at the full meeting two weeks later. Decisions of the Executive Committee were overturned resulting in two of the Class 2 referees who had failed to be promoted at the Grading meeting, now being promoted together with another Class 2 referee who had not even featured in the decisions at the Grading meeting. This referee had been recommended for promotion to Class 1 the year before but that had not been approved by the full committee. The power of the full committee over the Executive Committee worked both ways – at times it could scupper the work of the Executive but on other occasions it could work out in favour of those members who had lost the argument at the Grading meeting. Mowat would have been happy at a Class 2 referee finally getting promoted after losing out at the Grading meeting.

Over the next few years, Tom Wharton recorded dissent on numerous occasions. He was a dogged defender and proponent of his own referees and this was the basis of many of his arguments against other referees. In 1981, the Executive Committee was moved to express its concern at his having recorded dissent on a number of occasions, feeling that this could only have a divisive effect on the committee. The members were wary about Wharton's approach to discussions for a long number of years.

In 1977, consideration was given by the Supervisors to the timing of the Grading meeting relative to the subsequent meetings of the Referee Committee and the SFA Council. The view reached was that "*there seemed little suitable alternative to the current arrangements*". These were tied in to the formation of a new Council and new committees each season. This did not happen until the end of May. The Referee Committee met in July to approve the List. A factor not mentioned at all in the discussion was the Referees' Conference. The discussion groups at Conference were always based on the classifications of the season which had just ended, not those which would apply in the new season. Ayrshire RA had raised this point in 1973 - proposing that confirmation of the List be made earlier so that the Discussion Groups could be formed in line with the following season's List. The proposal was turned down in view of the administrative difficulties which were involved. It was not to be for more than another 20 years before the List was approved prior to the Conference and discussion groups could be arranged on the basis of the next season's classifications, which obviously made all-round good sense.

Annual Dinner

The Annual Dinner was introduced in the late 1950's and followed the first full committee meeting of the season. The hosting of this Dinner by the SFA for the Supervisors was a means of thanking them for all the work they carried out on its behalf. In 1971, the Executive Committee, responding to an enquiry made by Willie Allan, thought that the Dinner should be discontinued. However, the full committee was opposed to this suggestion and the Dinner carried on for a further two decades. A pianist was always hired to entertain those present at the Dinner, providing background music during the meal.

From the mid-1970's onwards, the Annual Dinner, and the preceding meeting, was regularly attended by the SFA President and Chairman of the Referee Committee and occasionally by other Office Bearers, as a mark of recognition by them of the work which the Supervisors carried out on behalf of the SFA.

Scottish Cup Final Luncheon

Another annual Supervisors' function provided by the SFA was the Luncheon held before the Scottish Cup Final. It was held to honour the officials appointed to the Cup Final with the officials present. Eating a three course meal less than three hours before a match was never the best preparation for any referee and many just picked at their meal.

Referee Committee

The Referee Committee met around eight to ten times per season depending on business to be considered. There was much on the disciplinary front to contend with. The main elements of referee business occurred twice a season –

receiving and approving the Supervisors' recommendations on the List in the summer, and the mid-season review with the Supervisors. Approving the Referee Tariff for each season was an annual task. Dealing with complaints from clubs was another regular feature of its business, along with the formality of being notified of any resignations from the List. Beyond these matters, other referee-focused business was included on the meeting agendas as and when required.

The committee was renamed the Disciplinary & Referee Committee in 1977 to better reflect the nature of the majority of its business – dealing with misconduct in the game.

Financial Cost

The creation of the supervisory system, together with financial support provided to the Referees' Associations in the later years of this period, brought with it an increase in the financial costs of the SFA. This was conscious decision by the SFA and a price worth paying to provide the necessary support framework for refereeing in Scotland - covering the costs of venues for meetings, training classes, physical training, Referee Supervisors' travelling expenses and the Summer School/Referees' Conference. For many years, in the SFA's accounts, costs were recorded under committees. The costs under the Referee Committee were generally much higher than for the other Standing Committees. The Referee Committee's only "competition" was from the International & Selection Committee, which occasionally had greater costs. It was not unusual in some years for the Referee Committee's cost to be greater than other the combined costs of the other committees and Council.

Referees' Associations

The Referees' Associations have played an integral part in the SFA's refereeing structure since their formation in 1945. Their role has been invaluable – attracting new recruits into refereeing for the training classes, holding monthly meetings and weekly physical training sessions, enabling bonds to be formed by referees and facilitating the sharing of knowledge and expertise amongst the memberships. The importance of the social side of refereeing cannot be under-estimated, as this strengthens the friendship and camaraderie amongst referees, with various social events organised on a regular basis by the associations. Referees have always been very loyal to their association.

The Development of the Referees' Associations
Following the creation of the new system, it quickly became evident that the structure of the association covering the wider Glasgow area was too large. Thus, Lanarkshire RA was made a separate association in December 1945. A further change in the west of Scotland came in 1948 when Renfrewshire RA was created, leaving the Glasgow and Dunbartonshire association to be styled as Glasgow & District RA. Within that association, the Supervisors agreed that, with the approval of the Glasgow & District RA, referees in Dunbartonshire should establish a sub-branch and hold meetings in Clydebank.

The formation of Edinburgh & District RA was approved during season 1950-51, replacing the former East of Scotland RA. A sub-committee of the Supervisors' Committee had been set up to deal with matters involving the East of Scotland RA and, by the end of the season, the constitution and rules of the new association were approved. Edinburgh & District RA submitted a letter to the Supervisors *"professing full support to the Supervisors' Committee and to its Area Supervisors"*.

The Aberdeen & North of Scotland RA was, in terms of geographical area, the largest of all of the associations. Overseeing and sustaining activities in the area was always going to be challenging for any Supervisor and the officials of the association. It was no surprise that a separate association, the North of Scotland RA, came into being in 1959. Issues regarding the size of each of those associations remained, evidenced in the case of Aberdeen & District RA when it received approval from the Referee Committee to change its name later that year to Aberdeen and District Referees' Association (incorporating Orkney & Shetland).

The last change to the associations came in 1981 when Moray & Banff RA was created out of the North of Scotland RA to serve the geographical area of the same name. Issues had emerged regarding the arrangements for the holding of meetings between the two centres of Inverness and Elgin. The referees of the Moray & Banff area made a case for becoming an association in its own right and won the approval of the SFA. The smallest of the 12 associations, it has worked hard to sustain itself and develop and, like all the other associations, it has provided an excellent service for the football played in its area.

Referees on Lewis & Harris were given permission to form a group to affiliate to North of Scotland RA in 1977.

Referees in Orkney tried to form a new association in 1981. After receiving information on the likely size of the proposed association, the Supervisors decided that this did not justify approval and that Orkney should remain within Aberdeen & District RA. Close contact is maintained with referees in Orkney and Shetland by the Aberdeen & District RA and regular visits are made to both sets of islands.

The associations are formally titled SFA Referees' followed by the individual name of the association in brackets –SFA Referees' (Glasgow). This style resulted from a suggestion made by Glasgow RA in 1952. The associations were advised that this style should be uniformly adopted. In the years that followed, Fifeshire RA changed to Fife RA in 1953 and Stirlingshire & Clackmannanshire RA dropped the "Clackmannanshire" part of its name in 1982.

When the structure of local government in Scotland was reorganised into regions in 1975, the SFA Executive & General Purposes Committee, in considering the impact of this restructuring might have on football, came to the view there did not seem to be any reason why the associations should not continue to function under their existing titles.

Constitutions

The creation of the associations brought with it a need to ensure that there was a commonality between all the respective constitutions. Once the constitutions were approved following the formation of the associations, any proposed alterations had to be submitted for the consideration of the Supervisors.

Proposals were considered from time to time – some were approved and some rejected. Whilst approvals of changes to the constitutions were never recorded within the minutes of the Supervisors' meetings, unsuccessful proposals occasionally were, particularly in the early years of the system. In 1949, approval was not given to the East of Scotland RA regarding a proposed alteration to the annual subscription and enabling referees to make a claim for payment in connection with matches being postponed due to the ground being declared unplayable. That same year, Aberdeen & North of Scotland RA failed to get approval for a fee to be charged to trainees. In 1952, Angus & Perthshire RA failed for a second time to gain approval for the introduction of a social fund levy on members.

Over the years, the approval of changes to constitutions slowly disappeared from view in the minutes. By 1970 however, after consideration of proposed alterations submitted by Angus & Perthshire RA and Fife RA, Willie Allan drew attention to discrepancies which existed between the various constitutions in certain areas which he considered should be uniform. The Executive Committee asked Allan to further investigate the issue and report back. However, such a report was never forthcoming and the divergence of the associations' constitutions continued. The subject of achieving uniformity of the constitutions was referred to periodically down the years but it was considered too big a beast to poke and was left untouched. The situation would not be addressed until the mid-2010's during the course of a review of the associations.

Membership Issues

The Supervisors gave great consideration to the important matter of the membership criteria of the associations. Their decisions were disseminated to the associations as and when required. Equally, many of the associations regularly sought clarification from the Supervisors on particular issues which had arisen.

One straightforward decision was taken in 1946 when the Supervisors decided that "*an official of any club cannot be allowed to hold office or membership in a Referees' Association*". This circumstance was further strengthened in

1948 when it was confirmed that club directors or officials should not be eligible for appointment as Honorary Office-Bearers of an Association.

A uniform application procedure for membership of an association was introduced in season 1947-48.

In 1960, arising from a letter from Edinburgh & District RA, the Supervisors recommended that it be left to each association to decide the minimum age of trainees wishing to attend training classes and that the same should apply to membership of an association. Where young referees were accepted into membership, it was further recommended that they should be accepted at a reduced membership fee, and that they should be indicated as *"under age referees"* in handbooks. It was understandable, due to such decisions being taken and the free rein being given to the associations to decide on such matters, that divergence in their constitutions resulted.

The Supervisors were always very protective, for good reason, of the required standards for membership when dealing with enquiries from associations. The need to undertake and pass the Entrance Examination was always a prerequisite for anyone returning or coming to Scotland from abroad who had a refereeing qualification gained elsewhere. If some time had elapsed between an individual ceasing to referee and wishing to return, passing the Entrance Examination was necessary to ensure an up to date knowledge of the Laws of the Game before being allowed to join an association.

The approach taken in these matters meant that it was impossible for any referee who moved to Scotland and who had been operating at a high level in another National Association, to progress to the List. In such cases, the Supervisors and the SFA passed the buck to the relevant association for it to make a decision on membership. This approach also meant that such referees coming to Scotland were restricted by age conditions and had to go through the same process as all other referees who were striving to get on to the List.

Secretaries' Meetings

Meetings of associations' Secretaries began to be held following a suggestion made by Glasgow RA in 1947. These meetings were held regularly over the years, and provided a very useful forum for the SFA to maintain links with the associations, particularly in trying to establish a common administrative framework. The associations' Secretaries fulfilled important roles and the part they have played in the organisation of Scottish refereeing cannot be under-estimated. Presidents of associations would come and go during their terms of office but a long-serving secretary was invaluable in providing a stable and constant presence within an association, dealing with all sorts of administration in the running of its business. The longest serving was Bill Mullan who was Secretary of Fife RA and then Edinburgh & District RA for a total of 21 consecutive seasons from 1957-58. Frank Crossley acted as the Lanarkshire RA Secretary for 12 seasons from 1950-51. Being a Secretary was long viewed as a good career move on the part of a referee seeking to demonstrate his commitment to the refereeing movement and many a Class 1 referee held the role down the years. Moreover, having been a Secretary was also a good foundation for being appointed as a Supervisor. Over the years, 16 Supervisors served as an association secretary. The knowledge gained by being a Secretary was an invaluable asset, as it gave a complete insight into the running of an association.

There were periods when Secretaries' meetings were not held, with the prevailing view of the Supervisors being that there was little purpose until such time as there was sufficient business to be dealt with. Convening annual meetings of the Secretaries returned from the mid-to late 1970's. They helped to ensure that a standardised approach was taken in dealing with the administrative issues of the day. There was a mutual benefit to be gained by both parties from such meetings.

Financial Support
From the start of the refereeing structure in 1945, the SFA provided financial support to the associations. Meeting the costs of training facilities and venues for meetings and training classes were the major areas where support was given.

Suspension of Referees
Being autonomous organisations, the associations could take action against their own members and suspensions and expulsions were reported to the SFA from time to time. On occasion, such suspensions impacted on referees who were on the List. During season 1953-54, the Supervisors noted a suspension imposed by Fifeshire RA on a Class 3B official. The official's time on the List came to a close at the end of the season. In 1987, Ayrshire RA's expulsion of a Class 3A referee from its membership automatically resulted in his removal from the List.

Minor Grades Advisory Panel
In 1952, George Graham outlined to the Supervisors a scheme being operated by Glasgow RA in amateur and juvenile leagues for the assessment of referees. The other associations were recommended to introduce a similar scheme. This was the birth of what became known as the Minor Grades Advisory Panel, which became instrumental in the identification of talented referees and assisted in their progress through the various grades of football to reach the point of being considered for admission to the List.

The SFA covered the costs. For season 1952-53, the Finance Committee reimbursed the princely sum of £3 12s 9d (£3.64) to Glasgow RA.

It is not recorded if other associations followed suit with their own schemes as details are scarce within SFA minutes. Lanarkshire RA had a Junior Supervisory Scheme in operation by the mid-1960's and in 1968 North of Scotland RA and Renfrewshire RA gained approval to start their own Junior Supervisory Panels.

In 1973, Edinburgh & District RA appointed a former Listed referee as a Referee Adviser to supervise referees at minor level. Financial assistance was given to the association to cover his expenses. Three years later, the association was given approval to appoint a former Class 1 referee who lived in the Borders as a Referee Advisor for Minor Association and Junior Referees within that area.

Attendance of Delegates at Minor Association Meetings

Soon after their formation, the associations expressed a desire to have a delegate attend meetings of local football associations to represent the interests of refereeing. The Supervisors were against the idea and offered to attend any such meeting themselves. The debate continued until the Referee Committee decided in 1948 that there should not be any exchange of delegates and that its decision was final. The Supervisors held to the position over the next few years, fending off other approaches from associations.

The matter lay dormant until 1977 when the Supervisors reviewed the situation. A change in policy resulted in 1979. The Supervisors decided that referees could attend minor football association meetings in an advisory capacity "*if requested to do so by the minor association and provided that the appointment is made by the local Referees' Association and the delegate appointed does not officiate in the association or league at whose meetings he will be in attendance.*" It may have taken a long time to reach this position but the use of referee delegates at such meetings has proved very successful at building relationships between associations and the minor associations in their area whom their members serve.

Social Activities

The social side has always played an important part in refereeing, with the position of Social Convenor being an integral role in the associations. The approach taken to dealing with social activities was such that a meeting of the Social Convenors of the associations was held in 1951. Two Supervisors, Willie Easton and David Turner, were sent to the meeting, presumably to keep a watchful eye on proceedings and to provide assistance if required. Dinner Dances, dinners, golf outings, the playing of inter-association football matches and various other activities have been a constant staple of the lives of referees for many years, providing opportunities for camaraderie and friendship.

Proposed Representative Bodies

The relationship between the SFA and the associations has been harmonious and on any occasion where they might not have been, the SFA has always brought its position of power to bear to settle matters back down again. One such issue occurred in 1957 when Glasgow RA, on behalf of all the associations, sought approval for the formation of a National Council of Referees' Associations. The Supervisors were the first port of call for the request and, understandably, they agreed that the matter be passed to the Referee Committee which bluntly *"did not consider that any useful purpose would be served by the formation of such a body, nor would they be prepared to give it recognition."* The thought of having to deal with a unified referee body, rather than separate, and thus weaker, associations was no doubt a prime motivation in refusing to give the proposal the time of day. The continuance of division rather than unity was the SFA's preferred option.

Feelings continued to be held within refereeing that a body was needed to represent them and these surfaced again in 1968. A proposed National Representative Council of Referees sought recognition from the SFA. The traditional conservative nature of the workings of the SFA came to the fore as the Referee Committee took the view that the Council did not have any contribution to make towards improving the standard of refereeing and decided against recognising it.

The Executive Committee discussed the position of the proposed Council. What the nature of these discussions was and what the Supervisors' view on the Council was is not known from the minutes of meetings. If they were in favour in some respects, the Supervisors also had to take account of their own position and standing within the SFA. It was a difficult period for refereeing with pressure being applied to abandon the proposals. By spring, Edinburgh & District RA and Fife RA decided to withdraw from the Council, with the former association taking the decision at its AGM.

The proposed Council stalled at this stage but similar proposals emerged in 1973. Willie Allan addressed the Supervisors on the possible formation of a Referees' National Council and outlined the attitude of the SFA, as he saw it, in relation to such an organisation. He viewed the proposed Council in a negative way and sought the assistance of the Supervisors to quell support for the Council at their associations.

Discussions continued over the next few months. The Supervisors declined an invitation to attend a meeting of Referees' Associations to discuss the proposed formation of a Liaison Committee. By February 1974, however, their position had changed to the extent that Frank Crossley and George Mitchell were appointed to attend a meeting of the Liaison Committee of the associations in March.

Things progressed over the next year and a request for recognition of the Referees' Liaison Committee was submitted to the SFA. In June 1975, the SFA Executive & General Purposes Committee declined to give it recognition. This brought forth a predictable response from the referees. Letters from the proposed Liaison Committee and the Aberdeen, Ayrshire, Fife and Glasgow associations, expressing disappointment that the request had been refused, were submitted to the SFA Executive & General Purposes Committee in October, requesting that it meet with representatives of all the associations to discuss the matter. That request was refused.

The Liaison Committee attempted to seek the assistance of the Supervisors in its cause. However, they considered that, given the SFA's refusal to recognise the Liaison Committee, it would be improper for them to have dealings with it. This position had an important bearing on the likely progress of the proposed committee. A dead end had been reached, with the Supervisors being forced into something of a corner to take the side of the SFA. By the spring of 1976, Edinburgh & District RA intimated that it was severing all connections with the Liaison Committee. The breaking of ranks continued and the Liaison Committee came to an end.

Over a near 20-year period, three attempts by referees, either through the collaboration of associations or a group of referees, to form a representative body for referees had come to nothing. The rigid, inflexible stance of the SFA had prevailed on each occasion. It was the classic "master and servant" situation. Having set up the refereeing structure, the SFA wished to maintain strict control over the refereeing movement to the extent that it did not wish to give approval to any form of grouping of referees beyond the existing structures. It did not wish to deal with a body which would operate similar to a Trades Union and for it to have any possibility of collective bargaining on a variety of matters, most notably fees and expenses. A good number of the associations had regularly submitted requests for increases to the fees for the SFA's Cup Competitions and travelling expenses. Normally, the SFA found it easy to bat such requests away, though, on the odd occasion, there was an acceptance that increases were appropriate. Referees, on the one hand, would have cause over the years to complain about how things were for them and how they might be treated and regarded by football but, on the other hand, there would have been a realisation that causing any difficulty would result in a problem being created for them. Effectively, the role they had was subservient to the SFA and they were reliant on the SFA, and the refereeing system, for their place in the game. That was understood fully by the SFA in its relationship with referees, hence the rigid approach taken in not recognising the requests from referees to form a unified body. It wanted to control refereeing through the system it had set up – the Supervisors and the Referees' Associations. Change can only take place at a pace which any organisation allows, and the SFA was a conservative body for much of this period. The scenario encapsulates the view that referees were part of the game, but apart from it.

Scottish Football Referees' Association

Early Issues
In the early period of the new structure's operation, issues were experienced, unsurprisingly, with the existence of two Referees' Associations – the SFA Referees' Associations and the SFRA. SFA referees were allegedly not being appointed by minor bodies and there was to-ing and fro-ing on this matter, with some of the bodies refuting the claims.

The Supervisors decided during season 1946-47 that they would be the body responsible for determining rulings on questions on the interpretation of the Laws of the Game and that such rulings would be disseminated to, and acted upon by, all referees within the SFA scheme to ensure uniformity of decision making. This eminently sensible decision illustrated the worth of the structure having been introduced – there was now a channel of communication open between the SFA and all referees within its associations. The fly in the ointment was the existence of the SFRA and its members. These referees would not be receiving any such communications and thus their interpretation of match incidents would not be the same as SFA referees.

During season 1946-47, a report was made on referees who had not transferred from the SFRA to the new associations, with the SFA being asked to ascertain from these referees the date when they last sat a referees' examination with a view to their being asked to sit a Refresher Examination.

A series of meetings between the Supervisors' Sub-Committee and the SFRA was held in 1949 and 1950 but nothing of note emanated from them. All went quiet thereafter as the two bodies co-existed for the best part of the next two decades. The possibility of the SFRA's integration into the SFA's associations emerged in the late 1960's.

Possible Integration
Edinburgh & District RA met with the SFRA (East) in 1968 to discuss possible amalgamation. By the end of the year, a number of SFRA associations had made approaches to their local SFA counterparts regarding integration. As it was apparent that there were misgivings in certain areas regarding the proposed integration, the Executive Committee met with the President and Secretary of those associations where the SFRA operated - Angus & Perthshire RA, Edinburgh & District RA, Glasgow RA, Lanarkshire RA, Renfrewshire RA and Stirlingshire & Clackmannanshire RA.

There was no expression of total opposition to integration, but apart from Edinburgh & District RA, which expressed the view that the passing of the Entrance Examination should not be a prerequisite, and Lanarkshire RA, which had an open mind, the other associations were firm in their stand that integration should entail the SFRA members undertaking an examination. Discussions between Edinburgh & District RA and the SFRA (East) continued that year, with proposals on integration being submitted to the SFA. Ultimately, in June 1969, the Referee Committee decided it was inadvisable to sanction any arrangement which did not make provision for the winding up of the SFRA (East) association. Not all the SFRA referees were wishing to transfer over to Edinburgh & District RA which meant that the SFRA (East) would continue to exist.

Problems caused for SFA referees
Members of the SFRA operated in minor football. Generally, this did not present a problem as the football played at this level could accommodate referees of both groupings. The highest level SFRA referees could operate in was Scottish Junior FA football, which impacted on SFA referees who were seeking to progress to the List. The gift of appointment to matches lay with the Junior Secretaries and they worked on the basis of getting who they held to be "good" referees, irrespective of which association they belonged to. Such issues arose in season 1972-73 when Renfrewshire RA referees experienced difficulty in receiving appointments in the Junior leagues as the majority of officials used in their area were SFRA members. Whilst the Supervisors appreciated the problem, it felt that there was little the SFA could do to alleviate it. The Renfrewshire RA Supervisor was advised to liaise with the Junior secretary to reach some agreement. That the Supervisors were of the view that the SFA could do little to address the issue was a reflection of the way things were in that era. The SFA's gaze was never particularly extensive below the level of senior football, other than maintaining and overseeing the regulatory framework and player registration issues, given the flow of players from minor levels to the senior game. A will to address the continuing existence of the SFRA took a long time to emerge.

Granting of Limited Recognition
The SFRA, for its own part, was conscious of its position within the game and, during season 1976-77, submitted a request for

recognition. This was refused by the SFA Executive & General Purposes Committee. Undeterred, the SFRA persisted and, by the autumn of 1977, preliminary talks on recognition were held between the SFA and the SFRA. This led to a meeting with the associations' Secretaries and Presidents to find out their views.

This dialogue with the SFRA took until March 1979 to reach an end point, when the Executive & General Purposes Committee, taking into account of the talks with the SFRA and the discussions with the associations, decided to accede to the SFRA's plea and granted limited recognition. Strict terms were applied.

The SFRA members would not be eligible to officiate at any match involving a member club of the SFA and would only be able to operate in the grades of football where they currently officiated; any SFRA member wishing to apply for inclusion in the SFA List would have to join one of the SFA's associations and pass the relevant examinations. The SFA would not seek to become involved in the administration of the SFRA nor to examine or grade its members. One small, but important concession was made: the SFA would keep the SFRA advised of any alterations to the Laws of the Game.

Within a couple of years, it became known that the SFRA had introduced a ruling that any SFRA member who enrolled in an SFA Referees' Training Class had to resign or be expelled from membership if they did not. Lanarkshire RA managed to get this topic included in the Discussion Points for the 1981 Referees' Conference. The general view which emerged was that an increase in the amount of publicity given to SFA Training classes would help alleviate the problem as there was clear competition to attract new recruits in the areas where the SFRA operated. Anyone wishing to take up refereeing would have had no real idea of the difference between the SFRA and the SFA's associations. This lack of knowledge served the SFRA well in attracting new members. The advertising of training classes in local newspapers was a key battleground.

The List of Referees

The First Two Seasons
The List for season 1946-47 was compiled by a five man Sub-Committee, chaired by Peter Craigmyle. Full powers were given to the Sub-Committee to revise the List for submission to the Referee Committee. As a general principle it was established that *"new applicants to the List must have had experience in the Junior grade of football and must thereafter gain considerable experience* [3 years was taken as a guide] *before being placed in Grade 1"*. As part of the process, the Sub-Committee met the SFL Management Committee to discuss the List and other matters. The Referee Committee approved the List in July 1946 following a meeting with the Sub-Committee. A Supplementary List was also approved in the early part of the season.

An indication of the SFL's influence arose when it suggested to the Referee Committee in September 1946 that John Cox should be added to the List at Class 1. The committee responded by indicating that it was prepared to ask the Sub-Committee to *"reconsider the position of this referee if and when he comes into line with the other referees on the List, undertakes to sit his refresher examination, and complies with the arrangements for training made by the Supervisor in his area."* It is likely that Cox was a loyal member of the SFRA and unwilling to transfer over to the new system. He was eventually admitted to the List as a Class 1 referee in December 1947. Cox was a referee of some standing, as he served as a FIFA referee in the first season of FIFA's International List in 1950-51and refereed the Scottish League Cup Final in season 1953-54. He resigned from the List in February 1954.

There was a state of flux with the List in these early seasons after the Second World War as civilian life returned to some form of normality. Revisions to the List were made in February 1947. On the basis of complaints from clubs and reports by Supervisors, four referees were downgraded from Class 1 to Class 2. Eight referees, one of whom was at that time a civilian (and in Egypt quite unbelievably), were accepted (temporarily) at Class 3. A number of referees who were still serving in the

Armed Forces were included on the List for season 1946-47 but were not given any classification.

Conditions for Application

The Supervisors decided that applications for admission to the List should only be considered twice a year, with the closing dates for applications being in mid-June and mid-December. Subsequently, 15 applications for Class 3 were accepted and 12 were refused in December 1947. Appeals were submitted by referees who had not been admitted to the List, but these were unsuccessful.

Conditions for admission to the List started to emerge. A "trainee" referee, on becoming a member of an association after having passed the referee's examination, was required to serve a minimum period of one year in minor football before being considered for inclusion in the List. Furthermore, all applicants for admission to the List were required to pass the Refresher Examination. This principle maintains to this day.

Another important decision on membership of the List was taken in November 1949, namely that all referees on the List *"must, irrespective of membership of a Referees' Association outwith the SFA scheme, be at all times in membership of an association within that scheme."* This indicates that it was possible at that time to have dual membership of an SFA association and of an SFRA Association.

Ensuring that referees on the List had an up-to-date knowledge of the Laws of the Game by passing the Refresher Examination was a regular concern in the early 1950's. All referees on the List had to sit the examination in November 1950 and in March 1954. A request was made to the Referee Committee in 1962 that all referees on the List should be required to sit the Refresher Examination at least once every five years but this was not progressed. The issue occasionally arose in later years but was never acted upon.

There was always competition in the 1970's and 1980's for admission on to the List at Class 3A. Not every applicant was guaranteed to win a place on the List. Further, there were invariably a number of referees who applied for the List each season who did not have the support of their Supervisor, a prerequisite in the whole process. To simplify its task in considering applications, the Executive Committee decided in 1985 that in years when there were more new applicants than places available at Class 3A, adverse assessment marks would be taken into consideration.

Numerous conditions developed over the years in regard to referees applying for the List, to the time that should be served in a Class before being recommended for promotion and to the assessment requirements to be fulfilled. The Supervisors had to comply with requirements placed on them. It was re-affirmed, in 1977, for example, that a Supervisor could only nominate a non-listed referee for inclusion in the List if he had seen him during the season. The supervisory requirements varied over time. In 1977, it was possible for a Supervisor to nominate one of his Class 3A referees even if he had not assessed him. At least two Supervisors were needed to assess the referee.

In the case of referees under consideration for admission to the List or promotion from Class 3A to Class 2, there was a regular late rush each season to achieve the number of assessments needed. In some instances, these things were not accomplished by some Supervisors, to the detriment of the referees concerned, and this always brought forth a "ticking-off" from the Executive Committee at the full committee meeting.

The Classification System

A new system of referee classification for the List was introduced for season 1948-49. The existing Class 3 was sub-divided into Class 3A and Class 3B. Classes 1 and 2 remained unchanged. Officials entered the List at Class 3A and operated as linesmen on the "far-side" at matches. Class 3B was the "senior" of the two classes and were positioned on the main "stand-side". The Class 3A official would take over as the referee if the referee had to come off injured or ill during a game. If a Class 3A referee did not progress to Class 2, he would be reclassified to 3B after a few seasons. This classification system served the SFA until season 1990-91.

The introduction of the new system resulted in a combined increase of 19 in Classes 3A and 3B compared to the previous number in Class 3. The numbers in Class 2 had however been trimmed for season 1948-49. The overall figures for the three seasons from 1946-47 were:

Table 1: Number of referees on the List of Referees 1946-47 to 1948-49

Season	Class 1	Class 2	Class 3	Class 3A	Class 3B	Total
1946-47	23	36	89			148
1947-48	28	45	109			182
1948-49	26	29		69	59	183

Turmoil with Referees' Ages
Turmoil broke out during season 1948-49 after it emerged that a number of referees had understated their age on their applications. As a consequence, all referees on the List had to produce birth certificates for inspection which resulted in the Sub-Committee putting forward a number of recommendations to the Referee Committee.

A Class 1 referee, Jim McLean, was re-classified to Class 3B as was a Class 2 referee. There were a number of deletions: one Class 2, three Class 3A and five Class 3B referees. A further 33 other referees who had understated their ages were informed of the committee's extreme disapproval of their action. A small number of referees were suspended until such time as they provided their birth certificate. From this point on, the submission of a birth certificate was an integral part of the List application process until the 2000's.

The issue concerning McLean reverberated through the system. The SFA Council referred his downgrading back to the Referee Committee, with a recommendation that *"he be placed in a grade which would enable him to be engaged as a referee."* The motion at Council had been proposed by a member of the committee, which indicates that there was dissention in the committee's ranks. The motion won by 15 votes to 13. The committee rejected Council's recommendation, taking the view that it had full knowledge of all the circumstances, albeit that the matter had gone to a vote with a 5-2 outcome. The committee pointed out that McLean would never have been promoted to Class 1 in the first place but for the *"wilful mis-statement of his age"*. For Council's benefit, it recorded that its decision had been taken in consultation, and by agreement, with the Supervisors' Sub-

73

Committee and that *"it was therefore faced with the alternative of departing from that agreement by unilateral action which would most certainly be resented or remitting the matter back to the Supervisors' Sub-Committee with the certain knowledge that their views would be unaltered"*. The Referee Committee won the day, as too did the Supervisors in terms of being able to carry out its business and being able to have the support of the Referee Committee in that. McLean remained at Class 3B until resigning from the List in October 1949.

Age Limits
The age issue during season 1948-49 is notable as the minutes are silent on any age limits from when the new system started in 1945. Some form of limit was certainly in use as in September 1948 Glasgow & District RA was informed of the age limits *"normally imposed"* on applications for inclusion in the List. The first reference to age limits was made in December 1950 when it was recorded that all new applicants for the List had to be under 36 years of age.

The possibility of adjusting the age limit for new applicants was mooted in 1959 by the Supervisors but they came down in favour of being able to use discretion.

The setting of a retiral age emerged for the first time in May 1977. The Executive Committee recommended to the full committee that 50 be introduced as the retiral age for Class 1 referees. It proposed that a Class 1 referee who reached 50 before 31st December of the season of application, would not be considered for the List. The recommendation was not accepted.

Despite this outcome, the issue was none the less still raised with the Disciplinary & Referee Committee. During the following season, however, that committee decided against the introduction of a retiral age. Matters were not allowed to lie and the issue was kept on the Disciplinary & Referee Committee's agenda. By the end of the season and with some good work behind the scenes, it was persuaded to change its mind. In the summer of 1978 it was confirmed that the retiral age of 50 would come into operation for the following season. Moreover, in October, it was decided that, as a matter of uniformity, the age limit would apply to every referee on the List. The introduction of the "31st December" cut off point brought the SFA into uniformity with FIFA's conditions for its List of International Referees. In May 1979, yet another change occurred, predicated on domestic circumstances to enable a better flow of officials through the List and to stop Class 3B becoming too large – the age limit for inclusion for Class 3B was reduced by two years to 48.

In 1987, the thought of relaxing the age limit emerged from the SFA-SFL Liaison Committee. It was the Supervisors' opinion that, if the age limit were to be waived, it could only be the case with the very exceptional referee and that each case would have to be judged on its merit and be reviewed each season. The Supervisors felt that should the SFA decide to alter the retiral age (an indication that it appreciated a final decision was out of their hands), then it would be preferable for them to be able to reserve the right to accept applications from referees who had reached the retiral age, and that anyone so selected could not be nominated for inclusion in the FIFA List of International Referees. The topic did not go away as it came to the fore again in 1988 at which point the Disciplinary & Referee Committee took the view that there was *"no great justification"* in departing from the existing retiral age.

Approval of the List
The approval of the List settled down to a standard pattern from the early 1950's onwards. The Referee Committee approved the List before the start of each season following the submission of recommendations from the Supervisors. A meeting was held in mid-season between the parties to review the List and to make any adjustments (additions, deletions, promotions) if necessary. Very occasionally, there was an alteration made to the Supervisors' recommendations by the Referee Committee but the individuals concerned were generally never revealed in the minutes. It can be supposed that these decisions pertained to referees other than Class 1, otherwise arguments and debate would have surely ensued. In February 1954 the Referee Committee rejected a recommendation that a Class 2 referee be deleted from the List and in July 1954 the recommendations of the Sub-Committee were approved after three amendments were agreed.

The full decisions regarding the revision of the List by the Sub-Committee were recorded for the first time in December 1953. 13 applications for inclusion in the List had been considered. All were refused on the basis that the referees needed to gain further experience. Six of these referees were admitted on to the List the following season (one of whom was a future Class 1 and FIFA referee – Alistair MacKenzie) and two were admitted on to the List the season after. Five of the rejected referees never made it on to the List. As a result of the high number of applications and their lack of experience, the committee decided that applications for inclusion on the List in future would only be considered in June each year.

Another factor for removing the December application spot was probably that, by this time, the List had matured in the numbers of officials included in it. The need to put more officials on to it twice a year had receded and this allowed the committee to be more selective in terms of which referees to admit to the List.

A significant divergence of views between the Supervisors and the Referee Committee arose in regard to the recommendations for season 1959-60. The Supervisors wished to reduce the number of Class 3B referees and accordingly made recommendations for deletion. The Referee Committee was not prepared to accept the recommendations as "*it was based on length of service only and did not take into account the ability of those concerned*". The Supervisors still wished to reduce the numbers in Class 3B and returned with a reduced list of 19 referees for deletion. This was accepted by the Referee Committee.

Numbers on the List

Over the 40 season period from 1948, the average number of referees on the List each season was 194. The table below sets out the average number of referees per class over that period, together with the maximum and minimum number in each class and the relevant season.

Table 2: Average number of referees on the List 1948-1988

Class	Ave. Per Season	Max. No.	Season	Min. No.	Season
1	29	32	See note	23	1950-51
2	26	35	1951-52	18	1962-63
3A	73	100	1958-59	57	1969-70
3B	66	79	1979-80	51	1949-50

Note: 1974-75, 1980-81, 1982-83, 1983-84, 1984-85 and 1987-88

The range between the maximum and minimum number for each class demonstrates that there was a fair degree of elasticity in how the List developed over the seasons. Numbers expanded and contracted as the movement of referees between the classes varied over time, dependent on decisions made at the Grading meeting, resignations and retirement of referees and the number of applicants admitted. Over the period, the numbers on the List became more settled with less of a significant variance each season from the previous one. Information is available from 1969-70 on the admissions to the List each season. On average, 16 referees were admitted each season. The highest figure was 24 in 1986-87 and the lowest was 9 in 1976-77.

The numbers on the List (by Class) were recorded for the first time for the 1971 Grading meeting and were compared to the figures for the previous season. This became standard practice.

In February 1977, the Supervisors had to explain to the Referee Committee a small increase in the number of Class 1 referees to 29 for that season (two more compared to the previous season) when the SFL had two years earlier asked that the numbers be reduced. In response, it was set out that as a number of Class 1 referees were nearing the age when they would likely have to retire, the opportunity had been taken to promote a higher than normal number of Class 2 referees (three) and to give them the chance to establish themselves as Class 1 referees. This approach heralded an early strategic approach being taken in respect of planning ahead for the future which came increasingly into use in the years ahead and which, in the current day, is ever present in the Referee Committee's thinking.

Deletion from the List

On occasion during the 1950's, the Referee Committee deleted referees from the List without reference to the Supervisors. These deletions were needed to be put into effect as quickly as possible with there being justifiable reason for acting on this basis.

The work of the Supervisors on the List generally passed unnoticed, other than the press reporting on the promotion of new Class 1 referees each season. However, a decision taken in December 1987 and approved by the Disciplinary & Referee Committee to downgrade a Class 1 referee, Kevin O'Donnell, to Class 3B created huge adverse press publicity. At the start of the season, he had refereed a Celtic v. Heart of Midlothian match and his performance generated a complaint from Heart of Midlothian, with the club making sure that much publicity was given to its very strong views. The perception held in the press was that the downgrading had been carried out as a consequence of the club's complaint and that the club had been able to wield some power. This was not the case at all – the referee's overall performance during the season had been the cause of his downgrading, not his performance in one single match. There was also one other Class 1 referee who suffered the same fate as O'Donnell at the time. A lesson was learned by the Executive Committee. It took the pragmatic decision not to downgrade a Class 1 referee during a season in the future.

At the Grading meeting at the end of that season, the Executive Committee firmed up this new carefulness in approach when it agreed that, in future, it would be better if all referees whose performances had fallen below the expected standard were to receive letters from the SFA drawing this to their attention, rather than having their supervisor speaking to them personally, as had been the case on occasions hitherto.

Scrutiny of Class 3A and 3B Officials

High standards were always expected of linesmen and acting upon unsatisfactory assessments was a relatively simple way of removing a Class 3A or Class 3B official from the List. Any official with two unsatisfactory reports during a season was automatically deleted from the List. This figure was raised to three from season 1977-78.

It was also expected that when not acting as linemen in the SFL, Class 3A and particularly 3B officials should regularly referee matches. From 1979, any official with less than 10 refereeing engagements throughout a season could be considered for deletion from the List. Nine years later, this view had to be re-emphasised to Class 3B officials. Evidence had become known of some who had just been acting as linesmen in SFL football and not officiating as referees in other grades of football.

SFL Issues

Compiling the List to suit the needs of SFL football was a continuous requirement. Occasionally, the Supervisors had to give consideration to possible adjustments within that approach. In May 1964, the Supervisors were requested to submit recommendations on Class 1 referees on the basis of 18 SFL matches per week (maximum 29 referees) and for 16 SFL matches (maximum 27 referees). Change did not materialise, however. The number of Class 1 referees for season 1964-65 remained at 29, the same as for season 1963-64.

The Referee Committee, during season 1969-70, wished to establish if the Supervisors would be in favour of introducing a separate List for each of the then two Divisions of the SFL. The Executive Committee did not support the suggestion but its position was overturned by the full Committee. It was recommended to the Referee Committee that two Lists should be created, with 15 referees being included in each List. The Referee Committee sought the views of the SFL on the proposals when the List was approved in July 1970, only to discover that the SFL was opposed to two Lists. This put an end to the matter. It would only be conjecture as to how the idea emerged in the first place. That aside, the thought of having separate Lists of referees for each of the League's Divisions recurred every so often in the Executive Committee's discussions, particularly at Grading meetings. The key deciding factor to maintain one group of Class 1 referees was the flexibility offered by having just the one group which enabled administrators to work unhindered in respect of making appointments.

Testing Class 2 Referees in SFL Football
During season 1966-67, the SFL agreed to a proposal from the Supervisors that certain Class 2 referees be appointed to some Second Division matches towards the end of the season. The scheme was an evident success as the three referees selected were promoted to Class 1 the following season. This was an indication of some progressive thinking to gain the chance of testing prospective Class 1 referees in the lowest SFL Division and to be assessed by Supervisors. The scheme was successfully repeated periodically in subsequent years.

Missing the Closing Date for Applications
The removal of referees from the List due to performance issues was a fact of life in refereeing. A few referees unfortunately suffered automatic removal due to entirely self-inflicted circumstances – failure to submit their renewal applications by the closing date. The Executive Committee maintained a hard line approach to this down the years. If a referee lost his place on the List by missing the deadline, the committee held that it was his fault and highlighted a weakness in his approach to administration. It also created a space for someone else to get on the List. Supervisors had to remind their referees constantly of the need to submit their applications in good time. A few failed to heed these words and paid the price. The most noteworthy casualty in this context was the Class 1 referee Andy Paterson whose renewal application in 1976 was received two days after the closing date. Despite Paterson, his employers and his Supervisor all making submissions outlining the background as to why the deadline was missed, the position of the Supervisors remained unchanged and Paterson's time on the List was at an end.

Service Referees
During the period from 1957 to 1979, the List contained referees from the British Armed Forces. This stemmed from a meeting of the four British Associations in March 1957 when,

arising from correspondence from the Royal Navy FA and Combined Services FA, it was agreed that referees with a Service classification should be accepted by the National Associations on to their national Lists with the caveat that the category of their classification would be held as a Services classification only. Four service personnel were admitted to the List for season 1957-58 – two at Class 1 Service, one at Class 2 Service and one at Class 3 Service. Over this 22 year period, 56 service referees held places on the List. The majority of these referees were stationed at Forces bases in Moray and officiated in the Highland League. Many of these Service referees served only a season or two on the List, with resignations submitted on a fairly regular basis as a consequence of a posting. In June 1975, the SFA Executive & General Purposes Committee, following upon correspondence with the North of Scotland RA and the RAF FA, decided that "Service referees" should be required to pass the SFA's Refresher Examination, as a pre-requisite to their inclusion, in their service category, in the List. This was a turning point in the continuation of these referees being on the List and within four years, none were left on it.

A Supplementary List
The need to have a Supplementary List of Referees disappeared quickly after the season 1946-47. Football circumstances in the north of Scotland emerged 40 years later to renew the need for one. Its purpose was to enable football to be serviced. The North Caledonian League, which had a number of SFA member clubs in membership and which necessitated their matches to be controlled by officials on the List, faced the real possibility of having to postpone matches given the lack of Listed officials in the area. Additionally, a similar situation was also being experienced by the North East of Scotland Youth Association (the precursor of the Highland Youth League) due to there being a small number of Listed officials in Moray & Banff RA.
To resolve the issue, a small supplementary List was created for use by the two bodies when Listed officials were not available for appointment. The composition of this Supplementary List was remitted to the SFA administration and compiled in

conjunction with the local Supervisors. The Supplementary List continued in the following seasons.

This was the first instance of such situations appearing in the game in the modern era. It was not to be the last, as local pressures would start to emerge in various parts of the country in the following years.

Assessment of Referees

Assessing referees has always been a crucial and integral part of refereeing. Assessments have a huge influence on the progress of a referee's career – from initial coverage to gain admission to the List to assessments which contribute to their promotion, reclassification or deletion. To the football clubs, the *raison d'etre* of the Supervisors was to assess the referees. That was their sole role, as they perceived it, regardless of the other duties which the Supervisors fulfilled at their association. Match days are the times when passions run their highest, especially after the games have been played, and in this context clubs have had a strong belief that the Supervisor had to "do his job right", which effectively translated to mean that they should view the referee's performance in the same light as they did i.e. awful, terrible or any other such comparable description, especially when they felt that decisions had gone against them. The Supervisor had, of course, to be independent in his assessment of referees and not be influenced.

Set against this background, the Supervisors were fully aware of the importance of assessment and they addressed the subject with the utmost seriousness. The underlying principle has always been that of improving refereeing standards and the quality of referees.

The Development of a Reporting System

Consideration of Supervisors' reports on referees featured from the very start of the supervisory system, with discussions at every meeting together with the planning of assessments of referees. A method for assessment was prepared by the Sub-

Committee in 1948 although it took until 1950 for a standard report form to be agreed.

Soon after becoming a Supervisor in 1960, Jack Mowat successfully proposed a new assessment system. Once he became Chairman, he was the driving force to develop assessment and set in motion the never-ending quest for the optimum method.

In the early 1960's the marking system for referees was simple: 2-Good, 1-Fair and 0-Unsatisfactory. Linesmen were assessed by under the following headings: Co-operation with the referee, Correctness of Decisions and General Remarks.

By the end of the decade, the following performance descriptors had come into use: Very Good, Good, Moderate, Poor and Unsatisfactory.

Changes continued throughout the 1970's. A new report form was used in 1971-72 but was revised four years later to *"give greater emphasis to the more important aspects of refereeing"*, particularly in respect of the marks awarded.

The marking system was:

Correctness in Decisions (good, moderate or poor and if moderate or poor, state instances) – 4 marks

Control (good, moderate or poor and if moderate or poor, state instances) – 4 marks

Personality (confident, uncertain, quick or slow thinking) - ½ mark

Physical Fitness (good or poor) – ½ mark

Co-operation with Linesmen (good or poor, if poor, state instances) – ½ mark

Appearance (bearing, dress, etc) – ½ mark

Any other remarks or suggestions which might improve efficiency

Another revised system put forward by Mowat was adopted for season 1977-78. Assessments were now marked entirely under "Correctness in Decisions" and "Control" with a maximum of five marks achievable in each section. All the other marks were dispensed with.

The percentage bands which applied to the descriptors throughout the 1980's were as follows:

Excellent - 90-100%
Good - 70-85%
Moderate - 50-65%
Poor - 30-45%
Unsatisfactory - 0-25%

Within that range, the following guidelines applied in relation to the type of match and the range of mark which could be awarded: Classification/Range of mark - Easy/70-75, Difficult/ 80-85; Very Difficult/90-100.

Uniformity of Assessment

Achieving consistency of assessment amongst the Supervisors was always a major aim. The first evidence of this issue is recorded in September 1964 when *"the question of the compilation of reports and attempt to reach a uniform standard"* was considered. A major discussion ensued at the following meetings. Willie Allan stressed *"the need for clear and concise reports"*, the merits of which comment have remained constant ever since.

Decisions were taken on match situations to enable Supervisors to carry out their assessments on a consistent basis. From season 1968-69 an unsatisfactory classification was given to any referee who should have sent off a player but did not do so.

A similar approach was taken on assessing linesmen. From season 1962-63 one bad decision in a game would merit "fair" and two or more an "unsatisfactory" assessment. The stakes were high for linesmen.

The need for Supervisors to take great care in wording their reports was regularly addressed. On occasion, quite simple things had to be raised with it once being conveyed to them that the overall classification of a referee's performance could not be "Very Good" if the standard achieved in each of the report's sections was "Good".

In 1973, the Edinburgh RA Supervisor, Andrew Wright, suggested that the SFA should either purchase a film which could be used as a means of instruction of Supervisors or, related to such a film, have all Supervisors complete the standard report form on the performance of the match officials. This was quite a far-sighted approach to take. The Supervisors felt that the aim of the proposal would be better achieved if they each assessed the referee in that year's Scottish Cup Final. This duly happened with the Supervisors assessing the performance of the referee, John Gordon, as either "good" or "excellent". Such an approach was to be repeated a few times in later years.

A major step forward was taken during season 1980-81 when, for the first time, assessment guidelines were developed to try to achieve better uniformity. Tom Wharton drafted the guidelines. On a general basis, where a player should have been cautioned, or was cautioned incorrectly, a half mark was deducted. Similarly, where a player should have been sent off or was sent off incorrectly, a full mark was deducted.

A further decision on deducting marks from a referee's performance was taken in 1984 as a consequence of a growing concern about the widespread increase of encroachment at the taking of a penalty kick. The Supervisors felt that referees were disregarding instructions issued during season 1981-82 and decided that marks should be deducted when referees failed to penalise encroachment.

During season 1986-87, a view was reached on the classification to be given to a linesman when he failed to take appropriate action by having a player cautioned when the referee did not observe the incident and when he carried otherwise out his duties satisfactorily. Failure to take action was classed as a major error of judgement and resulted in an "Unsatisfactory" classification.

Seeking Comments from Match Officials

In carrying out assessments, it would seem natural that a Supervisor should ask the referee or linesman for clarification of a match incident before completing his report. This, however, was not the case. In 1969, Willie Allan reported to the Executive Committee that it had become increasingly common for Supervisors to delay completing their assessment until they had been informed of the terms of a conversation between referee and linesmen. That practice had to cease.

During discussions at the 1971 Referees' Conference on the supervisory system, the referees said that they had no difficulty with a Supervisor visiting a referee after a match to clarify a particular point. However, the existing position of the Supervisors, who were fearful of potential difficulties which could arise in dressing rooms, won the day.

It took a further five years for a change to materialise, and the trigger for that was Jack Mowat needing to obtain clarification of a conversation between the referee and a linesman on a match incident. It was agreed that it would be acceptable for Supervisors to defer making an assessment, pending the result of any enquiry that was made. Speaking directly to each official after the match was, however, not the path a Supervisor had to follow. Everything had to be done by correspondence – the Supervisor requesting the SFA to obtain the information, the SFA then writing to the Supervisor of the official concerned to seek comment and once that had been received, issuing it to the Supervisor who had made the request in the first place. Often, it could take a few weeks to conclude all the elements before a report was eventually submitted. A speedy system it was not.

Club Reports

The views of the SFL clubs had a major influence on referees' careers from the very start of the supervisory system. With the SFL being the major "employer" of the referees on the List, its place as the major stakeholder was guaranteed and as a consequence it wanted a seat at the table in the consideration of referees' performances. The first reference to Class 1 and Class 2 referees in the club statistics is recorded in September 1948. Through the 1950's to the early 1960's, club statistics were considered separately from the Supervisors' own reports. A system developed to take account of the club reports. Referees whose percentages of good reports were below a certain figure (60% for Class 1 referees and 65% for Class 2 referees) were to be advised, by their respective Supervisors, of their mark and position. Referees whose percentage of good reports was not considered satisfactory were supervised more closely in the periods following meetings.

In the early 1960's two unsuccessful attempts were made to get the SFL to adopt the same marking system as the Supervisors so that there would be consistency in information provided to referees.

86

The combining of Supervisors' Assessments and Club Reports, to allow them to be considered in tandem, finally occurred for the Executive meeting of March 1964 when statistical tables were presented. It took until season 1970-71 before Supervisors' and Club reports were properly combined, with an average percentage of each category being calculated to determine the rankings of the referees.

Club marks carried the same weight as the Supervisors' marks in the consideration of the performance of Class 1 officials – it was a 50-50 split. A proposal to give more emphasis to the Supervisors' marks was raised in 1978 but was not accepted. The Supervisors gained success however in regard to the Class 2 referees. After seeking the abolition of club marks altogether for Class 2 referees, the SFL declined the proposal but conceded ground by agreeing to a 75%-25% split in favour of the Supervisors' reports. Whilst always appreciating the general overall worth of club statistics, and the hints and pointers as to how referees were viewed by clubs, the Supervisors always felt that there was a distinct possibility of rankings being skewed by a referee being, or not being, a favourite of clubs. This situation was accentuated for the Class 2 referees who received less supervision than Class 1 referees and because the person completing the club report was not always held to be appropriate to perform the task.

Scrutiny of Referees
By the early 1950's, the scrutiny of Supervisors' reports had become an important feature of the Supervisors' meetings. The Supervisors were issued with a copy of all reports to keep them abreast of the referees' performances and to assist in engendering a common and uniform understanding of assessment. It was common to request comments from match officials on various incidents to assist in the consideration of reports. Cases were referred to the Sub-Committee for further investigation, with referees being interviewed. Other cases were closed if the explanations offered by the referees were accepted. A favourable change in an official's assessment could result after the committee's review, following comments received from the official.

As part of the process of scrutinising referees' performances and their placing in the statistics table, the Supervisors adopted the practice of writing to the referees whose positions were a concern to advise them of their position. "Letter" became a constant feature of the minutes of meetings recording such decisions. Even worse for an official was to find himself being recommended to the Referee Committee for deletion from the List due to a review of his performances. This happened to a Class 3A referee in October 1962.

The Supervisors also balanced the "letter" approach by introducing a prior step in the process by deciding, when appropriate, to require a referee's own Supervisor to speak to him if he had a low percentage in the statistics. This applied in particular to club statistics but extended also to the combined statistics as the years progressed. By doing so, the committee was giving out a warning and covering itself if the worst came to the worst at the end of a season and deletion or reclassification was to be the outcome.

Each referee in Class 1 and Class 2 was advised by his supervisor of their Supervisors' percentages – their own and the Class average. On club percentages they were to be advised on the basis of the percentage of the markings of 2, 1 and 0, the system which applied for clubs.

In 1964 the Executive Committee decided that, when letters were to be sent to referees in future, no percentage figures would be given but that the referees would be advised that their overall performances were not considered satisfactory.

The decision to letter or speak to a referee invariably led to an increased level of supervision in the period thereafter, and particularly towards the end of a season. The statistics also informed the committee of the Class 2 referees who were performing well and were potential promotion candidates. These referees also came under greater scrutiny.

Performance Statistics
The table of performance statistics first appear as part of the minutes of meetings in October 1968. Taken in conjunction with the decisions of the committee, the information is revealing. 11 referees in total were to be advised by their

Supervisor that their overall performance had been disappointing and that the committee expected *"to learn of some improvement when they next come to review such tables."* Given the early stages of the season, supervisory coverage of many of the referees was still low, so some of the referees could justifiably feel aggrieved by this outcome. One referee being warned had only been covered once by a Supervisor (out of 5 appointments, given the club statistics) and a Moderate assessment had been recorded. Consideration of club reports had an impact on the overall view of the referees' positions.

Despite no statistics being considered on the performance of linesmen (Class 3A and 3B), performances were nonetheless reviewed, presumably on the basis the committee members' own knowledge of the official from seeing him in matches. In February 1969, the Executive Committee other than noting that a few linesmen fell short of the required standard and would be *"watched carefully"*, took no other action.

It was not until May 1981 that information on Classes 3A and 3B was included in the performance statistics. From this point on, these statistics were included in the end of season tables. The tables were considered by the Supervisors three times per season - November, mid-February and April, the decision to do this having been taken in the early 1970's.

When the recording of assessment marks became computerised for season 1984-85, the figures in the performance statistics were compiled to the nearest decimal point. This introduced greater differentiation in the tables as, until then, it was common for referees to share the same percentage mark.

Supervisors' Appointments and Issue of Reports
The motivation for the introduction of the supervisory system was to improve refereeing standards, but there was, for many years, an odd approach taken to the appointment of supervisors to assess referees and letting them know afterwards how they performed in matches. It is easy to make such a comment with the benefit of hindsight and it would be wrong to be over-critical. The system employed was of its time and reflected the prevailing thinking on these issues over the years.

Referees never knew when they were being watched in action. They would have had an expectation that a Supervisor would be appointed to major and important matches and, given where Supervisors stayed and the likely clubs they would regularly be appointed to within their geographical area, referees worked on the basis that there was a fair chance of that Supervisor being present at the match. At smaller grounds, referees would glance at the Directors' Box to try and identify if there was a Supervisor in attendance. Effectively, it was intended that a clear separation applied between the Supervisors and referees when it came to assessment.

This approach extended to what happened after games. It would have been thought that it would have been a natural part of the process to provide a copy of a Supervisor's report to a referee and to allow him to take stock as to how his performance was viewed. Not so. The system used was the following:

A referee who was assessed as having a good report would not receive a copy of the report, if there were no comments under the "Any other remarks or suggestions which might improve efficiency" section. If there were comments in that section, only that part of the report would be issued to the referee. The full report would only be issued if it was a moderate, poor or unsatisfactory assessment.

The same more or less applied to linesmen. Attempts to have moderate assessments on linesmen issued had been defeated on two occasions in 1976 and 1980.

Credit should be given to the Supervisors for providing referees with the opportunity of discussing the system at the 1971 Referees' Conference. They expressed the clear opinion that they should receive all their reports, irrespective of marking or classification. For whatever reason, no change in the system was forthcoming. On a similar theme (but again with a "no change" outcome), contact between a Supervisor and a referee before a match was raised by the Supervisors at the 1977 Conference, given that that was the practice in European football. The referees were generally positive to this happening, although a few wished it just to happen after a match. The referees also indicated that they welcomed constructive criticism.

It was theoretically possible for a referee to be assessed during a season, perform to a "good" standard in all of his assessed matches, not receive any comment in the "Any other remarks" section in every report and thus be blissfully unaware of how he was held to be performing. The only indication he would get would be from his Supervisor passing on his percentage mark, and that for his Class, at the relevant points during a season. Training nights generally provided the opportunity to the Supervisors to pass on reports to their referees. It was always ominous for a referee if his Supervisor indicated that he wished to have a word, particularly if there was an envelope in his hand containing a report.

A change for the better emerged for season 1984-85 when Supervisors received, for their information only, one copy of reports of Good and above on their referees who were assessed with the proviso that there were no grounds of appeal for such reports.

If a referee was never supposed to know which Supervisor was conducting an assessment, the system maintained this right to the end of the process. The Supervisor was not required to sign his report. Recognising handwriting was the order of the day for many years. At Discussion Groups at the 1973 and 1975 Conferences, the referees made a plea for reports to be signed. The pleas fell on stony ground. Change was still a number of years away.

With only a relatively small number of Supervisors, reaching a maximum of 16 during the 1980's, they fulfilled a remarkable role in regularly attending matches to assess referees. Assessing referees is crucial to the overall operation of the refereeing system. It effectively is the quality control of referees, building up a bank of information to enable the List to be compiled and reviewed during the season, whilst becoming aware of prospective candidates for promotion and admission. 468 assessments were carried out in season 1968-69 and there were 620 by season 1987-88. Generally, the number of assessments carried out each season during this period would have been in the region of 400-450.

Appeals against Assessment

If an objective was to achieve uniformity of assessment, a battleground where this was fought over was that of appeals. By season 1962-63 the increasing volume of requests from referees and linesmen to review Supervisors' reports and a resultant alteration to a number of classifications, led to the introduction of an appeal system. Appeals were possible for an assessment below the category of "Good".

A torrent of appeals was unleashed over the next 25 years. The number of appeals was dramatically high in the first few seasons. 20 were dealt with in season 1963-64, with nine being successful. 19 of 36 appeals were won during season 1964-65. An astonishing 43 appeals, the highest number of any season, were considered in season 1966-67. 13 were successful. The number of appeals per season never fell below 20 until 1975-76, and even then the numbers remained in double figures for the next five seasons. Appeals in the 1980's fell into single figures each season, with only three being received in two of these seasons.

The appeal process gave Supervisors the opportunity to fight on behalf of their referees who they felt had been harshly dealt with by the assessment. The outcome of a successful appeal would also, importantly, benefit the referee in the performance tables. Assessments of less than "Good" could be potentially damaging, particularly if a referee received a number of them during a season.

Procedures for the submission and consideration of appeals were developed and adjusted over the years. Dealing with appeals became a dominant part of meetings and took some time to dispose of. It took a while for the grounds of appeal to become part of the process. In 1969, the Executive Committee rejected a suggestion from Willie Allan that consideration of the grounds of appeal was an essential part of the process. The committee's views were that these were not of interest to them and that the referee's or linesman's comments were adequate for its purpose. Grounds of appeal eventually became part of the process within a few years. The grounds and the report being appealed against were read out, and the members debated the pros and cons before coming to a decision.

The processes surrounding appeals were hard fought over at times. Procedural and policy points were considered at length in 1971. Numerous appeals were deemed to be incompetent and not considered. The power of the full committee was demonstrated in May 1975. A proposal that decisions of the Executive Committee on appeals be final was defeated, with it being confirmed that any decision of the Executive Committee was subject to approval by the full committee.

The appeal process generated much debate and argument amongst referees. In September 1973, Edinburgh & District RA submitted a letter to the Supervisors intimating that the following resolution had been passed by the association: "*That all referees under the jurisdiction of the SFA be given the democratic right to submit a direct appeal against supervisors' moderate/poor/unsatisfactory reports, to the Secretary of the SFA. Thereafter, the appeal to be placed before the appropriate committee with a copy of the appeal to be sent to the local Supervisor.*" The committee did not see fit to change the existing procedure.

There was always risk attached to the submission of an appeal. Supervisors had to weigh up a few factors before deciding to submit an appeal on behalf of a referee or linesman, not least the chances of being successful. Some would also be wary of challenging an experienced Supervisor's assessment. On a few occasions, the committee decided that the classification should be lower than the one being appealed – a "Moderate" being changed to "Poor" and a "Poor" being lowered to "Unsatisfactory". Such appeals certainly backfired.

The thought of dispensing with appeals was raised at various times in the 1970's and 1980's, but not carried through. One change which occurred in 1979 was that the original assessment would stand if, after the appeal was determined, the committee's assessment differed only 5% in either direction from the original mark. Frank Crossley, always a considered voice, outlined his thoughts on the appeals system to the Supervisors in 1986. Notwithstanding that he recognised that the opportunity to appeal should exist, he considered that adverse assessments should be accepted in an honest fashion and in the interest of improving the general standard of refereeing. He wished that the number of appeals be reduced or hopefully cease altogether. Appeals were allowed to continue, given the relatively low number which had been received in recent seasons.

Examinations and Training Classes

Season 1945-46 saw the basic structures put in place for training classes and examinations. Venues were arranged by the Referees' Associations to hold classes, press publicity was given to the courses and the first Examination Sub-Committee prepared an examination paper, the key answer paper and a Guide for Marking.

The recruiting of new referees has always been crucial to sustaining the overall numbers of referees to service football. Becoming a qualified referee was not a straightforward process – the Supervisors set high standards from the start and undoubtedly operated on the basis of making sure, as best as possible, that prospective candidates were up to the job by having the required knowledge of the Laws of the Game, gained through attending the training classes and tested thoroughly by the examination. A very serious approach was taken. In 1960, in considering the number of failures in examination results, the Supervisors agreed that *"Referees' Associations should be more particular in the candidates whom they present for examination."* Little was to change over the years. By 1984, the Executive Committee's view was that it should be suggested to any candidates who failed the mock examination badly that they should not sit the Entrance Examination. This view was relaxed within a couple of years.

Examination Sub-Committee

A small Sub-Committee, generally comprising the Chairman and one or more members of the main Sub-Committee, was appointed on a seasonal basis to deal with examinations. The formal appointment of the Sub-Committee came to a close at the end of season 1962-63. Thereafter, it was set up on an ad-hoc basis as and when required.

Examination Conditions

Two basic but important principles were established towards the end of season 1945-46 – that to sit the Examination, a candidate had to attend the training class, and passing the examination was crucial to being accepted into membership, no matter how proficient the candidate might be at "*practical work*".

Further principles were established in August 1946. A Certificate of Acceptance was issued to candidates who passed the Class 3 Examination and anyone who failed the examination was given the opportunity to re-sit it. The term "Class 3 examination" was used through to the late 1950's when it was changed to "Entrance Examination" to more properly reflect that it was the examination required to be passed before qualifying as a referee.

In 1949, the Supervisors settled on 80% as the pass mark. A proposal from Fifeshire RA in 1952 that the pass mark should be 65% was rejected.

The opportunity to re-sit the Refresher Examination was provided from 1950.

It was decided in 1963 that all associations should only be advised whether a candidate has passed or failed - no marks were to be disclosed.

Notable developments occurred in 1964 when it was stipulated that all candidates had to attend at least 75% of the Entrance Examination classes. Only one re-sit was allowed in the event of a failure of either Examination. A two year gap between passing the Entrance Examination and sitting the Refresher Examination was introduced. Associations were to give 21 days' notice of an examination. This was to enable arrangements to be put in place – appointing a Supervisor and sending him the required number of examination papers.

In 1970 the full committee rejected a proposal from the Executive Committee that the Refresher Examination pass mark should be 85%.

A major change occurred in 1973 when the Executive Committee decided that different papers should be set for the Entrance and Refresher Examinations. It is remarkable that it took until then to decide that the Refresher Examination should merit a paper in its own right, given that it was meant to test the candidates' detailed knowledge of the Laws of the Game as part of the requirements for admission to the List. Mowat, Crossley and Willie Allan were appointed as a sub-committee to prepare new papers. The new Refresher Examination was devised with a higher level of questions than existed for the Entrance Examination.

A change to the principles of re-sits also occurred that year – candidates could now sit the Entrance Examination a maximum of three times and the Refresher Examination twice. The minimum number of candidates required for each Examination was set as four in 1976.

In 1977, the Supervisors re-affirmed a previous decision that attendance at classes was not compulsory for candidates for the Refresher Examination. A fair level of attendance at classes was felt desirable. The gaining of practical experience and a continual operating knowledge of the Laws of the Game were obviously deemed sufficient for the most part.

Throughout this period, the examination format was very much like those at schools and held under an invigilating Supervisor. The examination required a great deal of writing with the relevant Law having to be regurgitated to answer each question. The duration of the examination was generally two hours.

Minimum Age Conditions

In 1960 the Referees' Associations were given the flexibility to decide the minimum age of trainees wishing to attend training classes. This was always going to be tested for a definitive view. Angus & Perthshire RA did so in 1969. This resulted in 17 years being determined as the minimum age for membership of an association. It was further defined in 1973 when it was decided that a candidate could not sit the Entrance Examination until reaching 17 years of age. A final position was reached in 1976 when 16 years of age became the minimum age.

Training Classes and Examination Schedule

A standard schedule of training classes fell into place relatively quickly. The training classes ran for 10-12 weeks with each class lasting for about two hours per week. There were two examination schedules – autumn and spring, with it being determined in 1950 that they should be held during the first weeks of November and April. The smaller associations often just held their training classes in the autumn, there being insufficient numbers to warrant a course in the spring.

A firm line was taken with the examination schedule and this approach was rigidly adhered to through to the mid-1960's. Slowly and surely the schedule was adjusted and by the mid-1970's the standard window for Entrance and Refresher Examinations was set as the first 14 days of December and April. Even then, problems with dates were experienced and dispensation had to be given to hold examinations outwith these periods. A degree of flexibility for the holding of Entrance Examinations operated for the North of Scotland RA as it was advised that an Entrance Examination could be held in any month, the Supervisors realising that flexibility was necessary for the association given the size of its geographical area.

Up to 1961, the standard text book used in the training classes was the SFA's "Guide to the Laws of Football". Thereafter, the FIFA publication the "Universal Guide of Referees – Laws of the Game" came into use. IFAB had decided that year that such a book should be introduced to counter what it realised was a diversity of interpretation and a lack of uniformity in world football.

Marking of Papers

The marking of papers was always taken very seriously and diligently. A hard-line approach was adopted and maintained for many years.

The first instance of an appeal being made by someone who had not passed the Class 3 Examination is recorded in 1949. The Supervisors *"could not find any reason for dissatisfaction"* and considered that the paper had been properly marked.

In 1954, George Graham reported laxness in the marking of papers and asked the Supervisors to ensure that all answers were in accordance with the Key. Also that year it was decided that all future Refresher Examination papers marked between 75 and 82% should be rechecked. The same applied to Class 3 Examination papers with marks of between 75 and 79%. There was a realisation that, despite the existence of Key Answer Papers, there could be inconsistencies in the marking of papers and using a safety net of re-scrutinising papers between these marks would be beneficial and fair to the candidates.

Some serious issues emerged with the examinations conducted in December 1961. The papers of all successful candidates were returned to the respective Supervisors for consultation with the candidates concerned. As it became evident that discrepancies had occurred in the marking of papers, the Supervisors were reminded of their responsibility in marking. The Examination Sub-Committee conducted a review which resulted in fresh examination papers being prepared every year.

From 1963, a Supervisor could be given the paper of a candidate who had failed the examination so that areas where the candidate fell down could be identified to enable him to be better prepared for the next attempt. No objections to the marking of the paper could be submitted.

In 1973, an Angus & Perthshire RA coach enquired if it would be possible for a failed Entrance candidate to be given an oral examination to determine if they had failed primarily because of their inability to put pen to paper. Willie Allan replied pointing out that it was necessary for a referee to be capable of submitting written reports in a reasonable manner, and that from this point of view an oral examination would not be suitable. The Supervisors agreed. The view expressed by Allan summed up the approach taken by the SFA in this respect for many years. A good level of competence was inherently expected of referees.

Location of Courses

The Referees' Associations generally held their training classes in the main centres of population within their area. However, North of Scotland RA in particular held courses in a variety of towns across its large geographical area. Classes required to be held in areas where there was a need for referees to service local football, given the impossibility of having the candidates travel to Inverness for the training classes.

Courses were also organised in Stornoway, normally over a weekend with a Supervisor (often one from another association) being sent to conduct the course and invigilate at the examination.

This principle applied also to courses held regularly in Orkney and Shetland, under the wing of Aberdeen & District RA. A course was first held in Shetland in 1950. The Class 1 referee Charlie Faultless conducted the course, which was arranged to coincide with his visit to the islands to referee the annual match against Orkney.

Increasing the numbers of referees was a prime objective of the associations, but this possibility was denied Edinburgh & District RA in 1964. The association sought permission to hold a course in Berwick-upon-Tweed but when it was established that six of the seven prospective attendees lived in Northumberland, permission was withheld.

Examination Results

The results of the examinations were always reviewed by the Supervisors. Consideration of the results was heightened following the introduction of a new examination paper. Often in these instances, it was the candidates' fault, not the paper, when results were deemed to be poor. Consideration of the results would also lead to the conditions attached to the examination being reviewed, which sometimes led to an adjustment to the time allowed. When an association's results were held to be poor, the association's Supervisor was detailed to investigate the possible causes.

The examination results each season were recorded in the minutes of the Supervisors' meetings from season 1970-71. The following table, covering the period from 1970 to 1988 shows the overall number of candidates and passes in the Entrance and Refresher Examinations. There is no information on Refresher Examination results for season 1974-75.

Table 3: Entrance and Refresher Examination Results 1970-71 to 1987-88

Season	Entrance	Passes	Refresher	Passes
1970-71	236	164	68	53
1971-72	186	147	53	44
1972-73	136	112	64	57
1973-74	199	111	45	6
1974-75	202	130	-	-
1975-76	171	132	61	35
1976-77	272	224	72	41
1977-78	331	286	50	39
1978-79	161	131	36	29
1979-80	236	167	66	50
1980-81	284	206	79	61
1981-82	263	204	60	54
1982-83	302	239	45	38
1983-84	268	227	48	42
1984-85	210	171	51	44
1985-86	227	136	53	38
1986-87	225	158	41	32
1987-88	225	145	35	27
Average	230	172	52	38

The numbers coming into refereeing each season varied. An average of 172 new referees per year, spread over the associations, does not seem to be a very healthy situation to be in if the refereeing movement was to continue to flourish. There was almost an acceptance that people would come forward of their own accord to become referees, much in the same way as players would be generated automatically from playing in the streets. Taking a long term view was never particularly contemplated by the Supervisors. Consideration of the Entrance Examination results twice a year, and having a "feel" for how things were in each of their associations, was as close as they got to taking gauge of the health of the associations. A saving grace in this issue was the relative healthy numbers of referees taking the Refresher Examination. There were still sufficient referees wanting to progress to the List.

Educational Courses
From the 1970's onwards, refereeing attracted interest from schools and colleges as curricula developed into new fields.

That said, refereeing had long recognised schools as being a good breeding ground for referees. In 1947 Bob Carruthers introduced a scheme in Lanarkshire for the training of secondary school pupils as referees.

The SFA received enquiries from schools in Aberdeenshire and Lanarkshire in the 1970's in regard to the holding of courses with a view to the pupils sitting the Entrance Examination. The Supervisors decided that only those who had attended courses organised by one of the associations were eligible to sit an official examination.

Issues concerning the ability of associations to staff such courses, particularly during normal working hours, emerged also. Approval was given in 1979 to Jordanhill College of Education to hold a training class for PE Students provided that Glasgow RA could supply staff to service the course.

That same year, there was agreement in principle to the introduction of a training class for school teachers. Successful candidates would be qualified to referee in schools' football but they had to join an association if they wished to referee in other grades of football.

The 1980's saw enquiries being received from Colleges of Further Education as a consequence of a new educational syllabus for 16-18 year olds. The Supervisors determined that successful candidates should be issued with a letter stating that they had passed an examination held to be the equivalent of the Entrance Examination but that they would not be allowed to referee in authorised football until they applied for, and been accepted into, membership of an association.

Instructors/Coaches meetings

Refereeing is full of people deserving of the tag "unsung hero" for what they contribute to the well-being of the movement. Prime contenders for such a description are those who acted as Training Class instructors or Coaches, training the next generation of referees. Although it has to be recognised that there would have been a variance in the quality of the coaches, all selflessly gave of their time to take the courses and prepare the candidates for the examination. Whilst learning the Laws of the Game was generally a matter for more or less learning the various Laws off by heart (because they do need to be known!) the Instructors enlivened the classes by passing on anecdotes from games to illustrate the points being addressed.

The words used by Frank Crossley in a report he made to the Supervisors in 1978 following a coaches' meeting at the Referees' Conference sum up their contribution perfectly as he *"thanked the coaches for their interest and effort which they continued to provide for the benefit of the game"*. This was an extremely apt comment as it reflected, not just on the coaches, but on everyone who is involved in the refereeing movement, fulfilling as they do a variety of roles at all levels of refereeing – all for their love of, and commitment to, football. All of which would be entirely unseen by the vast majority of participants involved in the playing side and the followers of football too. In regard to the coaches' contribution, it was indeed football which benefited from their input. Without them, there would be no referees. And without referees, there would be no games.

The importance of having meetings of coaches, to generate a uniformity of approach, was recognised early, the matter being raised first in 1952. A meeting was held at the 1960 Summer School.

It was not all plain sailing however. The conservative nature of the SFA's approach to things had to be contended with on occasion. In 1968, the Supervisors rebuffed a proposal raised at the Summer School that a coaches' meeting should be organised, considering that it was not needed. This outcome encapsulated the workings of the time and the almost glacial movement to a point which should have been reached earlier. A coaches' meeting was held at the 1970 Conference with the aim of developing a uniform basis of instruction at training classes. These meetings became part of the Conference programme and the reports of the meetings from 1975 to 1978 are instructive as to the business conducted.

The coaching syllabus used by Edinburgh & District RA was considered in 1975, with all associations encouraged to adopt a similar system. Adoption of the syllabus became mandatory the following year after its praises were sung by those associations which had used it.

The coaches suggested that the SFA should give consideration to purchasing audio-visual equipment to enable special films to be made on refereeing to benefit the movement and which would also be useful at SFA Coaching Courses. (Jack Mowat obtained a film from FIFA). The suggestion that a practical examination should be part of the Entrance Examination was also raised. It would be another 25 years before this practice was adopted. The feeling of the coaches was that the written examination was fair, but clearly in favour of an academic student.

The method of selection of coaches was also addressed, with the feeling expressed that the system left much to be desired and in some instances was left to someone to volunteer. It was a firm view that the first priority should be the ability of the instructor to communicate and have a thorough knowledge of the Laws. On this point, Class 1 referees acted as coaches down the years in many associations, as they fitted the bill in this respect.

There was a feeling that more contact should be made between newly qualified referees and coaches to assist in the handling of issues in their early appointments. Varying ideas were bandied about the timescale which should operate, whether meetings should be held after three months or even after a season. Such views were indicative of an emerging realisation that more was needed to be done to support new referees in the early stages of their careers. Similar to the suggestion of an oral examination, these views demonstrated foresight on the part of the coaches.

The coaches also felt there should be greater feedback to them on Laws which were causing issues to candidates in the examinations and on any flaws in the coaching style of a coach. These points were well motivated and totally for the betterment for the development of referees. The time for addressing them was still some way away however.

Women's football was recognised by the SFA in the mid-1970's and that threw up the prospect of women seeking to take up refereeing. In the male dominated conservative world of Scottish football, that gave some pause for thought as to what would have to happen. A number of associations required guidance. For a while, it seemed that separate classes might have to be held for them (at extra cost to the SFA and extra time to coaches). The topic was debated by the four British Associations which initially decided against holding mixed classes, but this position was quickly changed. Women joined the male trainees in the classes and, to no surprise, the majority of coaches felt that mixed classes were satisfactory, although some felt the presence of females inhibited the male attendees. The women were deemed to be able pupils. Those early pioneers deserve great credit.

The possibility of an oral examination reared its head once more during season 1982-83 when the coaches again made the suggestion. This was not supported by the Executive Committee but another point put forward by the coaches – that there should be should be a Supervisor appointed who would have special responsibility for correlating coaching activities in Scotland - would play a part in setting in motion something which, a few years later, would have a lasting impact on refereeing in Scotland.

Scottish Football League

Having established a position of power in the game during the 1930's, the SFL continued to exert influence in the post Second World War period. Regular political tensions existed between the SFA and the SFL as the SFL vied for dominance and influence in the running of the game. Refereeing was often where such tensions collided. The dominant position of the SFL was such that refereeing had to be seen to be taking cognisance of the SFL and to be doing what was expected of it – improving refereeing standards.

The Post War Years

SFL issues featured heavily in refereeing matters in the immediate post war years. The SFL was informed that the Supervisors were prepared to investigate and to deal with any specific complaint against a referee. When complaints were received and where the complaint was of a specific nature, it was referred to the referee's Supervisor for investigation. The complaints and reports were considered and further action decided if thought necessary.

A system of team control operated in SFL matches for a couple of seasons in the late 1940's. Suggested by the Supervisors, it was intended as an experiment designed to improve close co-operation between referees and linesmen with such teams being appointed to matches on a continual basis.

The Supervisors' Sub-Committee, no doubt aware of the external scrutiny by the SFL and motivated by an aim of being transparent, decided in 1948 to suggest to the SFA that the SFL be invited to appoint a representative to attend Supervisors' meetings. The suggestion was never progressed.

Political Battles

Season 1949-50 saw a skirmish between the SFA and the SFL on refereeing. This stemmed from the Referee Committee's investigation of incidents and crowd misbehaviour during a Rangers v. Celtic match. Addressing the issues surrounding matches between the clubs, the Referee Committee, quite unbelievably, decided to ask the SFL *"to consider whether, owing to the frequency with which Scottish referees come into contact with the players in their various matches, it would not be advisable in matches such as between these two clubs where tension is likely to be great, to appoint a referee from another British Association; or if such a suggestion does not find favour, they should discontinue the practice of balloting the referee for these matches and appoint the referee by other means."* This was a staggering thought – the National Association, responsible for referees, suggesting that the country's major league should consider appointing a referee from another National Association to matches between two of its clubs.

The SFL quickly met the Referee Committee as a consequence. Various matters concerning control of matches, appointment, grading and inspection of referees were discussed, from which it emerged that the *"attention of referees be drawn to points of play upon which there would seem to be a lack of uniformity"*. The Supervisors' attention was also to be drawn to matters which fell within the scope of their duties. The issue of "foreign" referees was quietly dropped.

Subsequently, the Referee Committee had dialogue with the Supervisors on all of the points discussed with the SFL, with instructions passed on them.

At the end of season 1971-72, the Supervisors expressed strong disapproval and disappointment at an SFL decision to *"dispense with the services"* of two Class 1 referees, Ronnie Crawford and Jimmy McKee, in the latter part of the season. Taking up the cudgels, the Referee Committee called a meeting with the SFL to discuss the circumstances and implications of the decision. To reflect the important nature of the issue, Hugh Nelson, the SFA President, David Will, a member of the Referee Committee and Willie Allan represented the SFA. The outcome was not reported in the minutes but the fact that both referees were downgraded to Class 3B the following season indicates which body's views prevailed.

This was the forerunner of a similar issue on a bigger scale two seasons later.

Following the confirmation of the 1974-75 List, the SFL intimated that it would not appoint three Class 1 referees, Ian Grant, Tom Kellock and Alan Paterson to matches. A series of meetings ensued over the following months. Jack Mowat and Frank Crossley attended one Referee Committee meeting on behalf of the Supervisors to *"express the utmost concern"* at the unresolved position of the referees and were able to engineer their attendance at the Referee Committee's next meeting with the SFL. In a show of strength, the SFL Office Bearers, six Management Committee members and the League Secretary, Tommy Maule, attended.

David Will, now the Referee Committee Chairman, made it clear, following the approval of the List by the committee and then by Council, that the committee was not prepared to recommend to Council to change the classification of the three referees unless the SFL was able to advance convincing, and hitherto unknown, reasons why it should do. Will explained the functioning of the Supervisors, and the method employed by them in deciding upon their recommendations on the List to the committee. The reasons which had led the SFL to disregard the classification of the three referees were made known. Mowat and Crossley joined the meeting. They spoke forcibly of the anger, the ill-feeling and the resentment which had been generated among referees, and to the support expressed at a meeting of the various associations, by the SFL's refusal to appoint the three referees to matches. After the SFL's representatives met separately, the SFL President intimated that, as a gesture of goodwill, the SFL was prepared to appoint the three referees. The discussion concluded with Will re-affirming that, in future, there would be closer liaison between the SFA and the SFL in the compilation of the List.

That certainly happened. The SFL received a standing invitation to the Referee Committee meetings when the List was to be confirmed each season, meeting the committee once the Supervisors' recommendations had been approved. An invitation to the mid-season review of the List also became standard practice. It became customary for matters on referees and refereeing to be discussed at these meetings. The Supervisors had often reason to defend or explain the workings of refereeing to the SFL through the Referee Committee. Often, points addressed would reflect the tittle-tattle talk of Boardrooms and matters which were concerning club directors – the desire to curb cautions, the possibility of referees changing their diagonal to save wear and tear of running areas for linesmen, the methods adopted by referees in giving warnings to players and such like. In 1976 the SFL wished that a renewed instruction be issued to ensure that a Supervisor should not call at the referees' room before, during or after a match. A fear of potential influence by a Supervisor on a referee to the detriment of a club underpinned the request. When queried, no specific cases were cited.

Appointment Issues
The appointing of referees to matches by the SFL became an issue over the years. An early example of the views of the Supervisors is recorded in 1965 when the Executive Committee requested that an approach be made to the SFL that "*careful selection of appointments should be made for Class 1 referees in their first season*". The gap between appointments that some

referees experienced was a problem which often cropped up. When such points were raised with the SFL, they were generally fended off by a "mind your own business" explanation.

The Supervisors had concern as to when a Class 1 referee should first receive appointment to the SFL Premier Division, following league reconstruction in 1975. It was proposed to the Referee Committee in 1977 that the SFL should be requested not to appoint newly promoted Class 1 referees to that Division during their first season. This was declined by the SFL with the Supervisors repeating the request a year later. The proposal exhibited sound logic in protecting referees in the early stages of their developing career at Class 1. It was foolhardy to think that a referee would be ready to referee in the country's top league in his first year at Class 1. It took a few years for the SFL to accept the point.

Business Settles Down
There was a settling down of major matters from the mid-1970's onwards. Areas of discussion came to centre around the mechanics of the refereeing system – the marking system, the use of Club Reports marks, the appointment of referees, the possibilities of appointing Class 2 referees on a national basis to better assist in their supervisory coverage and the possible effects of a reduction in Reserve League football on the composition of the List.

Suspensions and Deletions

In the post-war period there was only one instance when a referee was suspended.

The unfortunate referee was Jimmy Callaghan, following a match between Celtic and Rangers in August 1969. The Referee Committee addressed the issue directly after Rangers submitted a letter. Callaghan and his standside linesman were interviewed. It was determined that Callaghan had failed in his duty as a referee and had committed a major error in failing to send off a Celtic player, previously cautioned, who was guilty of violent conduct. A two-month suspension was imposed on him.

Callaghan was one of the top referees in the country and had refereed that year's Scottish Cup Final between the two clubs. He was also a FIFA referee. The suspension did not impact on him as he served on the FIFA List until season 1972-73.

It was a different situation altogether in 1978 for another FIFA referee, John Gordon, when he and two other officials were deleted from the List in what was a shameful episode for Scottish refereeing. This happened just a few months after Gordon had officiated at the World Cup Finals in Argentina. The SFA had got wind that they had accepted excessive gifts from AC Milan before a UEFA Cup match against Levski Spartak. In terms of the amount of gifts which they had received, it can only be wondered how many suitcases were needed.

Ernie Walker, now Secretary, commenced an investigation by interviewing Gordon. This led to the SFA Office Bearers interviewing Gordon and the two linesmen, Rollo Kyle (Class 1) and David McCartney (Class 3A). The officials refused to respond to any questions on the matter, despite repeatedly being reminded of the importance to the SFA of giving their full co-operation and that the circumstances had been reported to UEFA. As the referees indicated that they were unable to attend a UEFA meeting, Walker and Tom Younger, the SFA Vice-President, attended. An interim suspension was placed on the three officials following the UEFA meeting and handling the affair moved to the Disciplinary & Referee Committee. The referees largely maintained their silence during the hearing. Given the circumstances, Tom Wharton represented the Supervisors by attending as a witness to proceedings. He retired from the meeting when the committee deliberated on the outcome.

Whilst the impartiality of the officials during the match was unquestioned, they were found to have been foolhardy in allowing themselves to be put in a position whereby their impartiality could be prejudiced. They were in gross breach of UEFA regulations governing hospitality by accepting an excessive amount of gifts well beyond permitted limits and had been uncooperative in the investigation despite repeated warnings as to the consequences.

The officials were deleted from the List and advised that no application for re-admission would be accepted from them before April 1981.

Gordon's name was automatically removed from the FIFA List of International Referees as a consequence.

UEFA found AC Milan guilty of a serious breach of its regulations but only imposed a modest fine. The SFA expressed strong views to UEFA on this outcome.

Appropriate comment on the sorry affair was made in that season's Annual Report. There were two telling sentences: *"There was no question of the three officials having been guilty of anything other than a remarkable imprudence coupled with a refusal to co-operate when the affair was investigated. Had co-operation been forthcoming it is probable that all three would still be on the List."*

In 1980, David McCartney submitted a letter to the SFA requesting that the suspension imposed on him be lifted so that he could apply for inclusion on the List for season 1980-81. This was a season earlier than set out. The Supervisors took no action. McCartney did not make any further applications for the List. He continued to serve his association, Edinburgh & District RA, for many years as a Minor Grades Panel member and helped many young referees with their development.

Summer School/Referees' Conference

Establishing a Success Story

The new refereeing structure promised that *"there will be a Summer school at a suitable centre open to all referees where lectures and discussions and interchange of ideas can take place under the Supervisors and other officials. The SFA will make arrangements for the Course and the Supervisors will arrange the programme of lectures and discussions."*

The first Summer School was not held until 1948, as a suitable venue could not be secured in the preceding years. The venue was Dounans Camp, Aberfoyle and held over a weekend at the end of May or early June given the dates of subsequent Schools. The programme included Practical Demonstrations, Group Discussions and General Talks. For the practical demonstrations, Willie Webb acted as the referee with David Turner and James Craig as the linesmen. A loudspeaker was used to *"enable the same interpretation of events to be available to all in attendance"*.

One major decision emerged from that first School. There had been a unanimous request from the referees to introduce the fixed diagonal system of control (the method of a referee running diagonally on the field of play to cover the areas not covered by each linesman) in place of the flexible system which was then in use and, on the recommendation of the Supervisors, the Referee Committee gave its agreement. The change took effect from the commencement of season 1949-50. But at the same time it was decided that all referees be entitled to practice either the right or left hand diagonal provided always that the flexible system is employed.

The Summer School warranted a mention in the SFA's Annual Report for season 1949-50. As the report had a narrow distribution to just the clubs and affiliated associations in membership of the SFA, the reference to the School served to explain the workings of refereeing to the membership. The comment was praiseworthy: *"These past two years, a Referees' Weekend Course has been arranged at Aberfoyle in an effort to arrive at uniform decisions on the Laws of the Game. It is felt that only by personal discussions and talks can the views of the different sections be obtained and under the guidance of the Supervisors these conferences have proved very fruitful. To encourage as many referees as possible to attend, the SFA agreed to refund railway fares in excess of 10/- and it is hoped to repeat this subvention this year. Those who have attended the course have expressed their complete satisfaction with the whole atmosphere in which they have been carried on and the evident desire of all to co-operate in improving the standard of refereeing"*.

The suggestion that refereeing standards would be improved as a result of the new structure and having a Summer School would have been a good selling point to clubs. They would be reassured that things were being done. The 1951-52 Annual Report offered further praise: *"The summer weekend for referees has now become an established institution and is eagerly anticipated by all referees. The course last year was held at Meigle and was well attended. Instruction, discussion and lectures occupied most of the time and proved of great value. The course was organised and carried through by the Supervisors who are due thanks for all their work during the season. The advance in standard of refereeing is steadily going on and there will be no let-up by the Supervisors in their efforts to provide the best type of referee."*

The Summer School established itself very quickly in a matter of a few years. It became the high point of the Scottish refereeing calendar, an event looked forward to by many. In 1969, it was renamed the Referees' Conference. Attendance was always open to all referees and this gave the gathering a great flavour – there was a great mix of referees from every association and young referees could meet and listen to, and speak with, the top referees. One of the great strengths of the School/Conference was the cross-fertilisation in the debates between referees of all classes at Discussion Groups.

There was also a great social aspect of the weekend and this was reflected in the contents of the programme. It was a weekend to be enjoyed with a mix of serious issues debated and some more relaxed fun. All the more fun was had on the Friday and Saturday nights when the referees hit St. Andrews and kept the pubs very busy. How many took advantage of the option of attending a church service on the Sunday morning, a staple part of the programme for many years, is open to question. The School/Conference was generally very well attended by referees. Although the actual attendances were not recorded for many years, there would have been around 150 referees present through to the mid-1960's and by the mid-1980's the attendance figure was around the 250 mark.

From the very early days of the School, Referee Committee members and SFA Office Bearers were regular attendees and over the years were joined by members of the SFL Management Committee. The Summer School/Conference provided them with the opportunity of meeting referees and Supervisors on an informal basis. It was also an ideal forum for educational purposes for these "football club people". An increased level of understanding of refereeing should have been easily gained by their attendance.

Venues

The Summer School was held in a number of venues during the 1950's and 1960's. Belmont Camp, Meigle was used in 1951. Butlin's Holiday Camp at Ayr was selected for 1957 as no other venue could be arranged. The choice was successful as the School returned there in 1958 and 1959. For the 1958 School, the Referees' Associations were asked which venue would be most suitable for their members – Dounans Camp or Butlins. The latter was a predictable majority choice! In 1960, the University of St. Andrews was the venue for the first time. St. Andrews became the spiritual home of the School/Conference once it became the permanent venue from 1970. Dounans Camp, Broomlee Camp, West Linton and Middleton Camp, Gorebridge were other venues used in the 1960's.

Format/Programme

Once a gathering such as the Conference becomes established over a number of years, the format and structure can often become repetitive each year. In 1972, Tom Wharton and Bert Sturgeon proposed the possible re-organisation of the Conference and produced a report which examined a possible change of time, venue, and the purpose and content of the conference.

After consideration of the report, St. Andrews was confirmed as the venue, in mid-June, and that its principal aim should continue to be educational with a social aspect. It was re-affirmed that the Conference was open to all referees and not restricted to "Listed" officials, one of the suggestions made in the report. Some elements of the report were accepted - the holding of a meeting of "Listed" officials during the Conference and making fuller use of the two days.

The 1973 Conference programme put into effect the agreed changes. Only two Discussion Groups were used – "Listed" and "Non Listed" referees. Wharton and Sturgeon led the "Listed" group and an active referee took the "Non Listed" referees. Wharton and Sturgeon addressed the conference on "*technical developments in football and the relationship of these to referees*".

The same format was used in 1974 but it did not go down as well as expected. Several Referees' Associations were critical of various aspects of the Conference. The Referees' Bulletin of April 1975 addressed the issue and made some pertinent points: "*It is generally acknowledged that the 1974 Conference did not measure up. If one were to judge by written and verbal comment, it would seem that individuals among the Supervisors cannot escape some of the responsibility. Criticism should not be aimed in only one direction. It might not be an exaggeration to say that a record number played truant from time to time. This is a situation which cannot be allowed to continue. Apart from other issues, the SFA is unlikely to carry on subsidising those who choose to attend only those sessions which take their fancy.*"

For the 1975 Conference, a revamped format was almost a necessity. Four Discussion Groups were formed: Classes 1 and 2; Classes 3A and 3B; referees operating in Junior football; and all other referees. Separate Discussion Group sessions were held for "Listed" officials and all other referees, and meetings of coaches and Secretaries were organised. The same format was utilised for the next few years. In 1980 a practical demonstration session was incorporated into the Programme.

In 1981 a novel approach was taken to the preparation of the Conference programme. The Executive Committee met with three association Secretaries to prepare the programme. Involving Secretaries was probably seen as a way of minimising the risk of any criticism of the programme format in the aftermath of the Conference. It was all quiet on that front that year.

Discussion Points

By the end of the 1950's, a report was compiled after each Summer School, recording the decisions taken at talks and discussion groups for distribution to the referee movement. These were much debated by the Supervisors before a final decision was taken. Final reports would on occasion be submitted to the SFA for approval and issues referred to the Referee Committee when required for its consideration.

The inclusion of the Summary of Discussion Points with the minutes of the Supervisors' meetings first occurred in 1971 and, although not repeated every year after, the documentation which does exist is very revealing as to the points which were covered at the Conferences.

In 1971, some of the discussion points focussed on the wider football issues of the day. In this respect, the views of the referees were always a handy sounding board for the Supervisors and the SFA. Other than through the Supervisors, the refereeing movement did not have a strong voice within football.

The disciplinary system was a major subject in the early 1970's. The referees were asked to debate what steps could be taken to curb field offences. All Discussion Groups were critical of the Referee Committee's perceived leniency and inconsistency in the issuing of suspensions. A call was made, very presciently given how matters worked out later in the decade, to adopt a system of penalty points for offence with a suspension applying on a player accumulating a certain amount of points, with suspensions being for a number of matches rather than for a period of time. That said, the referees also accepted that their concern should not be with the punishment method, as it was accepted that was the preserve of the committee and that "*a referee's responsibility was one of direct and impartial implementation of the Laws*". The referees also accepted the right of an appeal by a player.

On the point of representation within the SFA, the Class 1 referees were of the view that refereeing should be represented on the SFA Council by a Supervisor.

There was a discussion on the use of replays of match incidents during football broadcasts on television. This was generally favoured by referees as it was thought they would be useful to both referees and the public in proving the correctness of a referee's decision. The referees were strongly against the use of television footage as admissible evidence in a disciplinary hearing.

In his opening address, Jack Mowat made regular reference to points which would be discussed during the Group sessions. These points would without fail be generated from refereeing issues which had come to the fore during the season and many were to do with referees not applying the Laws in various types of incidents. The points were raised to remind referees to apply the Laws. The elimination of inconsistency in the application of the Laws, and reducing the discretionary ability which referees had in some respects in their officiating, was the desired aim. Conference was the only opportunity each year which provided the chance to address referees on the technical aspects of refereeing. Mowat made the most of that opportunity.

One particular point discussed in 1974 provides an excellent illustration of how refereeing was approached at that time. It concerned a player deliberately catching the ball to prevent an attack developing. For the World Cup that year, FIFA had decided that a player should be cautioned in such a circumstance, in addition to the offence being penalised by the award of a free-kick or penalty kick to the opposing team depending on its locus. The referees were asked if such an instruction should be issued by the SFA. Mowat acknowledged that he was aware that some were strongly opposed to such a suggestion but felt it essential that a greater uniformity of interpretation was achieved. He referred to having seen the offence being punished in three ways – a free-kick only, a free-kick and a warning and a free-kick and a caution. In similar vein, Mowat raised the issue of whether a caution should be given to a defending player who handled the ball to prevent it from going into his team's goal. He alluded to a wide diversity of opinion on these issues and urged the referees to reach a decision which *"may do something to obviate the present chaotic circumstances, which are unsatisfactory to players, managements, spectators and referees."* The outcome of the discussion was that the SFA should raise these issues with IFAB. Regardless of what came of that, referees of the modern era may have their eyes opened in terms of the type of incidents which were under consideration, given the current Laws, but referees would equally recognise the fact that debate on refereeing issues took place in that era in much the same way as happens now.

In 1981, the Supervisors expressed dissatisfaction with the application of the Law on the then "four step rule" when considering the Discussion Points summary. They felt that a change in the wording of the Law would be beneficial. Ernie Walker conveyed that IFAB had undertaken to look into the matter. Great faith was put into the outcomes of the Discussion Points. A "ruling from the SFA" carried great weight. The dissemination of information was a drawn out process, however, following the Conference. The Group Leaders/Secretaries had to prepare a report on their group's discussions and submit it to the SFA. The SFA administration then compiled a composite summary of Discussion Points for submission to the Supervisors at their October meeting, four months after Conference. The Supervisors approved a request from Glasgow RA in season 1986-87 that all referees who attend Conference should receive a copy of the Discussion Points Summary.

Guest Speakers
A traditional element of the programme was the attendance of one or two Guest Speakers. Much effort was expended to arrange suitable people. Notable Guest Speakers were Jock Stein (Celtic Manager, 1967), Harry Cavan (Irish FA President, 1968), Ken Aston (former English World Cup referee, 1973), Desmond White (Celtic Chairman, 1974), Archie McPherson (BBC Football Commentator, 1976), Fritz Siepelt (UEFA Referees Committee Chairman, 1979), Brian Marjoribanks (BBC Scotland Sports presenter, 1982) and Ken Ridden (UEFA Referees Committee, 1987). Attempts were made in three successive years from 1974 to get Denis Howell, then the UK Minister of Sport, to be the Guest Speaker, all to no avail.

Open Forum
The Open Forum was a regular and popular fixture in the programme for many years, held on the Sunday. The referees were presented with the opportunity to ask a small panel of SFA

and SFL representatives questions on the running of the game and refereeing matters. This was relished by the referees but probably less so by the panellists. Every Forum could be relied upon to have a "curved ball" question put to it. Polite diplomacy was generally the style of response.

Peter Scott Trophy

Peter Scott was a member of the Referee Committee for much of the 1960's, serving as Chairman for three of these seasons. He was also the SFA President from 1968 to 1970. As a gesture of appreciation towards the refereeing movement, he donated a trophy to be competed for at the Conference. The competition took the form of an inter-association general knowledge team quiz and became an integral part of the programme. It was intended to develop the social side of the Conference but it became very competitive with the associations very keen to win it. Ernie Walker compiled the questions and acted as the question master in the mid-1970's.

Sports

The Saturday of the School/Conference was rounded off in the late afternoon by the holding of a sports competition for the Referees' Associations. 5-a-side football and tug-of-war featured over the years. The football sometimes got a wee bit out of hand, which was just about the norm when referees played. A few individuals were cajoled into organising the Sports and the SFA met the cost of the prizes which were given out. A Referees' Golf Competition became a standard precursor to the School/Conference on the Friday, as those referees who were golfers wished to make a weekend of it. There were plenty of courses to play in the East Neuk of Fife.

Press Attendance

There was a degree of openness attached to the Summer School/Conference. Members of the press were allowed to attend. Publicity was generated to the wider public as to what was happening in the world of refereeing in Scotland. However, in 1967, Glasgow RA and Lanarkshire RA requested that the press should not be allowed to attend Discussion Group sessions. There was obviously a desire on their part not to show to the press the types of arguments and disagreements which could happen in the Discussions Groups and which could be used potentially to show refereeing in a bad light. The request was approved. The press were still able to attend the plenary sessions, but their main attention was always on the opening session of the School/Conference. Each year they reported on Jack Mowat's opening talk, which he used to review the season just ended and speak of points which would be addressed over the weekend. He also generally referred to the number of sendings-off and cautions for the season just finished. The Conference regularly generated stories and headlines for the Sunday newspapers, which, in mid-June, was always welcome for the journalists.

Any "doors open" transparency did not apply in 1976 when the SFA Executive & General Purposes Committee refused a request from the Players' Union for the association's Office Bearers to attend the Conference. The position did change, however. In the mid-1980's, Tony Higgins, the Players' Union Secretary, was invited to be a Guest Speaker. Bridges were now being built between referees and players.

Financial Support and Cost

As evident in the comments made in the Annual Report of 1949-50, the SFA recognised that it would be helpful to encourage the attendance of referees by refunding the cost of railway fares in excess of 10 shillings. The provision of such financial subsidy became an integral part of the School/Conference.

Meeting the accommodation costs of all referees under 21 years of age was introduced in 1954. From 1958 the cost of meals and accommodation was subsidised to the extent of £1 per person for those over 21 years of age in addition to meeting travel costs over 10 shillings for referees. Those under 21 had their subsidy increased to 50% of the cost in 1960. The £1 subsidy to other referees was halved in 1963 but returned to £1 in 1970.

The entire cost of travel of all referees attending the Conference was met by the SFA from 1977, and those referees under 25 years of age had 50% of the cost of accommodation and meals paid by the SFA. The £1 subsidy given to other referees ceased. As the School/Conference developed, so did the net cost to the SFA. The following figures, drawn from the SFA's accounts contained in its Annual Reports, provide a snapshot of the costs over a number of years:

Table 4: Net Cost of the Referees' Conference 1973 to 1988

Net Cost	£
1973	731
1978	2275
1982	3573
1984	5775
1985	6211
1988	7556

Physical Training and Fitness Test

Physical Training
The introduction of weekly physical training sessions at Referees' Associations was one of the main planks of the new refereeing structure. Arrangements were quickly put in place by the Supervisors. A few of the associations have more than one training centre given their geographical size. Glasgow RA operates with three training centres - East, South and West. Edinburgh & District RA had until recent years a second training centre in West Lothian in addition to the main one in Edinburgh. The grounds of SFL clubs were used for many years. The last ground to be used was Glebe Park, Brechin, where the local Angus & Perthshire RA referees trained.
During season 1945-46, due to an issue at Glasgow (East), it was agreed that *"all referees should be required to train as directed by the individual Supervisors"* and if permission were given to train elsewhere, *"each Supervisor should take steps to assure himself that such individual or individuals do so regularly."*
An integral part of the aims of the new structure was that attendance registers were to be kept and examined by

Supervisors. The register had to be signed at each training session by every individual present with a copy being countersigned by the Supervisor in charge, who was then required to send the register to the SFA. In 1979, the Supervisors introduced a requirement that, in general, all referees should have a 70% attendance at training.

Fitness Test
In 1974, compulsory physical fitness and health tests for international referees were introduced by FIFA. The fitness test was the Cooper Test, used by the US Military, and considered to be the best possible means of assessing referees' fitness. In spite of the Scottish referees having to do it each year as part of the nomination process for inclusion in the FIFA List, it took five years for the subject to be broached by the Supervisors. A suggestion that the test should be adopted for the fitness assessment of Class 1 and Class 2 officials was not agreed.

Within a year, however, the Supervisors came to the view that a referee should be required to prove his fitness before being accepted on to the List. Strangely, it was decided to refer the method of assessment to the Secretary, Ernie Walker. To no-one's surprise, the Cooper Test was chosen. The Disciplinary & Referee Committee approved the Supervisors' recommendation at the end of season 1980-81 that the Test be introduced. The successful completion of the test became a pre-requisite for all referees applying for re-inclusion or inclusion on the List. The test was taken prior to the referees submitting their renewal or application forms and was overseen by a Supervisor from another association. Each referee had to submit a form confirming the completion of the Test which had to be signed by his Supervisor.

Conducting the Test required the Supervisors to hire athletic tracks, with the SFA bearing the cost.

The delay in the introduction of a Fitness Test can be attributed to a fear that too many officials would fail it, which reflected how training was approached by referees in those days. This view is strengthened due to early requests being made by two Supervisors seeking an extension in the time allowed for the 400 metre run element of the test. The fear of failure and lack of fitness can be the only reasons for the requests being made. The point was discussed at length but an extension was not agreed.

A series of conditions soon required to be introduced to address issues which arose relative to the Test. The main ones were that a maximum of three attempts were allowed to pass the Test, a medical certificate had to be submitted by a referee unable to take the test through injury or illness; a referee who did not complete the Test by 31st December would have his name removed from the List and a referee who had not passed the Test would not be appointed to matches involving SFA member clubs.

Linesmen

The Supervisors always gave attention to the important role performed by linesmen. It was understood that they played a vital role in supporting the referee and were a fundamental element of the need for excellent teamwork in matches.

This was reflected initially in the short-lived operation of the team system of match control in the late 1940's. The scheme was based on the thought that a referee operating with the same linesmen in his matches would improve teamwork and increase the level of decision making.

Instructions

By the late 1950's, it was common for Instructions to Referees and Linesmen to be issued to the List prior to the start of each season.

The need to focus more on the role of the linesman led to the introduction of "Instructions to Linesmen" in 1962.

There was a long running debate for a few years from 1970 on the question of the position to be adopted by a linesman at the scoring of a goal. The Supervisors wished to make some adjustments to the established method of the linesman concerned immediately making his way to the centre line following a goal being scored. Several Referees' Associations expressing disquiet at the prospect of change. The instruction was hotly debated at the 1971 Conference. Classes 1 and 2 were completely opposed to any change in the existing instruction. All other referees, including those in Classes 3A and 3B, considered that the new instruction should assist in improving the game and was worth a try, although a suggestion was made to improve matters – by omitting any signal pointing towards the centre circle, as this was thought to likely to lead to confusion amongst players and spectators. Despite the difference in opinions, the Supervisors stuck to their guns and decided that its decision should be put into effect as from the beginning of season 1971-72.

When reviewed after the early part of that season and after all the ill feeling against the Supervisors' decision, it was generally held that the instructions were being operated successfully, much to their relief. However, the matter had not quite been put to bed. Things rumbled on to the extent that the issue was put to a vote in May 1973. The outcome was settled by Jack Mowat giving his casting vote in favour of a return to the old system. The heated nature of the arguments which would have taken place can be imagined.

"The Linesman"
This document came into operation during the mid-1970's and was updated on a frequent basis. One early instance followed the 1977 Conference. In his opening address, Jack Mowat conveyed that that few, if any, linesmen had carried out the signals for indicating offside, as illustrated in the Universal Guide for Referees. He indicated that it was imperative that the instructions be carried out especially in games played under the jurisdiction of FIFA and UEFA, intimating that Referee Observers at these games had deducted marks from the referee if his linesmen had failed to carry out the instruction. Referees were advised that the FIFA instructions should be carried out, with "The Linesman" being amended to suit.

The document was updated again following further debate at the 1982 Conference. The evidence from matches suggested that the majority of Listed officials did not appear to be in favour of the instruction on the position a linesmen should adopt at the taking of a free kick by the attacking team near their opponents' goal line. The majority confirmed that this was the case and sought greater flexibility for match officials with the referee being able to use his discretion where he and his linesmen should stand.

From 1977-78 a copy of "The Linesman" was sent to each candidate on passing the Entrance Examination. It also became standard issue to all new Class 3A referees.

Complaints from Clubs

The recourse open to clubs to convey their views on referees' performance has traditionally been by submitting a complaint to the SFA. There was always a consistent stream of traffic in this respect. The process more or less acted as a safety valve at times, as clubs assuaged their post match tempers on referees. The Supervisors in the late 1940's and early 1950's gave particular attention to complaints and were diligent in their consideration of them.

When complaints on referees were received and where it was of a specific nature, it was referred to the referee's Supervisor for investigation with further action taken if necessary. In most cases, this resulted in an increased level of supervision of the referee concerned. In some instances, the Supervisors considered that clubs were not specific enough in their complaints to allow action to be taken.

In 1959, the Greenock Morton Chairman/Secretary took it upon himself to start a one man crusade against referees, submitting a number of letters in which he was critical of referees. The Referee Committee's responses give a clear indication of the sensible and mature approach which characterised the SFA's handling of such matters. The sentiments expressed in one response still apply: *"The committee felt their duty to refute most vigorously, any suggestion that the integrity of referees is open to doubt, and to denounce those responsible for it. They expressed their conviction that responsible opinion does not believe that experienced referees consciously and premeditatedly show favour for their dealings with clubs. Furthermore, the committee consider that such ill-founded criticism cannot but be harmful to the game and liable to bring it into disrepute."*

Clubs did not just confine expressing their views to the performances of referees. Complaints were received on referees calling for floodlights to be used when clubs did not think it necessary. Complaints on matches being postponed after pitch inspections were another recurring theme. A club's idea of a playable pitch was often at opposite ends of the spectrum to that of a referee's. All such complaints required to go through the process of obtaining the referee's views.

The "heat" of a club's complaint would often be reduced hugely by the time gap between the match in question, the letter being submitted and the meeting at which it was considered. The passage of time generally cooled things down but that is not to say that the complaints were ever treated less seriously.

Points of Play

Deliberating on Points of Play and issuing a definitive answer to the refereeing movement was a hugely important facet of the Supervisors' business for many years.

Setting the Foundations

The Supervisors decided in 1946 that *"all questions discussed at Branch meetings or elsewhere concerning the Laws of the Game and of which there is any doubt or controversy as to a correct ruling be brought before the Supervisors. The question to be carefully considered by the Supervisors and a ruling given by them. This question and answer to be inserted in the following Bulletin as a guide to members and trainers. The Supervisors' decision to be accepted and acted upon by all referees under the SFA scheme."*

The first ever "Point of Play" was discussed at that same meeting: *"Circumstances: A player who has been off the field of play returns without notifying the referee. His return comes to the referee's knowledge only when that player's side is attacking and when that particular player is fouled inside the penalty area. Should a penalty be awarded? Decision: The ball should be dropped by the referee at the place where the player returned to the field of play and the player cautioned. Should the offence by the defender be sufficient to justify it, he too should be cautioned".*

Dealing with Business

The worth of keeping track of decisions on Points of Play was recognised in 1962 when a register of decisions was started.

There were times when arriving at a decision was not straightforward. A decision might not even be reached. In 1964, the Executive Committee chose to refer a Point of Play from Ayrshire RA to the full committee as it could not reach a unanimous view. The point was: *"A goalkeeper and an outfield player change places without the knowledge of the referee. The Law tells us what to do about the new goalkeeper handling the ball, but says nothing about the former goalkeeper taking part in the game, and we wonder what action a referee should take should this player score a goal before the change had been brought to the notice of the referee".* It was decided that both players should be cautioned for not informing the referee of the change of goalkeeper and that play be restarted by an indirect free kick at the spot where the offence was committed.

In November 1970 the Supervisors discussed two matters of note. Firstly, there had been an unorthodox free kick taken in an English match, Coventry City v. Everton, which had become a *cause celebre* - a player used two feet to loft the ball into the air. Secondly, the query was whether a match should be abandoned, if, for one reason and another, one of the teams were reduced to fewer than seven players. Willie Allan, demonstrating the power of the Secretary's position, made known his intention of advising referees, pending reference to IFAB, that in the first instance they should consider that the kick had not been properly taken and instruct that it be re-taken and in the second that, if, at the start of a match, one of the teams has fewer than seven players, the match should be abandoned, and that a match should not be abandoned if, after it has started, one of the teams is reduced to fewer than seven players.

Taking Points of Play to a Higher Level
The importance given to Points of Play was reflected in the fact that, on occasions, the SFA raised the point at a higher forum for clarification or determination. During season 1957-58 George Graham reported that the Secretaries of the British Associations had confirmed a decision taken by the Supervisors on a point of play query on Law 17. In 1969 the SFA referred a Supervisor's query on substitutes to IFAB.

In 1961, the Supervisors took the view that before any Point of Play decision was communicated to the Referees' Associations, the point should be referred to the SFA for approval. If the decision was not approved, the Secretary was to attend the next meeting to allow the point to be further considered. This again illustrates the power held by the SFA Secretary. Being a member of IFAB, his expertise in the Laws of the Game was held to be both invaluable and paramount.

In 1983, Lanarkshire RA submitted the following Point of Play: "*A goalkeeper standing within his own penalty area at a point close to the junction of the 18 yards line and the goal line receives the ball into his hands. He then rolls the ball outside the penalty area, dribbles the ball towards his opponents half of the field, then on reaching the end of his penalty area, kicks the ball back into the penalty area, picks the ball up and thereafter kicks the ball downfield.*" Bearing in mind the Laws of the Game at the time, the Supervisors' opinion was that the goalkeeper was committing no offence.

The decision caused minds to turn over and contemplate whether it was the correct view, because Ernie Walker took the query to IFAB in 1984. IFAB took a contrary view to the Supervisors and decided that: "*for a goalkeeper to act in the manner described would be a clear breach of the intention of Law XII 5(a) and that he should be penalised by the award of an indirect free kick to the opposing team.*"

Acting as a Sounding Board
The Supervisors provided a useful sounding board to the SFA in regard to Points of Play and the Laws of the Game. Prior to the 1986 IFAB meeting, Ernie Walker invited the views of the Supervisors on a discussion item at the meeting, namely at

which point is a substitution effected. He explained the IFAB Editorial Committee's view was that a substitution is completed when the referee blows his whistle to resume play, whereas the view taken by the SFA Executive & General Purposes Committee was that it is effected when the substitute crosses the touchline and enters the field of play (from which moment he becomes a player and the player whom he is replacing ceases to be a player). There were varying opinions taken on both points by the committee which appreciated the intricacies of potential situations and of IFAB's task in coming to a decision. When that point came, the SFA's view prevailed.

The Impact of Football Elsewhere
The impact of Points of Play and interpretation of the Laws of the Game were not just confined to Scotland, as evidenced by the English Point of Play in 1970. An incident during the 1986 World Cup led to a lengthy discussion on penalty kicks taken in extended time and to kicks from the penalty mark to determine the winner of a match. FIFA had allowed a goal to stand after the ball rebounded some three or four yards from the woodwork, struck the goalkeeper and then entered the net. The general opinion of the Supervisors was that a goal should not have been allowed, which aligned to the guidance given by training class instructors over many years. By the time the Supervisors discussed the point, however, FIFA (and UEFA) had issued instructions to the effect that in such case a goal should be awarded. On the advice of Ernie Walker it was decided to accept that interpretation.

The Place of Points of Play in Refereeing
There was a huge variety of Points of Play determined by the Supervisors over the years. Generally, they had happened in matches with the referees in question seeking to establish if they had acted correctly or wishing to find out how they should have dealt with it. Equally, some bright spark of a referee would seek to test a potential situation as a consequence of a change in one of the Laws. Discussing Points of Play became a staple part of the Discussion Groups at the Referees' Conference with a multitude of Points being considered.   Football has a

tremendous capacity of throwing up never-ending scenarios for a referee to deal with.

The Supervisors were looked up to as this all important body by the vast majority of referees and what they handed down as decisions would have been taken as gospel, although referees being referees there would always be some who would choose to disagree and indeed some associations took issue with a decision from time to time. The time taken to issue decisions was certainly not the quickest, particularly if the Point of Play had some significance, but the process was of its time and referees were kept up to date within the means possible of the day.

Kit

The Immediate Post War Years
In the period after the Second World War, rationing of all sorts of commodities, including clothing, was in place. This had an impact on the availability of kit for referees. Recognising the issue, the Board of Trade invited the SFA to indicate how many clothing coupons would meet the requirements of referees. A scheme was developed to gather and submit the information needed.

The Supervisors agreed in principle in 1946 that the most suitable dress for referees and linesmen was black with white shirt (collar exposed), black shorts, black socks with white top, and that this uniform should be utilised when possible. Arising from a Secretaries' meeting three years later, the Supervisors declined a suggestion that khaki be worn instead of black. Khaki was used, however, as an alternative colour to black for many years.

Moving Towards the Modern Age
Referees had to purchase their own kit and over the years there were many brands of kit worn, all the while adhering to the set uniform style.

The first hint of a desire for the referee and his linesmen to be kitted out in the same style emerged in 1976 when the SFA

Executive & General Purposes Committee responded to a query from Glasgow RA. It had no objection to the match officials appointed to the Scottish Cup Final being outfitted, free of charge, by a manufacturer. The door to the commercial world was starting to open.

As kit manufacturers started to develop ranges of referees' tunics during the 1980's, trying to latch on to the explosion of replica football jerseys, the conservative nature of the Supervisors was put to the test.

Pinstripe tunics came on the market in the early 1980's. The wearing of these tunics did not meet with the Supervisors' approval in 1983 as they wanted self coloured tunics to be worn. The topic was discussed again a year later as some referees had ignored their view and continued to wear pinstripe tunics. The Supervisors maintained their initial stance but added the caveat "*in matches which are played in Scotland*", which indicated that some FIFA referees were wearing pinstripe tunics. The tunics could be worn on their international appointments.

Kit continued to be a hot topic of discussion in season 1984-85. When a point was raised about which colour of socks should be worn by referees, the Supervisors chose not to come to a decision. In a bold move to ascertain the views of the referee movement on the uniformity of referees' dress, the Executive Committee chose to test the water by having the following as a Discussion Point at the 1986 Conference: "*It is the Supervisors' opinion that referees' standard dress should consist of black tunics with white trimmings, black shorts and stockings with, or without, white trimmings, and that red and white tunics should only be worn when the black tunic is similar to a team's strip. It would appear that this standard is not being adhered to by some officials. Why should this be the case?*"

It turned out that all but one of the groups concurred with the Supervisors' opinion. That lone group felt, within reason, that referees should be allowed to wear modern kits but should not draw attention to themselves unnecessarily (in terms of dress, not decision making, that is). A few of the groups thought that the SFA might be able to assist in the matter of referees' kit. The Supervisors did not wish to grasp this nettle on behalf of referees and considered that it would for the Referees' Associations to raise the potential supply of kit with the SFA.

International Matters

The horizons of Scottish refereeing extended beyond the domestic scene. Scottish referees developed a well respected reputation in other countries as a result of their performances.

FIFA List of International Referees
FIFA introduced a list of referees for international football in 1950. Responsibility for deciding on the nominations for the list lay with the SFA Executive & General Purposes Committee, rather than the Referee Committee. The Supervisors had no role to play in the recommendation process, the SFA wishing to ensure a clean separation of responsibilities so that the decision making process was independent of any possible influence being exerted by a Supervisor in favour of a particular referee. That said, there can be little doubt that that Jack Mowat, once he became Chairman of the Supervisors, had a significant role behind the scenes working in close co-operation with Willie Allan and Ernie Walker. Tom Wharton tried to address the issue in 1977 when, speaking on his own behalf, requested that the Executive Committee be allowed to comment on the nominations before being submitted by the SFA to FIFA.

Referees' Courses
There was an element of insularity displayed in British football for many years through to the middle of last century. One instance occurred in season 1947-48 when the Referee Committee decided not to send a representative to an International Referees' Course held in London. Similarly, invitations from FIFA and the Dutch Referees' Association were declined in 1959.
A positive response was forthcoming in 1961 when the Referee Committee selected Bobby Davidson to attend a FIFA Course for Active Referees in Italy. Frank Crossley attended a Referee

Instructors' Course organised by The Football Association that same year.

The four British Associations agreed in season 1956-57 that any association organising a referees' course should inform the others so that they could send observers if they wished. There is no real evidence, however, that this was carried through.

FIFA

In 1974, Jack Mowat was appointed as a member of FIFA's Referee Committee. Tribute to him was paid in a Referees' Bulletin newsletter during season 1974-75: *"Only those who are closely associated with him, have any real knowledge of the time, and energy, which he devotes to matters affecting referees and refereeing, and of assessing the worth of his contribution to the game, here in Scotland."*

He served on the Referees' Committee until 1981 when Tom Wharton was appointed by FIFA to replace him.

Each was given a Special Award and Diploma from FIFA for their services to refereeing. Mowat received his award in 1974 before becoming a member of the Referees' Committee with Wharton receiving his award in 1976. Later that year, Wharton was appointed to FIFA's Panel of Lecturers for Refereeing.

UEFA

UEFA formed its Referee Committee in 1968 to oversee referees' appointments and to organise refereeing courses. The first course was held in Italy in 1969, with Bill Anderson, Bill Mullan and John Paterson selected by the SFA Executive & General Purposes Committee to attend. This committee selected the referees to attend subsequent UEFA Referees' Courses throughout the 1970's.

During season 1968-69, FIFA and UEFA expressed concern at the general standard of referees nominated by their member associations for matches in their respective competitions. Both bodies were examining ways and means of bringing about improvement. Willie Allan was instructed in the nature of the replies to be sent. It can be imagined that the essence of the replies was that "our referees are of a high standard already, thank you very much".

The Supervisors concurred with a suggestion put forward by UEFA in season 1977-78 that a referee who is appointed as the senior linesman in a UEFA match, should be allocated a match as a linesman in a domestic competition match, prior to his UEFA appointment, and hoped that it would be found to be practicable. To achieve this however was well nigh impossible as the SFA had to gain the co-operation of the SFL to make adjustments to its appointments which were always issued for a six week period.

Controlling the Game

The expectations placed on referees to ensure that matches were played in a sporting fashion increased considerably over this period. In large part, this was due to the collapse in the standards of player behaviour from the 1960's onwards and the SFA trying in vain to stem the tide. The tone for controlling the playing of the game was set by the Referee Committee and the Supervisors, with the Secretary playing a very important role. Instructions were regularly issued. The idealism by which the early leaders of the SFA regarded football as a sporting art prevailed for many years.

A Turning of the Tide
In the immediate post war years, indiscipline was not hugely prevalent but a severe approach was taken to ensure that it stayed that way. *"Bad language and improper remarks"* by players was targeted in season 1947-48. By 1950-51, the Annual Report recorded that *"through the efforts of the Referee Committee and the Supervisors, a marked improvement in the standard of refereeing and match control has been noticeable during the season. The committee has been particularly severe in reference to dissent in any form being shown at decisions and they have practically eliminated this undesirable practice."*
By the end of the 1950's things were starting to change. The Referee Committee felt that some referees were failing to take adequate measures to curb dangerous and foul play. The need for *"firm control of matches at all times as an important factor*

in the elimination of undesirable practices from the field of play" was stressed to referees.

In the early 1960's, the SFA's finger was pointed at clubs for failing in their responsibilities to control their players, comment which would feature regularly in the years ahead. At the same time, it was wondered if the increase in misconduct was attributable to a *"measure of failure on the part of referees".* Annual Reports of the period wondered if referees *"by the exercise of a stricter control, might not provide a partial solution to achieving a desired improvement in standards".* The pertinent comment that the *"strong and efficient referee is not necessarily the one who resorts to ordering-off",* was made. These were the first references to referees coming under the spotlight.

The Inexorable Rise of Misconduct

In the second half of the 1960's, the disciplinary statistics steadily got worse. During season 1969-70, the SFA convened a meeting with the SFL, the Players' Union and the Supervisors to try to address the problem. If the involvement of the Supervisors in these discussions was a good sign of their being given their place in the game, it was a different story in 1972-73 when the SFA formed a Joint Consultative Committee comprising the SFA, the SFL and the Players' Union. The Supervisors were not included on the Committee and their exclusion provoked disappointment within the refereeing movement. The issue ran for over a season. At the 1973 and 1974 Conferences, strong views were expressed by the Discussion Groups that the refereeing movement should be represented on the committee. Refereeing eventually won its argument and, in the early part of season 1974-75, the SFA confirmed that the Supervisors would be represented at any meeting of the Joint Consultative Committee when disciplinary matters were discussed.

The disciplinary figures continued to increase significantly during the 1970's and the crisis in the senior game was becoming greater each season. A series of meetings were held, with one involving the Players' Union, the Executive Committee, and the Presidents and Secretaries of the Referees'

Associations, the inclusion of the latter group being a demonstration of the SFA's willingness to cover all sections of the game in its efforts to improve things.

The 1976-77 Annual Report reviewed the background to the whole disciplinary context and offered excellent commentary on the perceptions prevalent in football on referees: "*It is increasingly fashionable in some quarters to blame referees, publicly, for a club's failure to win a match, to hold them responsible for field misconduct, and even, on some occasions, to suggest that they are responsible for the misbehaviour of spectators. The notion is absurd. The referee is the neutral, acceptable arbiter appointed by an objective organiser to control a match. Without him there would be no match. His knowledge of the Laws of the Game is infinitely superior to that of his critics. That he might make mistakes at times is obvious, although quite irrelevant to the issue, and until such time as some of our players learn to accept his decisions without resorting to boring displays of dissent which, in any case, are quite futile, and serve only to cast doubts on the intelligence of those concerned, and some managers learn to accept defeat with a degree of dignity, there can be little hope of a marked improvement in behaviour patterns. The problem is a serious one and the frustrating aspect of it is that, unlike some other problems with which football is beset, the remedy is in our own hands.*" To any current observer of football, it would seem that nothing has changed.

In an effort to manage the explosion of misconduct, in 1977-78, the SFA adopted a system of penalty points/suspension threshold for offences and automatic suspension for sendings-off to replace the long trail of players appearing before the Referee Committee. It did nothing to stem the tide as player misconduct continued to rise inexorably. The new system effectively minimised the importance of a caution. Referees came under criticism for having "*been caught up in the general change of attitude and, however unwittingly, were cautioning for offences which might have been dealt with in another fashion entirely.*"

Further comment was made in the 1979-80 Annual Report: "*It is said that the new system encourages referees to caution players much more indiscriminately than they might have done in the past, although many objective observers of the position dispute that this is the case and lay the blame for the deterioration in behaviour, fairly and squarely at the door of the clubs and players and blame the apparently ever-increasing determination to win.*" The report also commented on a growing problem which was impacting on the game and on the authority of referees - the increasing tendency amongst managers to blame the referee whenever they were defeated.

The Field Discipline Campaign
Ernie Walker, appointed Secretary in 1977, became the primary force in the drive to improve the standard of discipline in the game. His career had run parallel with the decline in player behaviour and he was well versed in the issues. By the early 1980's he was determined to improve the standards of behaviour and decided to launch what became known as the "Field Discipline Campaign". Referees were at the forefront of it.

Instructions were issued to them for the start of season 1983-84 to deal with players delaying the taking of free-kicks by kicking the ball away or standing over the ball and encroaching. Walker and the Disciplinary & Referee Committee Chairman met with Scotland's seven FIFA referees in mid-season to seek their opinions on the continuing high levels of misconduct. Given their experience of refereeing in European football, Walker considered that they were ideally placed to contribute to the debate. The referees reported that the offences targeted at the start of the season had been virtually eliminated, after an initial spate of cautions led to the penny dropping on the part of players. The level of dissent was deemed excessive, with the view expressed that if dissent were eliminated, coupled with the improvement already achieved, a further all round improvement would follow. It was also conveyed that managers and coaches were showing an increasing lack of restraint on the touchlines and that this was impacting on player behaviour.

Dealing with dissent became the focus of the campaign's second season. Referees were instructed to act more firmly in dealing with it. Players soon realised that a caution would quickly come their way if they showed dissent. An improvement in behaviour resulted.

The third season of the campaign turned attention on removing over-physical aspects of play from the game. The Executive Committee was given the opportunity to meet the Disciplinary & Referee Committee to discuss the approach to be taken. To set the scene for the season ahead and to allow them to express their views, managers and coaches were invited to meet the two committees. Instructions were then spelled out to referees: they were required to ensure that all forms of violence were punished in accordance with the Laws of the Game. The intent was that football skills should prevail against the crude physical challenge.

When the Supervisors reviewed the situation a few months into the season, they felt that some referees, particularly in reserve football, had over-reacted to the instructions and that in some cases it had appeared that referees had forgotten that verbal warnings could be given to players before being cautioned. On the playing side, it was evident that the behaviour of players had, to some extent, improved and that it seemed that they had taken heed of the instructions issued.

Over its three season period, the campaign resulted in a marked improvement in player behaviour. Referees had played their part in the effort to ensure that the game was played in a disciplined environment. The 1985-86 Annual Report considered that, *"by and large, the majority of referees had carried out the SFA's instructions tolerably well. Most of them adjusted to the new way of things sensibly enough, but as always, there are a few who appear to be struggling to meet the SFA's requirements adequately. This has nothing in particular to do with any increasing demands which may have been placed on them, but rather is it confirmation of the fairly obvious fact that in any group of referees some will always be better than others."* Some ire was directed at referees for *"their persistent failure to deal with the constant flow of complaint from a few of the most prominent players in the game"* with the view expressed that *"an intelligent and capable referee should realise that if he succeeds in making the star players comport themselves in a reasonable fashion, the rest should be easy."*

All this was said in an era when the game at the top level in Scotland had become really competitive, with Aberdeen and Dundee United out-performing Celtic and Rangers. The expectations placed on referees to control the game had never been higher. The landscape in which they operated had changed. The stakes had increased.

Referee Training Officer

Sowing the Seeds
The thought that the SFA could do more to develop refereeing by using films and modern teaching resources, was first aired at a coaches' meeting at the 1976 Conference. Although debated by the Supervisors in its aftermath, nothing happened. The coaches returned to the theme in 1982-83 suggesting that a Supervisor should be appointed with special responsibility for correlating coaching activities in Scotland. However, the Supervisors decided that there would be "*no benefit*" in such an appointment. The conservative approach had won again, although another coaches' suggestion was accepted, namely that there would be benefit in making refereeing films or videos available to Referees' Associations. They agreed that the SFA should investigate the possibility of producing these.

Another trigger point for considering future action emerged from a SFA-SFL Liaison Committee meeting in 1985. The SFL suggested that more could be done in referee development and raised the possibility of quarterly seminars being held and the closer monitoring of referees.

The suggestion was passed to the Supervisors, who felt that the supervisory system, together with weekly physical training and monthly meetings, adequately fulfilled any needs which the SFL thought might be required. The situation changed relatively quickly, however, as the question of holding seminars or courses for referees arose at the following month's Conference and prompted action. The Executive Committee was specially convened in July to address the subject.

A number of points emerged. The case for the introduction of seminars, in addition to the Conference, was accepted and that their purpose should be to develop refereeing and to work towards achieving greater uniformity in decision making. The seminars would be arranged as and when required and would cater for "Listed" or "Non-Listed" officials at either national or regional level. The Supervisors were held to be best placed to staff the courses with four to act as "staff coaches" and be paid for fulfilling these duties. The benefits of using films showing examples of fouls and misconduct in matches was recognised, with it being thought that such material would form the major part of the content of the seminars. The possibility of conducting practical demonstrations and fitness tests at seminars was broached.

Given these outcomes, this was quite a considerable turnaround in the committee's position within a matter of months. The Executive Committee appreciated that these were initial thoughts and that more time was needed for further discussion. This took place at the full meeting in December.

Then, it was generally agreed that more could be done for the refereeing movement by the SFA at both national and local levels in terms of the training of referees. Some Supervisors felt that associations were failing to get an adequate response to courses which they were attempting to organise. It was recommended to the Disciplinary & Referee Committee that the SFA should organise courses for Classes 1 and 2 and that instructional films for referees should be produced, depicting various incidents from football matches and how they should be dealt with by referees.

Grasping the Nettle

The realisation that more should be done to develop refereeing had finally emerged within the Supervisors. Momentum to create a specialist position was building up. Given the voluntary nature of the roles they fulfilled, it must have been obvious to them that they did not have the wherewithal to properly carry through their proposals. However, for whatever reason, their recommendations were not progressed within the SFA and the issue lay dormant for a year. Another coaches' meeting at the 1986 Conference reignited the discussion.

The views of the coaches were, in many ways, damning of the current state of affairs in refereeing. It was held that the standard of candidates for the Entrance course was becoming poorer and the average age of the candidates was increasing; the examination paper was not in keeping with modern day standards, with far too much writing required; support systems for new referees were needed; coaches should not be selected at random by associations; courses should be held for coaches to standardise coaching methods and be overseen by a Coaching Officer; group discussions should be held at monthly meetings; instructional films and other modern resources would be invaluable to further develop refereeing; the introduction of lecturing at schools on the Laws of the Game was suggested, given the apparent poorer quality of candidate.

The Executive Committee took on board the points made by the coaches. Given their nature, it would have been a dereliction of duty had they not. The issues raised were stark. Thus, in February 1987, the committee recommended to Ernie Walker that consideration be given to the appointment of a Coaching Officer.

When the Supervisors came to review the results of the April examinations, the issues raised by the coaches quickly came to the fore. Whilst the number of candidates for the April diet was always lower than for December, the results were not great – only 44 out of 70 candidates had passed the Entrance Examination. A general discussion developed on refereeing issues.

Some Supervisors considered that poor coaching was evident in the answers to particular questions in the examination papers and that this lent support for coaching methods to be standardised across the associations. The style and content of the examination papers was discussed in the context of modern educational standards and practices. The calibre of candidates coming forward for the training classes was also questioned and it was felt that improved publicity by the SFA and the associations on them would be beneficial in attracting more people into refereeing. The low level of fees and expenses paid to referees was mooted as having a possible bearing on the quantity and quality of persons entering refereeing, whilst doubt was expressed as to the desire of new referees to seek advancement in the game, given that many seemed to be content to officiate at the lower levels of football.

The focus of the Supervisors had always been the List, with everything below that level being of a lesser significance. The discussion altered the dynamic. Whilst individual Supervisors always had an awareness as to the health of their associations, on an overall basis it was almost taken for granted that people would come forward to the training classes and that there would be sufficient numbers wanting to progress to the List. The examination statistics provided a hint that perhaps that the referee movement was not quite in the rude health that was imagined.

All these points gave impetus to the recommendation that consideration be given to the appointment of a Coaching Officer.

The Appointment is Made

Ernie Walker brought these matters to the attention of the Disciplinary & Referee Committee in November, reviewing all that had been discussed and put forward by the Supervisors. The appointment of a full-time Referee Training Officer was agreed.

In February 1988, Jack Mowat reported to the Executive Committee that George Cumming, a Class 1 referee, had been appointed to the role and would commence his duties in mid-April. The principal roles of the appointment were outlined: the co-ordination of recruitment and training activities of the Referees' Associations, to provide modern teaching aids for the associations; to examine and improve referees' physical training; to collaborate with educational authorities with a view to introducing courses on the Laws of the Game into the curriculum; to stimulate the interests of players in the Laws of the Game.

In the 1987-88 SFA Annual Report Ernie Walker set out the context and background of the appointment:

"Over a long period of years now, the SFA's attitude and approach to many areas of its work have undergone radical changes. This applies particularly in the fields of coaching,

youth development and commercial activities, but for one reason or another, one aspect of its function has remained virtually unaltered in every respect for just about as long as anyone can remember, and that is the subject of referee recruitment and training. That the methods of recruitment and training which are used today are more or less the same as were used 30 or more years ago, perhaps reflects the fact that the standard of refereeing in Scotland, generally speaking, would appear to be as good as in any other country, and for certain, our top referees are held in as high regard by both FIFA and UEFA as are their counterparts in any other countries. One other possible reason for this lack of change, of course, could be that many people feel that referees are born rather than made and that no amount of training will turn any man into a great referee. There may be some validity in this argument but of course it could be applied to players equally well and the SFA invests large sums of money in attempting to improve player coaching and training programmes. It is accepted that improved training will not turn bad referees into good referees, but it is reasonable to hope that it could turn good referees into better referees. At any rate, the Disciplinary & Referee Committee has decided that a re-vamping of the whole refereeing movement is long overdue and as a first step the SFA has engaged the services of a full time Referee Training Officer who will take up his duties in April, 1988. He is Mr. George Cumming, a relatively young man, whose background would appear to provide him with impeccable credentials for the job. He was a player of some note himself, achieving Amateur international and Olympic representative honours before turning professional and playing for a number of Scottish League clubs. At the end of his playing career he took up refereeing and at the time of his appointment to the SFA's staff, was one of our more promising young referees on the Class 1 List. In addition to that football background, he is Deputy Rector at Lesmahagow High School. It is difficult to argue with these credentials. Mr. Cumming's principal role will be to co-ordinate the recruitment and training activities of the various referees' associations throughout the country, to provide modern teaching aids for these associations, to examine and improve the physical fitness aspects of referees' training, and generally work with a view to raising the standards of refereeing throughout Scotland. The SFA recognises the naivety of imagining that any form of training will bring about a situation whereby all of our referees are regarded as being satisfactory. That is just not in the nature of things and it will never happen, but it is recognised that more can be done to attempt to improve the situation and it is hoped that this appointment will bear fruit in the not too distant future."

The modern era was about to begin.

Part Five

1988-2023

The Age of the Referee Specialist

George Cumming - 1988-2000

When George Cumming attended his first Supervisors' meeting in May 1988, he presented a paper on a multitude of topics: coaching and training, training classes, audio visual material, coaching seminars, monthly meetings, young referees, communication, publicity, match visits, Referees' Associations, contact with clubs and other associations, education, spectators, fitness, recruitment drive.

The range of these topics demonstrated to the Supervisors that the creation of the role opened up opportunities which were virtually impossible to progress under them. The stark reality was that they were fulfilling voluntary roles with limited ability to take referee development forward in any meaningful way. Now, there was a full time specialist employed by the SFA to do just that. Whilst the refereeing structure provided a firm foundation to build upon, it also presented a blank canvas to Cumming to implement his ideas.

Cumming used his first year to take stock of the situation and in 1989 produced a major document, "Refereeing in Scotland: The Way Ahead", which set out various proposals on the Supervisory System/Assessment of referees/Reports, Entrance and Refresher Examinations, Fitness, Meetings of Listed officials, Association Coaches, Referees' Conference, Resources and the SFRA.

It was natural that tensions would emerge during the consideration of the document, as the innate conservatism of the Supervisors was tested with fresh and modern ideas. The specialist had to learn to work with the Supervisors and the Supervisors had to learn to work with the specialist. Progress was achieved, as it had to be. From this point on, there was a period of unprecedented activity in refereeing. The initiatives put in place by Cumming benefited from the improved financial ability of the SFA to provide the appropriate support. Commercial income had greatly increased during the 1980's and enabled the SFA to devote resources to develop football in Scotland in a way which had not been possible previously. The football landscape in Scotland and throughout the world has been completely altered from the late 1980's. There has been a huge change in many aspects of football since then. Refereeing has changed dramatically also during that time. Cumming played a pivotal role in that process. He brought a determined and forceful approach to his role and undoubted benefits followed.

There was a constant drive to improve refereeing with many schemes and initiatives introduced. This was exemplified in 1997-98 when Cumming led a representative group to conduct a review of refereeing in Scotland to identify ways in which the refereeing structure could be strengthened and improved. The recommendations of the report, "Refereeing in Scotland – Towards the New Millennium", covering the classification of all referees, support systems for referees, referee instruction, the functions of Referees' Associations, insurance and medical cover, were largely adopted.

Cumming's appointment was indicative of the progressive nature of the SFA under the stewardship of Ernie Walker in the 1980's. The SFA was among the first National Associations to appoint a Security Adviser and to have an in-house Travel Department. The appointment of a Referee Training Officer was another example of innovation and came to be copied quickly by other National Associations. Within a couple of years of being appointed, Cumming's job title was changed to Development Director (Referees and Education). With the SFA being a member of IFAB, Cumming became an important part of the SFA's operations in this respect and developed a close working relationship with FIFA. He played a key role in a re-write of the Laws of the Game in the mid-1990's. His burgeoning reputation led to his becoming a regular port of call for many National Associations seeking guidance on Laws of the Game queries. FIFA benefited from Cumming's input on a number of educational fronts, producing resources and films on its behalf. He was appointed to the FIFA Panel of Referee Instructors in 1991, which led to his taking courses in many parts of the world on behalf of FIFA. He received many invitations to lecture at numerous courses held by national and other associations. In 1998 FIFA appointed him as a Technical

Adviser for the World Cup in France, tasked with making an instructional film for referees.

Given the close connections he had with FIFA, it was no surprise when FIFA appointed him as its first ever Head of World Refereeing in 2000. In his time with the SFA he revolutionised the whole approach to refereeing. It had been modernised.

Donald McVicar - 2000-09
When the "Refereeing in Scotland – Towards the New Millennium" report was considered, George Cumming took the opportunity to seek an additional member of staff with a refereeing background to help him to implement the various recommendations, a not unreasonable request given the workload. The staff numbers at the SFA had grown considerably during the 1990's but, given the inherent support that the SFA had traditionally given to refereeing, it was odd that additional staff support had been slow in forthcoming.

The request was successful and Donald McVicar, a former Class 1 referee and a member of the Executive Committee, was appointed as Referee Development Officer in April 1999. On Cumming's departure to FIFA, McVicar was promoted to succeed him. The job was renamed Head of Referee Development.

The groundwork put in place during the 1990's was developed further by McVicar during his tenure. Bringing a collaborative approach to the job, further changes were brought to the supervisory system with the introduction of Executive Supervisors in 2002 (coinciding with changes to the Referee Committee structure), and a complete revolution in 2005 by replacing Supervisors with the positions of Referees' Association Managers and Referee Observers, to better reflect the reality of the circumstances as they had developed over time.

Issues with gaining a replacement Referee Development Officer unfortunately returned and it took until 2005 to gain approval to fill the position. Bobby Orr, a former Class 1 referee and the Stirlingshire RA Manager at that point, was appointed in the summer of 2005. Tragically, within a couple of days of starting his role, Orr took seriously ill and died in February 2006. Hugh Dallas was appointed as his replacement in September 2006. He had been appointed to the Referee Committee when he had retired from refereeing at the end of season 2004-05. UEFA appointed him to its Referee Committee at the same time.

When Donald McVicar retired in the summer of 2009, the Referee Committee appointed him as a Referee Observer and as a member of the Referee Committee. These were sensible appointments which enabled refereeing to benefit from his experience. He served six seasons on the Referee Committee and was a Referee Observer for seven seasons.

Hugh Dallas - 2009-10

Hugh Dallas moved into the post of Head of Referee Development in 2009 on McVicar's retirement. His time in the position was short-lived as he was dismissed by the SFA in November 2010 as a consequence of getting caught up, along with other staff, in the sending of an offensive email. It was hard to leave any sort of a mark having been in position for less than 18 months but Dallas continued to serve UEFA as a Referee Committee member and as a Refereeing Officer, playing an influential role in the progress of Scotland's FIFA referees at UEFA level for the next decade.

John Fleming - 2010-19

It was a smoother process filling the vacant Referee Development Officer when Dallas moved to the main role. John Fleming was quickly appointed and was in place by August 2009. Fleming was another former Category 1 referee (and a former FIFA Assistant Referee) who was, at the time of his appointment, Manager for Renfrewshire RA and a Referee Observer. He succeeded Dallas as Head of Referee Development. Fleming continued to build on what had gone before and oversaw big changes to the operations of the Referees' Associations. Existing programmes were developed and refined. New initiatives, such as the SQA Course, were introduced. He was a graduate of the University of Life and brought to bear managerial skills developed at British Telecom. Rather than have one person fill the post of Referee

Development Officer, Fleming secured two Class 1 referees, Steven McLean and Craig Thomson, as Recruitment and Education Officers on a job-sharing basis in 2011. Progress was made on a few fronts over the next few years. Due to a promotion in his main job, Thomson resigned in 2016. His successor, on a full-time basis, was Tom Murphy, a former FIFA Assistant Referee who had been on the Referee Committee since 2104. The experience he brought to the appointment gave further impetus to developing initiatives and programmes for assistant referees.

John Fleming sadly died in October 2019 after a long battle with cancer. His time as Head of Referee Operations had been very positive and fruitful, marked by a real consolidation of the professional structure which had been developed over the years.

Crawford Allan - 2020-
Crawford Allan was appointed Head of Referee Operations in early 2020. A former Class 1 referee and a past Secretary and President of the Scottish Senior Football Referees' Association (SSFRA), his prime aim was to continue to steer the ship on the course which had been set and to oversee the introduction of the refereeing side of VAR into Scottish football.

Refereeing within the SFA Administrative Structures
Before George Cumming's appointment in 1988, the refereeing function within the SFA's administrative structures was carried out through one dedicated post and a typist, serving disciplinary matters as well as refereeing. When Departments were introduced at the SFA in 1990, the Development Department and the Disciplinary & Referee Department were formed. This remained the case until the SFA was admitted into the UEFA Referee Convention in 2007 when the SFA was obliged to separate the two functions of the Disciplinary & Referee Department. The Referee Administration Department was created, along with a separate Disciplinary Department. The two refereeing Departments existed side by side, working extremely closely, for the next five years until they were unified in 2012 under the leadership of John Fleming. From that starting point of a one/two person administrative approach,

there is now a Referee Operations Department of 10 posts to cover all aspects of referee development, referee appointments and administration.

Referee Supervisors

Increasing the number of Supervisors
In his paper "Refereeing in Scotland – The Way Ahead", George Cumming proposed that more Supervisors should be appointed, with the aim of increasing the assessment of referees. There was a long and hard debate on the issue. There was a strong element of resistance on the part of some of the Supervisors, with the view being expressed that there would be no benefit in enlarging the committee's size. Protection of their position lay behind their thinking – being a Supervisor was held to be a very exalted and privileged position and that would be diluted if more were appointed. If there was to be an increase in their number, the Supervisors thought it should be a gradual process over a few years and would be dependent on the quality of personnel which might become available, something which was always held by the Supervisors, and indeed the SFA, to be a crucial part of any selection process.

Cumming recognised that there was no point in making the committee unwieldy by enlarging it too much, but held to his position that increasing the number of Supervisors was needed. Although there was a gradual easing of the position of the Supervisors during the consideration of the proposals, a deadlock was reached. There was also scepticism of an inherent aim of the proposal, that of having all SFL matches attended by the Supervisors, something which had been raised from time to time over the years. The feasibility of this was challenged given the geographical location of certain clubs, the likely journey times involved and the resulting increase in costs to the SFA.

Undeterred by the impasse, Cumming took his proposals to the Disciplinary & Referee Committee which promptly gave him the support it had promised him when he was appointed. The proposals were adopted, with the number of Supervisors being increased from 16 to 21. Ernie Walker attended the meeting to lend support and to explain the expansion of the supervisory system. He referred to the aim of achieving coverage of all SFL matches, with the increase in the number of Supervisors being the first step towards achieving this. It was envisaged that increasing the number of Supervisors to as much as 30 would have to be carried out over a period of time and be dependent on finding persons of suitable quality.

As resignations were received from Ian Foote and David Wilkie, seven new Supervisors were appointed in total. With a couple of "transfers" between associations, the changes were put into effect early in season 1989-90. Bill Crighton was appointed to assist Robbie Harrold in Aberdeen & District RA, Bob Valentine and Colin Sinclair were appointed to replace Wilkie in Angus & Perthshire RA, Eddie Thomson was appointed to share duties with Bill Mullan and Douglas Downie at Edinburgh & District RA, Tom Gray was moved from Glasgow (East) to Glasgow (West) to replace Foote, Ian Barbour was moved from Renfrewshire RA to take over from Gray at Glasgow (East), Mike Delaney was appointed to assist Frank Crossley at Lanarkshire RA and Ian Byars and Ian Marshall were appointed to replace Barbour at Renfrewshire RA.

Valentine had retired as a Class 1 referee at the end of the previous season, Delaney the season before and Crighton and Sinclair resigned from the List, at Class 3B and Class 1 respectively, to accept their appointments. Various other positional changes of Supervisors with associations took place in October 1990.

An end of an era

In October 1990, Jack Mowat retired at the age of 84 after 30 years as a Supervisor and 28 as Chairman. He had presided over 250 meetings. A great era had come to an end. As a lasting tribute to his remarkable contribution to and influence upon the refereeing movement, spanning 60 years, the SFA commissioned a trophy – "The Jack Mowat Trophy" – to be presented to the referee who finished top of the Class 1 Referee assessment table each season. From 1994 the Trophy has been awarded to the referee of the Scottish Cup Final.

151

Mowat was succeeded by Tom Wharton as the Chairman. In 1994, he stepped down as the Supervisor for Glasgow (South) which allowed him to assume wider responsibilities commensurate with his role as the Chairman.

Updating the Duties and Powers of Supervisors

In 1995, Jim Farry, the SFA Chief Executive, initiated a review of the role of the Supervisor, conveying the view that it needed to be redefined due to some issues which had arisen in some associations. A small committee was formed to review the role of the Supervisor.

As part of the exercise, the views of the Supervisors and the Referees' Associations were obtained on how the role was perceived and what was expected of Supervisors. Revised Duties and Powers of Supervisors were approved in 1996.

The most significant change allowed Supervisors to attend all meetings within their association to enable them to provide an appropriate level of guidance to ensure that the SFA areas of responsibility and involvement could be put into effect. This strengthened the role of the Supervisor (and the SFA) and addressed the difficulties which had been experienced.

Modernising the system

In 1997, Cumming presented a paper on the supervisory system to the Executive Committee. His proposals envisaged a further increase in the number of Supervisors and the creation of three types of Supervisor – Match Supervisor (responsible for assessing referees), Association Supervisors (to have overall responsibility within the association) and Executive Supervisors (the Executive Committee members who would have oversight of the two or three Referees' Associations). Association and Executive Supervisors would also act as Match Supervisors.

With the composition of the Executive Committee having evolved during the decade with a "younger generation" of members now in place, the old conservatism of the committee had ebbed away. The proposals were welcomed. It was recognised that their implementation would result in the further development of the supervisory system and bring enhanced benefits to the refereeing movement. It was felt that that the proposals related directly to the real basis of a Supervisor's role - assessing and developing a referee's potential. The Referee Committee approved the proposals.

One element of the proposals attracted concern when they were presented to the full committee – the possibility of Match Supervisors retaining a non-conflicting role within their own association. Reservations were expressed by some members on this potential situation, with the feeling being that any supervisory function should be divorced from any association role. However, the proposals prevailed.

Two years were to pass before developments took place in regard to implementing the proposals. In February 1999, four new Supervisors (all former Class 1 referees) were appointed – Sandy Roy (Aberdeen & District RA), Colin Ross (Edinburgh & District RA) and Gerry Evans and Bryan Robertson (both Glasgow RA). Two Match Assessors, Joe Timmons and Hugh Williamson, (both former Class 1 and FIFA referees) were appointed, the term Match Assessor having been chosen to replace Match Supervisor. In terms of their function, Match Assessors were to assess match officials and submit recommendations in the same manner as Supervisors. They were to have no direct connection with a Referees' Association.

Further changes were made that summer. Bill Mullan, Archie Webster, Eddie Thomson and Bill Crighton moved from being Supervisors to Match Assessors, Sandy Roy was appointed the main Supervisor for Aberdeen RA, Douglas Downie moved to Fife RA to replace Archie Webster as its Supervisor, Drew Fleming moved from Glasgow RA to Stirlingshire RA to take over from Eddie Thomson and Douglas Hope moved from Glasgow RA to take charge at Renfrewshire RA.

The summer of 2000 saw more changes in personnel. Jim McCluskey, newly retired as a referee, was appointed as Ayrshire RA Supervisor in place of Hugh Alexander, Colin Sinclair retired as a Supervisor for Angus & Perthshire RA, Bill Crighton resigned as a Match Assessor and Bill Mullan, Eddie Thomson, Archie Webster and Hugh Williamson were retired from their roles as Match Assessors. Martin Clark and Jim Bruce were appointed as Match Assessors.

For season 2002-03, Donald McVicar was able to put into effect the proposals concerning Executive Supervisors which had been first raised in 1997. The existing Executive Committee became Executive Supervisors. They stepped down from being a Supervisor for their association and became responsible for fulfilling a liaison role with a group of three associations (with the exception of the Chairman) to assist in the creation of development plans and to develop a greater knowledge of the potential pool of referees for the future. They were also to encourage consistency in the organisation and operation of the associations and to assist the Head of Referee Development in various aspects of development work and education. Tom Wharton continued to have no direct connection with an association to maintain "neutrality" as Chairman. The position of Match Assessor was discontinued with those in the role invited to become Supervisors.

The Duties and Powers of Supervisors were further revised to take into account of the introduction of Executive Supervisors. The document was also issued to clubs, leagues and associations in order to increase the level of understanding of the many and various duties carried out by Supervisors.

Tom Wharton retired following the Referees' Conference in June 2003. He had served 56 years in the referee movement and 32 as a Supervisor.

Referee Supervisors' Committees

Full Power to the Executive Committee

As a consequence of the increase in Supervisors in 1989, there was one significant outcome from the consideration of the "Refereeing in Scotland: The Way Ahead" paper. The Disciplinary & Referee Committee gave the Executive Committee full power to compile the List, with the ability of the full committee to outvote its recommendations being removed. The change was designed to allow the Executive Committee to work unhindered and for the process to function effectively.

The introduction of Seminars

The four meetings per year schedule of the full Committee was well settled by the late 1980's. The "Refereeing in Scotland: The Way Ahead" paper put forward that there was not enough regular meetings and that it would be beneficial to have other meetings focussed on refereeing topics. Seminars were thus introduced to either complement or replace meetings and these provided the chance to address refereeing issues in more detail than was possible during a normal business meeting.

Seminars were held more regularly from 1997, following the review of the supervisory system. The topics covered assessment, match incidents and how to deal with them, the role of the Supervisor in his association on recruitment and retention, involvement in support schemes and the relationship with the association Council or Executive committee. The Seminars proved worthwhile and formed the basis for the way things would develop in the years ahead. It is indicative of the progress made that eight Class 1 referees attended a Seminar in 2003 to provide a contribution from the referees' perspective on the discussion points.

Sub-Committees

Appointed as SFA Chief Executive in 1990, Jim Farry's commitment to refereeing was undoubted and was reflected in his regular attendance at Supervisors' meetings. He capitalised on his position to the full and gave George Cumming the necessary support and backing to get various proposals adopted. In 1990, Farry announced the creation of five sub-committees to assist in the operation of the full committee: Coaching, Liaison, Laws of the Game, Planning and Development, Entrants and Examinations. An Executive Committee member was appointed as Chairman of each sub-committee.

The committees were forums where much more detailed work was undertaken than was possible through either the Executive or full committee. They provided an avenue for Cumming to test ideas on initiatives before taking them forward to the main committees. A revised sub-committee structure was introduced from season 1996-97: Instruction & Coaching, Planning & Liaison, Examinations & Laws of the Game. The sub-committees operated successfully but drew to a conclusion at the end of season 1997-98.

Connecting the Supervisors' Committee to the Referee Committee

Adjustments required to be made to the Referee Committee's Standing Orders due to legal action brought against the SFA in 1996, which required reference to the Supervisors' Committee to be included in them for the first time.

As part of this process, guidelines for Supervisors, introduced some years before, were also revised. Notably, these set out that the Referee Committee "*shall approve, or otherwise, in consultation with the Chief Executive*" the appointment of Supervisors, the Executive Committee and the Chairman of the two committees. A retiral age of 70 years for Supervisors was introduced to maintain parity with the retiral age of SFA Council members.

Following on from these changes, the Referee Committee confirmed, in June 1997, for the first time, the composition of the Supervisors' Committee, the Executive Committee and the various Sub-Committees. As a further consequence of the changes to the Standing Orders, the minutes of the Supervisors' Committee meetings were now submitted to the Referee Committee for its information. This had never happened previously.

The process of linking the Supervisors' Committees to the Referee Committee was brought to a conclusion in 2003 as a result of the change to the Referee Committee structure and, more importantly, to changes to the Articles of Association which enabled committees to form sub-committees. The Referee Supervisors' Committee now became known as the Referee Supervisors' Sub-Committee. It operated for a further two years when further significant changes to the refereeing structure were implemented. The last Supervisors' meeting was on 27th May 2005. The Supervisors' Committees had undoubtedly served refereeing well since their inception 60 years previously. A new chapter was about to unfold.

Scottish Cup Final Luncheon

From 1998, the Luncheon continued without the presence of the Cup Final officials, the Supervisors having been persuaded that it was not in their best interests for pre-match preparation to attend. A Dinner was held in honour of the officials at the Referees' Conference until that came to a close. The Cup Final Luncheon still continues with the referees occasionally taking up the option given to them to briefly meet the Referee Observers and RA Managers during their lunch to receive their congratulations on their appointment to the Final.

Referee Committee

The return of a Referee Committee

By March 1993, it had become evident that the business of the Disciplinary & Referee Committee had been ever increasing on both sides of its responsibilities. Splitting its functions was agreed and two separate committees came into force following the SFA AGM in May.

The Standing Orders of the new Referee Committee were:

a) to compile and issue the Official List of Referees and to make any amendments as appropriate

b) to deal with all questions of the remuneration of the Official List of Referees

c) to oversee the promotion of refereeing through the Referee Supervisors' Committee and the Referees' Associations

d) to liaise with appointed Referee Supervisors, assign their duties and co-operate with them in any development projects to improve refereeing and control of matches.

e) to deal with the nomination of officials to the FIFA Lists of International Referees and Linesmen

f) to consider alterations to the Laws of the Game and to make recommendations in this regard to the Executive Committee.

g) to deal with all other relevant matters concerning referees and refereeing.

The formulation of these Standing Orders meant that for the first time in its history, the SFA had a Referee Committee which was focussed entirely on referees and refereeing and enable it to do justice to its task. All responsibility for player and club misconduct, which it had held since the formation of the very first Referee Committee in 1886, was now the preserve of the Disciplinary Committee.

Whilst not stated in the Standing Orders, the Supervisors' Committees reported to the Referee Committee through the Chief Executive. It did not take long for that connection to have to be made.

The SFA had to give attention in 1996 to formalising the structure of the Referee Committee due to the outcome of a Judicial Review sought by a referee, George McGuire, following his deletion from the List the previous year. This required the Referee Committee's Standing Orders to be revised to connect the Referee Supervisors' Committee to it for the first time and to make that link clear. That such a structure had not been defined until then offers an example of how football operated for many years – on the basis of a common understanding and custom and practice. The McGuire case was an example of emerging legal challenges which the SFA was starting to face in regard to how it carried out its business and how it was being obliged to react.

The Changing Structure of the Referee Committee

The first indications of a more modern approach being taken by the SFA to its business operations appeared in the late 1990's, coinciding with the appointment of David Taylor as Chief Executive in 1999. The Standing Committees were empowered to co-opt a member to provide some expertise and specialist knowledge into the consideration of business. The options of who to appoint were considered over season 1999-00. This resulted in Jim Herald, a Class 1 referee nearing the end of his career, being chosen. He resigned from the List in April 2000 to accept the appointment. He served as a co-opted member for three seasons. Tom Wharton became a co-opted member of the committee for two seasons from 2001-02.

A decision of huge significance was made by the SFA Executive Committee in June 2002. It decided to disband the Referee Committee as it was constituted and to effectively make the Supervisors' Executive Committee the new Referee

Committee. This momentous decision arose from a FIFA directive on the Organisation of Refereeing within National Associations and UEFA indicating that it planned to conduct an audit of refereeing structures within its members. The SFA was obliged to take heed of what was being conveyed by these two bodies. Maintaining the system was not an option. A National Association's Referee Committee had to comprise a majority of former referees, something which was commonplace in almost all other National Associations. The change was put into effect following the SFA's AGM at the end of season 2002-03 as part of other planned alterations to the organisation and structure of the SFA. The Chairman and Vice Chairman of the "new" Referee Committee continued to be members of the SFA Council. The appointment of Council members was the SFA's means of maintaining a "club" connection with the new committee and the refereeing movement.

John Smith, the SFL President, was the Referee Committee Chairman in season 2002-03 and he was re-appointed in that role to the new committee. Sandy Stables, the Aberdeenshire FA representative on Council, and a committee member the previous season, was appointed as Vice-Chairman. As the SFA Committees were now being appointed for a two year term, it was prudent not to appoint Tom Wharton given his stated intention of retiring at the end of season 2002-03. The four remaining Executive Committee members, Drew Fleming, Kenny Hope, George Smith and Bob Valentine, became members and were joined by Douglas Hope and Jim McCluskey. The committee had eight members. As part of the changes being introduced, Valentine was appointed as the Chairman of the Referee Supervisors' Sub-Committee for a two year period.

As a consequence of major organisational restructuring by the SFA in 2011, the most extensive in its history, the committee system was disbanded with the exception of the Referee and Licensing Committees. Both committees had to be retained to comply with FIFA and UEFA requirements. The disciplinary powers held by various committees, including the Referee Committee, were assumed by a new Judicial Panel to deal expediently with all disciplinary matters across SFA jurisdiction. The age limit for committee members was also removed as part of the raft of changes.

John Fleming successfully proposed to the Referee Committee in 2014 that a former assistant referee should be appointed to the committee to broaden its scope and to bring appropriate expertise to discussions on assistant referees. Tom Murphy was appointed on this basis.

The last major change to the structure of the Referee Committee occurred in 2016 and was a hugely important one. The SFA Board was persuaded by representations made to it that the Chairman and Vice-Chairman need not be appointed from the List of Congress members (Congress having replaced Council in 2011). This change opened up the possibility of the specialist members being appointed to these roles. The milestone of a former referee becoming Chairman of the Referee Committee was finally achieved in 2017 when Willie Young was appointed. The Referee Committee was however mindful of being seen to maintain some connection with the game, rather than being entirely separated from it. It was not an unreasonable position to take and doing so still complied with FIFA and UEFA regulations. Thus, a further change was effected to enable two Vice-Chairmen to be appointed to the committee. These appointments may be made from the List of Congress members or co-opted from outwith that list, thus providing a degree of flexibility.

These changes brought the composition and structure of the Referee Committee to its present state. The Chairman and the Vice Chairmen are appointed by the Board following a recommendation from the Office Bearers and Chief Executive. The number of former referees on the committee has to be no less than six. When a new former referee has to be appointed, the Referee Committee submits a recommendation to the Board for its approval. The Referee Committee is mindful that the future appointment of a former female referee to the committee would be appropriate when a suitable candidate is identified.

Committee Objectives

At the first meeting of the new Referee Committee in season 2002-03, John Smith reported that the Board had requested the

Standing Committees to prepare objectives. Such a move, which had never happened previously, was a real breakthrough moment for the refereeing movement given that former referees were now on the committee and could bring experience and knowledge to bear. The following objectives were agreed and approved by the Board:

- the recruitment and retention of referees
- in consultation with the relevant leagues and associations, to work towards the SFA becoming the central appointment body for senior football and, ultimately, for this function to extend to Junior football
- to review the structure of the List in the context of servicing the game as set out by Article 113
- to improve the perception, within football, of the role of the referee

A "Working Committee"

During season 2008-09, the committee had a major discussion on the conducting of its business, prompted by its then Chairman Alan McRae. The discussion was wide-ranging, covering its current operating structure, the composition of the committee, the responsibility of the staff, the potential for the committee to become a "working" committee, the structure of meetings and finance. It was recognised that future strategy would be founded on the SFA's membership of the UEFA Referee Convention, achieved in 2007.

The creation of a "working" committee, involving the former referees on the committee, happened in 2014 following proposals from John Fleming. The areas of responsibilities were:

Education/Recruitment -

- Recruitment and monitoring of education pathway
- Monitoring intake of recruits, identifying areas of concerns and devising initiatives for improvement

Grassroots

- Monitoring Introductory Class pathway

- Integrating recruits into refereeing and improving retention
- Overseeing development of programmes for instructors and coaching co-ordinators

International Referees
- Coaching and mentoring FIFA Listed Referees, including FIFA Development Referees

Assistant Referees
- Coaching Category 3 Referees identified as prospective Category 3 Specialist Assistant Referee Development
- Identifying and coaching future FIFA Assistants from the Specialist Assistant Referee group

Mentors & Talent
- Identifying talented referees in conjunction with RA Managers
- Coaching and mentoring through education programmes

Female Referees
- To enhance recruitment, retention, talent identification and development of female referees
- Coaching and mentoring FIFA Listed Female Referees

Referees' Associations
- Reviewing and monitoring the operation of the Referee's Associations

These areas of responsibility have evolved in the seasons since, as has the membership of the committee and the allocation of responsibilities, but the principles remain the same. Each member works closely with the relevant Referee Operations Department staff and provides regular updates on progress at committee meetings. The liaison roles which the referee specialists have with the Referees' Associations continued to operate from the change of the style of the Referee Committee in 2003.

Referees' Associations' Managers and Referee Observers

The Introduction of a new structure

The process of adjusting the supervisory system structure, first put forward by George Cumming in 1997, was concluded in 2005. Donald McVicar had introduced Executive Supervisors in 2002 which had proved very beneficial and paved the way for the changes which followed. After a further review, the role of Supervisor was replaced by two new roles – Referees' Association Manager (RA Manager) and Referee Observer. The motivation behind the changes was to streamline the structure by utilising resources, both human and financial, to best effect to bring appropriate improvements to meet the needs of a modern refereeing movement.

A Manager was appointed to each of the 12 associations to fulfil the "managerial" role performed by the Supervisor(s). The referee assessment function of the Supervisors was taken over by a group of Referee Observers. The Referee Supervisors' Sub-Committee was replaced by two new sub-committees: the Referees' Associations' Managers Sub-Committee and the Referee Observers' Sub-Committee. The term "Executive Supervisor" became redundant, although the function continued to be carried out by the former referees on the Referee Committee.

All existing Supervisors were appointed as Observers, with the exception of one who chose to retire. 11 other appointments were made. Two were of Class 1 referees who were about to retire, Brian Cassidy and John Rowbotham. One Class 2 referee resigned to take up his appointment. The other eight appointments were Referee Development Advisers. In total, 34 Observers were appointed.

A key aspect of the new structure was that an RA Manager could also operate as an Observer. The creation of the roles of an RA Manager and an Observer was underpinned by the belief that the traditional function of the Supervisor had become outdated. Different skill sets were required for each role. It was not always the case following the expansion of the supervisory system that all new appointments had the necessary abilities to perform the managerial role now being required. For those associations which had more than one Supervisor, the system had become overloaded with Supervisors who were there in name only as their real purpose was to assess referees, and operating under the person who had been designated as the main Supervisor for the association.

To avoid any potential conflicts of interest arising, Observers cannot hold any position within an association. They are expected to regularly attend associations' meetings to keep abreast of current and topical refereeing issues, including the application of the Laws of the Game.

One important aspect of the change of emphasis introduced by the creation of the role of RA Manager was the moving away from the traditional role a Supervisor had at his association's training night when he would have one to one coaching with his referees when discussing assessment reports. The best person for a referee to speak with on these matters was the person who did the assessment, the Referee Observer. The new system also allowed greater opportunity to a Manager to observe his own referees more regularly than was the case under the old system.

The adoption of the new system streamlined and modernised the refereeing structures and better reflected the way things should be. It was groundbreaking in regard to giving direction for the future development of the refereeing movement in Scotland and was certainly very timely given that the UEFA Referee Convention was looming on the horizon. The creation of the roles of RA Manager and Observer has been an unqualified success, as they have undoubtedly strengthened the means by which the SFA carries out its refereeing operations. The RA Managers, in particular, exemplify the commitment so many bring to the refereeing movement.

Meetings

As a consequence of the adoption of the changes, some immediate adjustments to the standard end of season arrangements were carried through. There was no longer any need for a RA Managers meeting to be held on the evening prior to the Cup Final in the same way as a Supervisors' meeting had been held. A summary of the Grading meeting decisions was issued to the RA Managers when the List was published.

The need for regular business meetings comparable to the days of the Supervisors' Committee quickly diminished. Within a couple of years, the Referee Committee reached the view that the appointment of a Chairman to the two Sub-Committees was redundant. There is an annual meeting of the RA Managers and RA Secretaries which is attended by the Referee Committee. Other meetings are called as and when required. These meetings provide an excellent forum to debate all the issues which refereeing generates.

The Referee Observers' Sub-Committee has never formally been convened as a business meeting. The Observers attend Seminars at least twice a season, regularly in conjunction with the Class 1 referees, to consider and debate assessment issues. Attendance at a match is often part of a seminar.

RA Managers Payment System

A system of administrative payments to RA Managers was introduced in 2007, based on a combination of an equal flat rate payment and a per capita element for each member of his association. The Referee Committee was pleased to recognise the time and commitment the Managers give on a voluntary basis. The scheme was funded from savings from the existing budgets for RA Managers and Observers.

Payment System for Observers

A lengthy process was gone through before a match fee payment system was introduced in 2015 for the Observers. Up until then, the SFA was one of the few National Associations in UEFA membership not to make any payment to Observers. Information was obtained from European associations to provide a basis of consideration. A few options were considered and dialogue was entered into with the SFA Board to reach the final outcome.

Assistant RA Managers

By 2010, thoughts started to emerge about the possible appointment of an Assistant RA Manager for some associations, given their size of membership and the workload of the Manager. Succession planning was also an important factor. Glasgow RA was the first association to have an Assistant Manager (Alan Cunningham) appointed in 2011. Four years later, George Drummond was appointed as Assistant Manager for Lanarkshire RA. The benefits of these appointments were quickly realised and the possibilities of making further appointments were addressed during the course of the Referees' Associations review which was then being conducted.

For season 2015-16, Assistant Managers were appointed to Ayrshire RA, Edinburgh & District RA, Fife RA, North of Scotland RA and Stirlingshire RA. Appointments of Assistant Managers were made to Aberdeen & District, Angus & Perthshire RA and Renfrewshire RA in the early part of that season.

Assistant Referee Observers
In another step forward in terms of referee development, for season 2014-15, four Assistant Referee Observers were appointed to assess assistant referees. The intention was to improve the quality of these assessments by using persons who were experienced former assistants which, in turn, would allow the Observer to concentrate on his assessment of the referee. After a successful first season, the number of Assistant Referee Observers was increased to 10. This innovation has proved a great success and has greatly benefited the Referee Committee's consideration of assistant referees' performances and informs decision making at the Grading Meeting.

The role of the Assistant Referee Observers was changed for season 2022-23 to enable them to observe referees up to Category 2. This was to help achieve the required coverage of referees in the lower categories.

The Categorisation of Observers
The introduction of Observers brought with it a better opportunity of focusing attention on their training, the quality of their reports, possible categorisation, the optimum number needed and the identification of potential new Observers.

As had been the case for many years, all Observers' reports were reviewed by the Development Department prior to issue and, where appropriate, points are raised with Observers on aspects of reports. This system was reinforced by the Referee Committee agreeing that any issues with an Observer's report should be raised if the reports are considered to be below an acceptable standard.

All candidates being considered as an Observer come from the pool of Referee Development Advisers, the category of referee assessor operating below an Observer. Any Class 1 referee who retires and wishes to become an Observer has to act as a Referee Development Adviser for a period of time as determined by the Referee Committee. It is not always a given that a candidate under consideration automatically becomes an Observer.

An informal two-tier system of categorisation of Observers operated from season 2010-11, with a formal categorisation of Observers being introduced for season 2014-15:

- Referee Committee Observer: Observer at all levels of domestic football.
- Scottish Premiership Observer: Observer at all levels of domestic football.
- Scottish Championship Observer: Observer at all levels of domestic football, excluding the Scottish Premiership.
- Specialist Assistant Referee Observer: Observers for Assistant Referees at all levels of domestic football. Observers for Assistant Referees may attend a match in conjunction with or without an Observer.

Observers were allocated to either category on the basis of their ability and standard of report. The categorisation of Observers is intended to ensure that a referee is assessed by an Observer of appropriate quality commensurate with the level of the match. It also opened up a pathway for Observers. Progress can be made from a Championship to a Premiership Observer.

SFA Regional Committees

In 2011, as part of the SFA's Football Development Strategy, refereeing was given the opportunity of nominating representatives on the SFA's six regional Committees to provide input from a refereeing perspective and to assist in the growth of the game. This was a rare example of football connecting refereeing to the game's development at grassroots level. It was important for refereeing to be given a voice at such forums to provide expert knowledge.

RA Managers were identified as the most appropriate persons to serve on these committees. Whilst the boundaries of the Regional Committees do not match those of the Referees' Associations, those RA Managers appointed have to liaise with their neighbouring colleagues to keep them abreast of developments. With great strides being taken to develop the structures of grassroots football in the last couple of decades, the refereeing input has provided an informed balance in discussions and helped the football representatives on the committees to better understand likely issues and problems in servicing the growth of the game. The committees have also provided funding for the Referees' Associations which has been a decided benefit for their own development purposes.

Scottish Football Referees' Association

Initial Negotiations

One of George Cumming's first priorities was to address the situation with the SFRA and to find a way of incorporating that body's members into the SFA's associations. He and Tom Wharton entered into discussions with the SFRA Office Bearers in the latter half of 1988. Whilst some progress was made, it was apparent that reaching a satisfactory conclusion would take some time.

As the SFRA had not responded to the SFA by the end of 1989, things were allowed to rest.

Engaging with the SFRA membership

Cumming returned to the issue in early 1991. He decided to by-pass the SFRA Office Bearers and go directly to the members to move things on. The differences between the two associations were set out to them together with the benefits they would receive by transferring over to the SFA's associations. They were invited to transfer during the course of summer 1991.

The direct contact initiative brought success – enough to cause the SFRA to respond given the loss of members which it started to experience. By the end of the year there had been a good integration of SFRA members into the various associations. However, the SFRA response was not a positive one, with the Supervisors' view being that there would be no purpose in the SFA having further discussions with the SFRA.

The SFRA remained active and was still proving to be a thorn in the flesh to the Referees' Associations in the areas where it operated. It had been successful in attracting a good number of candidates to a training class in Angus to the detriment of Angus & Perthshire RA.

The Final Stages

As the national Registration Scheme for Referees was in the throes of being planned and launched by the SFA in 1992, clearing the impasse with the SFRA became even more crucial. The issue was taken to the Disciplinary & Referee Committee and then to the SFA Executive Committee. The SFRA's intransigence towards creating a unified refereeing body resulted in its being told that its recognition as a refereeing organisation would be withdrawn from 30th April 1993. The support of the Affiliated National Associations was enlisted to ensure that priority for their appointments was given to members of the Registration Scheme.

More power to the SFA's elbow came along in December 1992 when FIFA communicated to its member associations in connection with National Refereeing Organisations. It was made clear that there should only be one such body within a National Association. The SFRA's position had become untenable.

As the SFRA had been selective in disseminating information to its members regarding the SFA's proposals, the SFA organised meetings in Glasgow, Edinburgh and Dundee for SFRA members so that the SFA's schemes and proposals and the nature of the change being affected by FIFA's directive could be explained to them. The fact that only registered referees were permitted to officiate in authorised football was a hugely important factor for the SFRA members to contemplate.

These developments forced the SFRA to the table. The SFA President chaired a meeting of SFA and SFRA representatives in March 1993. The need for the SFA to comply with FIFA's directive was outlined. The opportunity was given to the SFRA to decide how to comply with the directive and with the SFA's schemes. Unless the SFRA did so, it would be declared an unauthorised body and its members would be unable to officiate or be involved in any way with the authorised game. FIFA's directive would be enforced from the start of season 1993-94 and only referees who were registered with the SFA would be permitted to officiate at matches played under its jurisdiction.

The game was almost up.

In the aftermath of the meeting, the SFRA wrote to FIFA, which confirmed that its position was untenable. In one last futile throw of the dice, the SFRA failed in an attempt to obtain an interim interdict against the SFA in respect of the implementation of the FIFA directive.

The desired outcome had been achieved. By the early part of season 1993-94, the SFRA was virtually out of existence as a result of large numbers of its membership transferring to the Referees' Associations. The Affiliated National Associations and their member leagues and associations provided excellent co-operation by ensuring that only registered referees were appointed to matches.

The SFRA members were well accepted into the associations. They were quick to appreciate the opportunities which were now open to them, primarily the chance to progress to the List. Many had their eyes opened by joining their new association, not even having understood in some cases that such associations existed. It had all boiled down to which advert or publicity – SFRA or SFA - someone had responded to in terms of going to a referee training class.

The Registration Scheme and Classification of Referees

Registration Scheme
It took until 1992 for the SFA to decide to have a proper register of all referees. There had been no need to do so previously. If a total number was ever needed, a check could be made by asking each Referees' Association to confirm its membership. There was also limited scope for the administration to deal with such a task. Football at senior level was the SFA's historical focus and a throughput of referees always emerged from the associations to service the List. There never seemed to be any call emanating from the Affiliated National Associations saying there were not enough referees for their matches. The game managed to get by. Referees were effectively split into two groups: those on the List (the "Listed" referees) and all the other referees who were known as either the "Non-Listed" or "Unlisted" referees.

George Cumming had the great foresight to realise that a having a register of referees was an absolute prerequisite for the SFA to have to be able to have direct contact with them to aid the development of refereeing. The idea anticipated the requirements of the UEFA Referee Convention 15 years later.

Approval was given to the annual registration of all referees in Scotland with the SFA, to enable accurate records to be kept and provide a means for the issuing of information concerning alterations to the Laws of the Game and other refereeing matters. The use of the terms "Non-listed" and "Unlisted" came to an end. These referees were categorised as Class 5 and were recommended for appointment as referees or linesmen in football played under the auspices of the Affiliated National Associations.

The Registration Scheme was launched for season 1992-93, although it was entirely on a voluntary on the part of the referees if they wished to register. It met with a fair degree of success as over 50% of the referees had registered by the middle of the season. To encourage registration, the full fee for attending the 1993 Referees' Conference had to be paid by non-registered referees. The worth of ensuring that all referees should be registered became apparent during the season. Registration became compulsory.

The Registration Fee was incorporated into the annual subscription which a referee paid to be a member of his association. The associations retained the fees for their members, confirmed the number of members to the SFA and received the appropriate financial credit in their budget statements, budgets having been introduced in 1991.

The first Registration fee was £6. Referees were issued with a membership card, a copy of the Laws of the Game and a copy of the Amendments to the Laws. The fee also included an element for insurance cover. The issuing of a membership card ceased after some 20 years as it was eventually deemed superfluous. The current fee is £10. The level of insurance cover provided through the Registration Scheme has been increased periodically.

One area of slight difficulty came to the fore, namely that of the position of "non-active" referees. These referees were either members of Minor Grade Advisory Panels or retired from refereeing but who wished to retain membership of their association. It was decided that these members should not pay a registration fee.

Making registration compulsory had the desired effect. By September 1993, 1850 referees were registered, a considerable increase compared to the first year of the scheme. The following year, in December 1994, the number of referees was 2173.

A List of Registered Referees was regularly issued to the Affiliated National Associations to keep them alert to those who were registered. There was always going to be a risk of non-registered referees, those who for whatever reason chose not to continue in membership of an association but who still continued to referee, officiating in minor football. The Scheme's effectiveness and purpose was illustrated when, in 1994, the Scottish Amateur FA ordered two cup ties under its jurisdiction to be replayed because the matches had not been refereed by registered referees.

Over the years, the registration processes have been improved upon and consolidated. Nowadays, a report on all registered referees is issued on a weekly basis to the Affiliated National Associations and each association receives a weekly report on its membership. The associations are required to submit a list of its members to the SFA by 30th June each year.

Classification of Referees

Early in season 1997-98, the Referee Committee gave authority to George Cumming to review the structure of the List and the classification of referees within the Registration Scheme. He formed a group from a cross section of Scottish refereeing to conduct the review. A consultation process was undertaken with the Supervisors, Referees' Associations, the SFL and the Affiliated National Associations. The report, "Refereeing in Scotland – Towards the New Millennium", was produced by the end of the season and its recommendations were largely adopted.

A starting point was the consideration of the classification system, where there was a clear and stark imbalance. That season, the List (comprising Classes 1 to 4) numbered 177. There were 1993 Class 5 referees (at 1st November 1997). Class 5 referees formed 92% of the List of Registered Referees. A more equable classification system was sought to try to redress this imbalance.

A number of common features on the grading of referees emerged from the consultation process, including attendance at association meetings and training, ability to pass a fitness test, specialised assistant referees, passing the Refresher Examination, Probationary referees, Youth referees, recognition of non-active referees as a separate grading, defining a clear promotion structure (both upward and downward) and recognition of the prominent role required of senior officials within their association. These points informed the structure proposed by the group:

- Class 1 – the List would be collapsed into this Class, with a number of sub-classes within it to reflect the hierarchy – Class 1 Referees, Class 1 Specialist Assistant referee and Class 1 Assistant referee. All these officials would continue to officiate in the same grades of football as before.

173

- Class 2 – these referees would have their classification approved annually by the Referee Committee on the recommendation of their Supervisor. They were to referee regularly in Junior football. For the first time, the category of referee to officiate in Junior football had been designated.
- Class 3 – they would referee in recreational and youth football and be classified by their Supervisor. They were expected to regularly attend meetings and training and be encouraged to attend the Referees' Conference.
- Class 4 - they would referee in recreational and youth football. If they did not meet the criteria for Class 3 they would become Class 4 referees. Such referees were deemed to be the ones who did not attend meetings or training. Progress to Class 3 was possible if they met the criteria.
- Probationary Referees – these were to be referees over the age of 18 who passed the Entrance Examination. They were expected to fulfil the criteria for Class 3 referees within two full seasons otherwise they would be made Class 4.
- Youth Referees – the minimum age for this classification would be 16 years. After reaching the age of 18 and having been a Youth Referee for at least two full seasons they would be reclassified to Class 3 if they fulfilled the criteria.
- Senior Associate referee – non-active referees who actively support the work of their association by attendance at meetings and by fulfilling a particular role within it.

The Class 1 and Class 2 referees were all expected to have a 70% attendance at meetings and training and to attend the Referees' Conference. The Probationary and Youth referees were to pay a reduced Registration fee, with no fee paid by Senior Associates.

A proposal to reduce the retiral age of Class 1 Assistant Referees from 45 to 40 was not adopted, although the Class 2 retiral age was reduced from 48 to 45.

The report was pivotal and resulted in the formation of a proper structure for refereeing in Scotland. A pathway between the classes had been created and the issues with the previous Class 5 had been addressed. By creating Probationary and Youth Referees, recognition was made of these important entry categories into refereeing. The need to give more focus on such referees had instantly come about. Encouragement could be given to them to progress in the structure. It was in the movement's interest to do so.

The introduction of this structure set the template for modern refereeing in Scotland. Things evolved over the years but the basic form of the structure has remained relatively constant.

During season 2000-01, two of the classifications were adjusted. A problem had existed from the start of the new system – the identification of the former Class 2 referees. They had been included in the Class 1 Assistant Referee grouping and, for the purposes of reflecting their status for match appointments, were identified as Class 1 Assistant Referee (Selected). This issue was resolved by renaming them Class 1 Referee (Category 2). Consequentially, the Class 1 Referees had (Category 1) appended to their classification. The remaining two Class 1 categories remained unchanged.

A desire arose to consider the classification system more fully and to make further adjustments. During season 2003-04, the Referee Committee formed a Sub-Committee to review the structure of the List. The proposals from the review enlarged the List, for the purpose of better servicing of the game, and extended into the overall classification system. The following changes to classifications resulted:

Table 5: Changes to Classification System 2004-05

Existing Classification	New Classification
Class 1 (Category 1 Referee	Category 1 Referee
Class 1 (Category 2) Referee	Category 2 Referee
Class 1 Specialist Assistant Referee	Category 3 Specialist Assistant Referee
Class 1 Assistant Referee	Category 3 Referee
Class 2 Referee (Senior)	Category 4A Referee
Class 2 Referee (Junior)	Category 4B Referee
Class 3 Referee	Category 5 Referee
Class 4	Category 6 Referee

The classifications of Youth Referee and Probationary Referee were not changed.

The new categories expanded the range as set by the previous terminologies and brought greater clarity to the classifications. It aided a better understanding within the game, as there had been some difficulties expressed on the terminology. The Class grouping was designed for the professional leagues which had the effect of matches in senior regional football being refereed by a Class 1 Assistant Referee rather than a "referee", something which stuck in the craw of some in the refereeing movement. As there was no alteration to the levels of football in which the referees officiated, the new classifications were easily accepted.

The last main changes to the overall classification structure happened for the start of season 2012-13. The basis for the change was the SFA's new strategy for football which had, amongst many targets, the goal of doubling the number of registered football players by 2015. Achieving this goal had implications for the servicing an increase in matches. To address it, the classification Category 8 Referee (Quality Mark Awareness) was created. The referees were to be generated from people attached to clubs with the SFA's Quality Mark Standard and, once qualified through the Awareness Course, would be able to referee small-sided games played under the jurisdiction of the Scottish Youth FA. The classification is valid for three years. If the person wishes to maintain the category they must undertake the Awareness Course again to ensure an up-to-date knowledge of the Laws of the Game.

The categories of Probationary and Youth Referees were dispensed with as three new categories – 7, 7A and 7B – were introduced. The latter two categories were required to track the entry point of referees, either through the SQA course offered through schools and colleges (7A) or the Introductory Course (Parts 1 and 2) provided by the associations (7B). Both classifications are valid for three years. Once they lapse, the individual has to undertake the Introductory Course if they wish to become a Category 7 referee.

A Category 7 referee is someone who has passed Part 3 of the Introductory Referee Course set by the SFA, assessed refereeing a match, completed the recognised Disclosure Scotland Checks, and accepted into membership of a Referees' Association. The classification applies for a maximum of 12 months from the date of membership before being re-classified by the RA Manager. Within the List, a Category 2 Development classification had been introduced informally during season 2010-11 as a means of identifying and testing Category 2 referees in the SFL Third Division. Given its success, other Development Categories were introduced, thus creating a much clearer pathway for progression.

Referees' Associations

The Referees' Associations play a very important part in the refereeing structure, providing a crucial and indispensible vehicle through which the SFA has been able to develop and progress refereeing in the modern era. Change has been at the forefront of all the various component elements of refereeing over the last 30 years. The associations have had to change and evolve too, often acting on direction given by the SFA. In the last decade the SFA conducted a major review of the associations which resulted in a significant modernisation of their operations.

Secretaries' Meetings

The annual Secretaries' meetings fulfilled an important purpose and allowed a forum for the SFA to progress its plans for developing refereeing. It was a two-way street, with the Secretaries doing an excellent job in reflecting views and concerns arising from their memberships on a variety of issues. They were never slow in expressing disquiet at the feelings of referees that disciplinary decisions on so-called high profile cases involving players and managers were on occasions too lenient and harmful to the refereeing movement.

These meetings enabled agreement to be reached on a wide variety of refereeing and administrative issues so that information could be shared and passed out to the memberships.

Issues would crop up within an association and addressing them meant that a consistent approach could be adopted by all the other associations. Best practice could be developed.

By 2006, the agendas for these meetings had become lighter, perhaps as a consequence of the general progress made. As a result, the meetings were merged into a joint annual meeting with the RA Managers.

Monthly Meetings

Given his time as a referee and a teacher, George Cumming was ideally placed to address the associations' monthly meetings. The harsh reality was that much could be done to make improvements. Little on actual refereeing matters was dealt with at the meetings. Rather, there was a bureaucratic structure to them as the focus was more on dealing with the business of the association.

There was also an obvious variance in the format of meetings. Guidelines were therefore issued, via the Supervisors, for the conducting of business in order that a more structured format could be achieved. The quality of venues, and the facilities provided, was also addressed as some were not best suited for purpose. Over time, a number of associations changed their meeting venue to a much better facility than they had been using.

A change in emphasis to provide greater discussion on refereeing matters quickly resulted following the introduction in 1990 of the position of Coaching Co-ordinator in each of the associations. The Co-ordinators led discussion on refereeing topics provided by the SFA. The placing of the Co-ordinator's slot was an important early element in modernising the meetings.

The desired improvements were achieved within a few years. Each association had an instructional section at each meeting which proved beneficial to members and which made it worthwhile for them to attend. This view was reinforced early in season 1998-99 following the introduction of the new classification structure. Increased attendances at meetings and training resulted at all associations.

The coaching topics at meetings were standardised in 2004. Helped greatly by advances in technology, the SFA produced DVDs of coaching material covering instructional points and topical match incidents, with guidance notes provided. The move proved successful. Clear and consistent messages could be advanced by the Coaching Co-ordinator when discussions on a topic were concluded, thus ensuring a uniform interpretation among all referees. A library of material was developed as a consequence which meant that a topic could be returned to when required to maintain an emphasis on it.

Despite improvements in the format of meetings, a focus continued to be given to them. At a Managers and Secretaries meeting in 2009, Donald McVicar raised for discussion the timings, programme content and attendances. In some associations attendances were not reaching 40% of the membership. The Referee Committee debated on which night meetings should be held. A few associations held them on Fridays, which was not thought to provide ideal preparation for a referee for a match the following day. The relevant associations were encouraged to think of moving to another evening. It was a tricky problem to address. A variety of factors relating to referees' availability, association business and football fixture scheduling were provided as reasons for these associations continuing to favour Friday evenings for their meetings. Departing from that approach was not a straightforward exercise.

Financial Support

The SFA introduced a budgetary system in 1991 to replace the piecemeal submission of countless invoices. An annual payment was made to each association based upon a submitted budget covering the core areas of expenditure including the cost of venues for meetings and training classes, physical training facilities, training class instructors and minor grade advisory panel members' expenses.

Any surplus or deficit which accrued was taken into account by the SFA when determining the following year's payment. Within two years, the credit function relating to the associations receiving Registration Scheme fees from their memberships was built into the budgetary process.

Budgets were replaced by a financial grant system in 2008, operating in parallel with the SFA's financial year. An important factor in the change was that each association could now focus on the cost of its operations, with the possibility of creating savings within the grant payment for use elsewhere within other refereeing activities.

In addition to the systems which have been used to provide financial support to the associations, the SFA has also provided support in kind by providing laptops, projectors and screens for use at meetings and training classes, together with training gates for fitness tests.

In 1995, to recognise the 50th Anniversary of the founding of the associations, the SFA gave a contribution of £1000 to the relevant associations for a development project as and when their anniversary was reached.

Disciplinary Processes and Appeals to the SFA

The SFA carried out major changes to its Articles of Association in 1994. Many of these changes resulted in the incorporation of "referee" into many of the Articles for the first time, which had a consequential impact on referees and the associations. One such change led to the SFA requiring the associations to introduce into their constitutions a procedure for referees to appeal to the SFA if they had been subject of disciplinary action. A regular stream of appeals from referees to the SFA Appeals Committee ensued. Despite being the persons in a football match who applied the Laws of the Game, referees, being human, also managed to breach rules and regulations. There was a mixed bag of appeal outcomes – some were dismissed, others upheld in whole or in part. In those instances where a referee's appeal was upheld, it was often the result of a procedural issue not having been handled correctly by an association or too severe a sanction being imposed.

The associations were required to alter their disciplinary and appeal processes following the introduction of the Judicial Panel in 2012.

A Review of the Associations

Despite the improvements in the format of monthly meetings, concerns were still held about them. Comment was made at a Referee Committee meeting in September 2012, with a desire expressed to standardise the structure of the meetings to ensure that best practice was being followed. This discussion set in train a mammoth undertaking over the next few years to review the operation of the associations in conjunction with delivering grassroots coaching to the referees in a completely different manner.

The initial proposals were extremely ambitious and bold. The 12 associations were to be disbanded and replaced by six Regions in line with the six regions introduced by the SFA for football development purposes. The monthly meetings were to be replaced by four regional coaching meetings per year for grassroots referees. Each Region's Manager would conduct all business and financial matters under the aegis of the SFA. All referees were to operate under one set of national regulations, rather than the varying constitutions of the 12 associations, and the membership fee was to be reduced or dispensed with.

Giving attention to grassroots referees was almost the "final frontier" for the SFA to address, given all the other changes and programmes which had been introduced in previous years. These were essentially all directed at the List, with the view being widely held that the volume of meetings for the various categories had become too high. The attendance of grassroots referees at the monthly meetings was low in most associations. Introducing the regional coaching meetings was reckoned to better cater for the grassroots referees, making it more attractive for them to attend rather than the monthly meetings. They also provided the opportunity for activities on the field of play, compared to being in a room for coaching purposes.

The Referee Committee approved the proposals in principle and gave the go-ahead for a major review to be conducted, taking the view that a rigorous approach to effecting change would be beneficial given the many other developments which had occurred in Scottish refereeing.

A Working Group, comprising a cross section of the referee movement, was formed by John Fleming to explore and progress the proposals. Due to magnitude of the task to be undertaken, it was recognised that it was impossible to set any timescale for the project's completion and implementation. A number of sub-groups were also created to consider particular aspects of the review. A rigorous root and branch review of the refereeing structures and operations took place through these sub-groups.

John Fleming visited all the associations during the autumn of 2013 to explain the basis for the proposed developments. The visits were well received and helped to eliminate potential points of issue.

One specific item of business required to be addressed as an outcome of the review at this stage. It had emerged that provision for the dissolution of an association was absent from virtually all the associations' constitutions. This omission was corrected where required at the associations' AGMs held in the spring of 2014.

Internal SFA discussions on the legal and financial implications of the proposed new structure proved to be crucial to the review's progress. It transpired that the 12 associations, being separate legal entities, required to remain in existence, rather than potentially be dissolved as had initially been envisaged. It was also advantageous for the SFA to maintain the existing structures between it and the associations to allow it to conduct its operations in an appropriate way.

If the implementation of the original proposals was not going to be possible, it was always appreciated that other elements would emerge which could be acted upon and assist in progressing the development of refereeing in Scotland. The principal aims of the review were therefore revised.

Beyond retaining the associations, the aim was now for them to adopt a uniform and simplified constitution and to introduce a national set of regulations for referees, with disciplinary cases being referred to the Judicial Panel. It was proposed also to reduce the number of monthly meetings and to provide the two sets of regional coaching meetings per year for grassroots referees. Assistant Association Managers were to be appointed to the majority of associations. To address an untidy area of refereeing business, a standardised fee for the Introductory Course was planned, together with uniform fees for instructors.

Once revised proposals were fully prepared, including the determination of the most suitable methodology of providing financial support to the associations, a further round of association visits took place in spring 2016.

The final proposals were presented at a Managers and Secretaries meeting in January 2017. The proposed reduction of "monthly meetings" to four was accepted.

It was now a matter of implementation. As the uniform constitution had to be adopted by all the associations to allow the new operational structure to become active, an anxious wait had to be endured as each association held its AGM during a two month period from March to May. One by one the results came into the SFA. Any fears which may have been held were allayed. The constitution was resoundingly accepted. The associations were thanked by the Referee Committee for their hard work in enabling such an important and progressive change. John Fleming conducted another tour round the associations to reinforce that message of thanks.

The adoption of a simplified constitution was a terrific success. Over the years since the associations were formed, there had been an unwitting divergence of their constitutions. Now, every referee in Scotland, regardless of the association, is governed in exactly the same way by the same rules and regulations (particularly in respect of disciplinary cases being dealt with by the Judicial Panel). Since its adoption, there have been some amendments made to the Constitution. To ensure that uniformity is maintained, each association is required to adopt the proposed amendment, otherwise the amendment falls. One area where an association can operate "individually" is that of Membership Rules. These are separate from the Constitution and are designed to suit local circumstances.

The national set of regulations is entitled "Refereeing in Scotland: A Guide to the Organisational and Operational Structure" and contains all relevant information required by referees in regard to refereeing in Scotland. This means that a newcomer to refereeing has exactly the same starting point of knowledge regardless of which association the person is a member, something which had never been the case previously.

The number of meetings has increased from four to five, which was in response to views expressed by the associations.

The review was a major undertaking which has proved its worth. At the outset, it was recognised that a fluid approach would have to be taken and that the aims and objectives would adjust and evolve as the project progressed. That is what happened, and although the initial ambition of collapsing the associations into the geographical area of the SFA's six Regions was not achieved, there was still a huge amount of modernising change effected. Refereeing is the better for it.

The List of Referees

A Changing Structure

1991-92
After operating on a very stable basis for over 40 years from the late 1940's, the List has gone through a number of structural changes since 1991. These changes were a combination of a desire to improve refereeing and also as a result of having to respond to changing demands within the game to ensure it was serviced with officials.

The first restructuring in 1991-92 stemmed from George Cumming prompting the Executive Committee to consider how it decided the composition of the List and the objectives it had in that task. Adopting a more rigorous approach was suggested. The committee appreciated that its previous operating principles would have to be re-appraised if that were to happen.

Cumming's proposals worked their way through the Supervisors before being approved by the Disciplinary & Referee Committee in March 1991. The SFL was consulted on the proposals and gave its full support. The proposals were underpinned by a desire to establish a system which allowed the quality of referees and linesmen to develop and improve. It was a case of "less is more". The target was a planned reduction in the size of the List which would mean an increased frequency of appointments for referees and linesmen and lead to an increased quality in performance.

The changes were:

- Class 1 and Class 2 referees were to be regularly used as linesmen in appropriate matches
- A new Class 3 was created from the existing Class 3A and Class 3B, with the new Class being smaller in size than that of the two previous grades
- The existing retiral age for linesmen was reduced from 48 to 47 years at the end of season 1990-91 and thereafter to 46 and 45 years in the following two seasons, and
- A new Class 4 was created to incorporate the Supplementary Lists which had been introduced so that some leagues had an adequate pool of referees to use for their fixtures. These officials would not be appointed to SFA and SFL competitions.

The use of Class 1 referees as linesmen was revolutionary in the context of domestic football. Developments in international football at that time had a clear influence on the decision to deploy them in the role. The 1990 FIFA World Cup had not been the best for refereeing and FIFA chose to do something about the quality of linesmen. The category of FIFA Linesman was introduced in 1992, with these officials being experienced linesmen, thus leaving the FIFA referees to concentrate on refereeing rather to have to run the line in international matches. The Class 1 referees only experience of running the line once they were promoted to Class 1 was when they were appointed to an international club match, which was infrequently. Using them as linesmen in domestic football would give them that added bank of experience for potential appointment in international matches, whilst making use of their abilities as referees to monitor and control touchline behaviour. A good number of Class 1 referees were selected as FIFA Linesmen over the next five years.

The decision to use Class 2 referees as linesmen was an inspired one. Up to this point, on becoming Class 2, such a referee, by the nature of the appointments they received, was divorced from any involvement in first team football until either being promoted to Class 1 or re-classified to Category 3B. Using them as linesmen kept them connected to first team football, and allowed them to bridge that previous gap in their career development. They also, importantly, benefited from operating with Class 1 referees and were able to gain a better understanding of what lay ahead of them in the event of being promoted to Class 1. Additionally, their faces became known by players and coaching staffs.

The changes were regarded as keeping the SFA abreast of wider developments in refereeing which FIFA was instigating, prime of which was encouraging a trend towards younger, experienced referees and linesmen. The view was that Scottish refereeing would be in a favourable position to progress, not only domestically, but on the international scene as a result.

The changes relative to Class 2 had implications for Scottish Junior FA football, where Class 2 referees were the highest class that could be used. Co-operation with the Scottish Junior FA was developed on the use and appointment of referees in that grade of football.

The changes to the List were aimed entirely to benefit SFL football and, consequently, impacted on senior regional Leagues which appointed their referees from those who were free from SFL appointments. The new system reduced the availability of local Class 1 and Class 2 referees for these leagues, the Highland League in particular. To counter the problem, the SFA put in place a scheme whereby the League appointed Class 1 and Class 2 referees from outwith its area to cover the absences of the local officials from time to time during the season. Similar schemes were introduced for the East of Scotland and South of Scotland Leagues.

The new structure operated well and was positively received. Referees benefited from an increased level of appointments and Class 1 referees, the experienced ones in particular, were considered to have applied themselves well to acting as linesmen. A greater degree of team work had developed due to regular contact, and interchanging of roles, between Class 1 and Class 2 referees due to the system of appointments. On the downside, at Class 3, there were some complaints regarding the reduction in the number of appointments, particularly from older officials.

Problems were experienced with the new Class 4. It worked successfully in those areas where it had superseded the Supplementary Lists but elsewhere resignations were prompted by either a lack of appointments or lack of attraction of the appointments open to the officials. The resignations were generally from referees who were put to Class 4 when the List was compiled and who lived well away from the areas where they were intended for use. Difficulties were experienced by the East of Scotland League in appointing referees as a consequence. The functioning of this Class settled down after review and better focus on its compilation.

1998-99

The next restructuring of the List came from a further desire to evolve and change, influenced once more by international developments, and the anticipated change in League structures in Scotland. The creation of Specialist Assistant Referees was the major development, with the days of Class 1 referees being linesmen coming to a close.

The threat of rebellion by the country's top clubs had been a constant theme during the 1990's as money became an increasing and all important factor. A potential breakaway from the SFL was the dominant theme of season 1997-98 in the politics of Scottish football. The talk of previous seasons finally crystallised when the Scottish Premier League (SPL) was formed for season 1998-99.

Running in parallel with the negotiations on the potential formation of a new league was the work being conducted by the Referee Development Group formed by George Cumming to review the structure of refereeing. The proposals which emerged in relation to the classification structure had one eye on the league negotiations. As a consequence, the outcomes of the review ideally positioned the SFA when the league was approved at the end of the season and strengthened the ongoing drive to professionalise refereeing.

Classes 1 to 3 were collapsed into the Class 1 grade, with sub-categories.

Only the Class 1 Specialist Assistant Referees would officiate in the SPL. Class 1 assistant referees would not be appointed to the competition. Class 1 Assistant Referees (Selected) would continue to act as assistant referees in the SFL Divisions. Class 4 became Class 2.

A new role beckoned for the Class 1 referees: that of Fourth Official. After years of the SFA having raised the issue with the SFL, the SPL had agreed to have Fourth Officials appointed within its league.

The creation of Specialist Assistant Referees opened up a new career path for officials. As only a small proportion of referees achieve the ambition of making it to Class 1, the possibility of being an assistant referee in the country's top league was now something to aim for. Additionally, the route to become a FIFA Assistant Referee was now also open.

In the early part of season 1998-99, problems quickly came to the fore. 10 Class 2 "Junior" referees from Edinburgh & District RA referees were moved into Class 2 on the List to assist in the servicing of the East of Scotland League. As the SFL was experiencing difficulties in appointing referees to its Youth Competitions, 12 referees were admitted to Class 1 Assistant Referee on the List. It was a good intake – six of these referees became Class 1 referees.

2005-06

In the seasons which followed the restructuring in 1998-99, issues concerning the servicing of the game at regional senior and junior levels became a recurring theme. Referees were added regularly to either Class 2 – senior or Junior, in whichever areas of the country they were needed. Local circumstances had given rise to variances within the overall general policy for the categorisation of referees in Junior football. Greater scrutiny was given to the Class 2 "senior" referees to ensure that they were properly fulfilling the purpose of their category - to service Leagues such as the East of Scotland and South of Scotland rather than their officiating in Junior football. Such points fed in to the resultant process of the Referee Committee's carrying through its objective, set in 2003, of restructuring the List in the context of servicing the game and to surmount the difficulties which had been experienced in preceding seasons. The outcome was put into effect for season 2005-06.

The simple solution was to enlarge the List. This was done by including the Class 2 "Junior" referees within it. As part of the overall renaming of classifications, they became Category 4B referees. The Class 2 "senior" referees became Category 4A referees.

In terms of movement within the List, a Class 1 (Category 1) referee, if being downgraded, could not be re-classified automatically as a Specialist Assistant Referee but was re-classified as a Class 1 Assistant Referee to have the opportunity of gaining at least a season's experience as an assistant before being nominated as a Specialist. The same pathway to Specialist Assistant Referee was adopted for Class 1 (Category 2) referees a year later.

2007-08

Further changes to Categories 4A and 4B were implemented for season 2007-08 following a revision of the relevant criteria. Category 4A became the entry point for the List for potential future progression to Category 3. Category 4B referees became those officials who were on the List to essentially service the game, whether in senior or Junior football, and would not have the chance to progress to Category 3. A referee older than the normal upper age limit of 35 for admission to the List could be included at Category 4B specifically to service the game. To ensure that the needs of the East of Scotland, South of Scotland, North Caledonian and Highland Youth Leagues could be met, the retiral age of Category 4B referees was set as 50 years. Category 4B referees over 45 years were not permitted to referee in Junior football unless in exceptional circumstances when there are no other referees available for appointment. If a Category 4A was not going to progress to Category 3, reclassification to Category 4B would occur.

These changes meant that a good number of referees switched between these two categories when the List for season 2007-08 was compiled. This was a necessary correction to populate the categories in the right manner.

2012-13

Other changes to the List's structure were put into effect following an overall review of the classification system. Following the success of the informal creation of a Category 2 Development group during season 2010-11, Development Categories were introduced for Category 1 and Category 3 Specialist Assistant Referee. To better fit into the structure and to better illustrate the clear pathway which was now in place, Category 4A was renamed Category 3 Development. Category 4B was changed to Category 4.

2021-22

Category 2 Development was removed from this season, as it as it was felt that it had become counterproductive.

For Category 1 and Category 3 Specialist Assistant Referee, each group is divided informally into three sub-groups – Select, Performance and Development with the intention that these reflect a tiered basis of match appointment issued to the officials in the Scottish Professional Football League (SPFL) i.e. Premiership, Championship and Leagues 1 and 2. Category 2 and Category 2 Development were merged.

Admission Age

35 was long regarded as the maximum age for admission to the List although this was not formally confirmed until 1995. There were instances in 1990 and 1995 when a relaxation was introduced to allow an older referee with exceptional ability to be admitted to the List but in each case it was anticipated that the frequency of this happening would be relatively low. Very few referees, if any, gained admittance to the List due to this mechanism.

As the years passed, the upper age limit became redundant as the programmes put in place by the SFA, combined with the restructuring of the List, resulted in the average age of admission tumbling quite dramatically, especially once Category 3 Development was introduced. It is common for referees to be admitted at that category when they are either side of 20 years of age.

Retiral Age

Addressing the retiral ages of referees became a recurring theme within refereeing, and football, from 1990 onwards. In a parting flourish before his retirement, Jack Mowat unsuccessfully raised the possibility of increasing the retiral age of 50 years for Class 1 referees.

The retiral age of the new Class 3 was an important factor in the changes introduced in the restructuring of the List in 1991. It was reduced from 48 to 45 over a three season period. The motivation for this was to reduce the numbers of referees in the Class 3 and to create greater competition for admission to the List.

Increasing the Class 1 retiral age was raised by the SFL in 1994, but this was not supported by the Supervisors and the Referee Committee. The prevailing argument was that it felt that to selectively choose certain referees to continue beyond 50 years of age would give rise to more problems than might be anticipated and, at the same time, reduce the opportunity for other referees to gain promotion to Class 1.

Raising the retiral age beyond 50 ran counter to the approach being taken by FIFA, as it had dropped the retiral age of FIFA referees to 45. Maintaining the retiral age at 50 had everything to do with having an experienced supply of referees to serve the SFL and to keep the clubs happy. It was only a matter of time before the argument moved in the opposite direction – reducing the retiral age.

George Cumming flagged up the possibility of lowering the Class 1 retiral age from 50 to 48 in 1999, but nothing was progressed.

In 2002, Bob Valentine suggested to the Executive Committee that Scotland was largely out of step with all other UEFA National Associations in having 50 as the retiral age for referees. His view was that the retiral age had contributed to young referees not being able to break into the top group, thus curbing their enthusiasm and, on the wider scale, limiting the opportunities for referees to develop lengthy international careers in comparison to other European referees. He proposed reducing the retiral age on an incremental basis to 47 years, being of the belief that reducing the retiral age would be compatible with development objectives and avoid stagnation with the Category 1 group.

The issue was hotly debated by the Supervisors. At both the Executive Committee and the full committee, the topic went to a vote. On each occasion, the proposal won. When the recommendation went to the Referee Committee, it was tested to the full by the majority of members and, with their looking at things from a football perspective and being fearful of losing experienced referees in the 45-50 age bracket with whom they were familiar, it was no surprise that the recommendation was defeated after a vote.

The change in the structure of the Referee Committee in 2003-04, when the former Supervisors' Executive Committee became the committee, altered the dynamic. Carrying though one of its agreed objectives to review the structure of the List, it decided in 2004 that the retiral age be reduced from 50 to 47 years over three seasons from 2005-06. Seven referees would be retired over that period – one after the first season, four after the second season and two after the third. The SFA Board accepted the recommendation without comment.

In November 2005, the recently formed Scottish Senior Football Referees' Association (SSFRA) wanted the Referee Committee to review the retiral age of the Specialist Assistant Referees and raise it from 45 to 47, to maintain parity with the Class 1 referees. Whilst valid reasons were explained to the SSFRA for the damaging impact this would cause, the SSFRA then solicited the support of the SFL. The Referee Committee re-affirmed its position that there should be no adjustment to the retiral age of assistant referees.

The SSFRA made further representations a year later, referring to new age discrimination legislation which had been introduced and its potential implications on retiral ages.

In October 2008, the SFA Board requested the Referee Committee to review the retiral age. This was much to the committee's surprise given that the Board had straightforwardly approved its recommendation to reduce the retiral age three years previously. The Board's opinion was that a number of good experienced referees had retired in recent years and were not being replaced. The committee considered that the recent retirement of referees who were well regarded by clubs was a factor in the Board's request. It was football politics at play. It was a short term club view versus the longer term strategy of the committee. The Class 1 group of referees had become younger than their predecessors – more were being promoted to Class 1 in their early to mid-30s compared to years gone by when the majority of promotions of referees would have been in their late 30's. The committee stood firm and conveyed its views on its rationale to the Board.

During 2009, the SSFRA persisted with its request to have the retiral age reconsidered, continuing to seek parity between Category 1 and 3. Its case was becoming stronger, and the committee's position started to change. Age discrimination legislation had become an important element of the issue's consideration. In December 2009, the committee raised the age limit for Category 3 Specialist Assistant Referee and Category 3 to 47 years, to be consistent with the Category 1 referees. The retiral age of Category 4B referees was also raised to 47 years and the maximum age of 35 years for admission to the List at Category 3 and 4A was dispensed with.

The SFA President, George Peat, met the committee in September 2010 to discuss the issue. The thought of abolishing the age limit was beginning to emerge. After a period of deliberation, the Referee Committee recommended to the SFA Board in December 2011 that there should be no age limit for referees included on the List from season 2012-13.The committee felt that it would be rare for a referee or assistant referee to be able to continue for many seasons beyond the limit of 47 years due to the demands of the Fitness Test, if at all, and more crucially, that it, and the SFA, ran the risk of falling foul of the age discrimination legislation if the current system did not change. The committee also appreciated that retaining a mandatory age limit ran counter to the SFA's Equality Policy and that the age limit of 70 had been removed in regard to membership of Council.

The committee recognised that, in dispensing with age limits, its levels of scrutiny and objectivity in compiling the List would have to increase and that its decision making processes would have to be guided by a referee's competency and his ability to pass the Fitness test.

Putting a Strategy into Practice

The genesis of a strategy occurred during season 1990-91 when the Executive Committee reviewed the ages of the Class 1 referees. A high number were to retire over the next few seasons. By the end of season 1991-92 only five Class 1 referees under the age of 40 years would be on the List. The realisation dawned that measures had to be taken to plan ahead and to correct this apparent imbalance. The first steps to correct things happened mid-season when three Class 2 referees were promoted to Class 1.

If any strategy had operated prior to that season it worked on a short term basis and operated in a natural way, conditioned to some extent by the number of any Class 1 referees who were retiring. Retirals and deletions created the spaces to fill with promotions and that approach cascaded down through to the other Classes. It was a relatively rare day if the Executive Committee ever looked much beyond the season it was dealing with. The numbers in each Class were much the same season by season and were predicated by the needs of the senior game, which were stable for many years. As well as providing an adequate pool of referees to referee in Reserve football, the size of Class 2 was also influenced by these referees being appointed to handle the 16 ties in Round 2 in the Scottish Qualifying Cups (North and South).

The List's restructuring for season 1991-92 laid the foundations for the strategies which have developed since then.

At the outset, it was recognised that the List would be entering a period of transition and that existing principles regarding the compilation of the List would, by necessity, require to be reviewed so that a greater degree of flexibility could be introduced. The scrutiny of promotion candidates and applicants for the List was intensified. This applied also to referees in Classes 3A and 3B given the merging of these into the new Class 3 and the planned reduction in the numbers. The principle of accelerated promotion for referees who showed potential was also introduced. To assist in this aim, the time period between passing the Entrance Examination and sitting the Refresher Examination was reduced from two years to one year.

A rigorous approach was adopted at the Grading meeting when the 1991-92 List was compiled. It was a meeting of wholesale changes. Two Class 1 referees were reclassified to Class 4. Four Class 2 referees were promoted to Class 1, with one deleted, two reclassified to Class 3 and two reclassified to Class 4. 18 Class 3A referees were promoted to Class 2, with one deletion. 12 Class 3B referees were reclassified to Class 4. 16 applicants were admitted to the List, six of whom were to become Class 1 referees. The numbers at Class 2 were increased by six to 37 from the season before to allow a suitable pool of referees to operate as linesmen in SFL matches along with Class 1 referees. When the process was concluded, the numbers on the List from Class 1 to Class 3 had been reduced from 194 to 171. The number at Class 3 was 100, 30 less than the combined Class 3A and Class 3B total for season 1990-91.

At the following season's Grading meeting, the first notable case of accelerated promotion occurred. John Rowbotham was promoted to Class 2 after only one season at Class 3. He repeated the feat the season after when he was promoted to Class 1. He served 12 seasons at Class 1 and became a FIFA referee, more than justifying the committee's decisions.

Progress was made in introducing younger Class 1 referees. This also happened within the other categories. A focus was kept on reducing the numbers of officials included within Classes 1 to 3. This applied particularly to Class 3. The committee's efforts to reduce the numbers of the List are shown in the following table, covering seasons 1991-92 to 1997-98.

Table 6: Number of referees on the List of Referees 1991-92 to 1997-98

Season	Class 1	Class 2	Class 3	Total
1991-92	34	37	100	171
1992-93	36	36	95	167
1993-94	37	35	93	165
1994-95	39	30	88	157
1995-96	33	28	88	149
1996-97	34	27	83	144
1997-98	34	25	85	144

The List's restructuring for season 1998-99 saw the introduction of the Specialist Assistant Referee, which brought a new dimension to the continuing strategy in terms of identifying the appropriate number for the group and candidates. The general ethos of exercising a rigorous approach to the composition of the Class 1 group continued. The need for long term planning was now a fixed component of the overall approach which meant that the Referee Committee had to be aware of the likely progression of referees through the categories. Various elements of developments in the refereeing structures aided this – the formation of Development Plans, the assessment of referees, the use of Development Categories, the development of the Referee Analysis and the Referee Committee being in receipt of all Supervisors'/Observers' reports. After 1998-98, the strategy of reducing the numbers on the List loosened considerably as the need to service the game returned to be an important consideration.

Since 1991-92, the aim of introducing younger referees to Class 1 has been a constant theme of the strategy. This has been an undoubted success and proof of the benefits referees have received from the development programmes that the SFA introduced. The average age of the Class 1/Category 1 group was successfully reduced and maintained at a lower level, even allowing for the graded reduction in the retiral ages by three years from 2005-06. The following table covers the period 1992 to 2012, the year age limits where removed, and sets out the average per year, taken at 31st December.

Table 7: Average Age of Class 1/Category 1 referees 1991-2012

Year End	No.	Average Age	Year End	No.	Average Age
1991	34	41.26	2002	36	39.63
1992	35	41.25	2003	38	39.39
1993	38	40.76	2004	36	39.22
1994	39	40.10	2005	38	38.21
1995	33	40.54	2006	34	38.56
1996	33	40.48	2007	34	38.24
1997	32	40.05	2008	35	37.63
1998	32	39.68	2009	35	37.57
1999	34	40.26	2010	32	38.09
2000	36	38.94	2011	30	37.50
2001	36	39.94	2012	29	36.62

An abiding principle in the strategy is "don't let the team get too old". Exactly the same applies to football teams. If a team is allowed to grow old together, the harder it can be to effect change and, if it has been a successful team, to maintain the standards set in level of performance. Refereeing understood the ethos. Clubs did not fully appreciate it and, on the occasions when they say that decisions have gone against them, the youthfulness or perceived inexperience of the referee can often be the first thing to be referred to. It has been a recurring issue over the last 20 years or so at all levels of the game.

With age limits being removed in 2012, the Referee Committee, in compiling the List, cannot rely on referees retiring through age limits and spaces on the List being created naturally. Its focus is completely on the use of criteria such as competence and ability to pass the Fitness Test to determine which referees should be removed or promoted.

Grading Meeting

The Grading meeting was the forum through which the strategy was put into effect. Bearing in mind the principles it was working to, the task was not an easy one for the Executive Committee to apply itself to. The meeting to restructure the List for season 1991-92 accomplished the rigorous task it had been set. The List was changed dramatically.

The strategy of reducing the size of Class 3 continued and was an aim of the 1994 Grading meeting. At the conclusion of the meeting, the number had been reduced by five. To get to that stage, there was much debate and argument, especially as 14 referees were admitted to Class 3. New blood still had to be introduced to the List.

The rigorous approach to addressing the composition of the List was repeated across all the Classes. Debate and argument was constantly gone through to reach decisions. They were not easy meetings, particularly as the drive to reduce the numbers on the List continued. There was a perception that the Class 1 referees were still not receiving match appointments frequently enough and this fed into the thinking. The 1995 Grading meeting saw a reduction of five Class 1 referees and two Class 2 referees.

The 1997 Grading meeting was particularly difficult. There were no demotions or deletions at Class 1. Three Class 2 referees were promoted due to the natural creation of vacancies at Class 1 due to retirement and resignations. Tensions between George Cumming and the Executive Committee rose as he considered there was a slackening off in the required approach and that a reluctance to act was delaying decisions for a year. On the other hand, the committee considered that its task was not made easy by factors such as the assessment system, which did not lend itself to introducing differences between referees in the statistical tables.

The following year's Grading meeting saw another major restructuring of the List, with the selection of the new Class of Specialist Assistant Referee. There was also a further reduction in numbers. The combined total of Specialist Assistant Referee and Assistant Referee, 104, was six less than the previous combined total of Classes 2 and 3. Such an outcome rebounded very quickly as the impact of servicing the game hit home. The focus on the List was entirely on SPL and SFL first team football. The SFL soon experienced difficulties in appointing referees for its Youth Division competitions. In December, 16 new Class 1 assistant Referees were added to the List to help.

At the 2000 Grading meeting George Cumming presented recommendations for the Executive Committee's consideration to help guide its deliberations. The submission of recommendations has been repeated every year subsequently by the refereeing specialist. The Referee Committee has come to rely on these as the foundation of its discussions at the Grading meeting. A great deal of supporting information was always made available to the Executive Committee but in the years since 2000, the level of information increased considerably. With a constant flow of information issued to the Referee Committee specialists throughout a season and regular discussions, including the mid-season review, the committee comes to the meeting with a very full and rounded understanding of the circumstances with which it has to deal with. There is a maturity to its outlook. The task to be conducted at a Grading meeting is unchanging but the processes involved over the years have evolved to deal with the situations presented at the time. Different generations of former referees have borne the responsibility of compiling the List and they have done it very well, often in difficult circumstances. Arguments and debate take place at every Grading meeting. Deciding on a referee's future has never been easy and discussions of that nature have always been full and frank. It was once said by a member that, in all his years on the committee, he felt that a referee had not been missed, in terms of making it to Class 1. There is some truth in that.

Numbers on the List

Up to 1991-92, when Class 4 became part of the List, the List was always regarded as being Classes 1 to 3. The "true" List was that which served SFL football, then the SPL and SFL and what is now the SPFL. Focus was placed on those referees in these categories. Achieving a reduction in the numbers was the constant theme during the 1990's. This was achieved and maintained for some 20 years, although at some cost as the impact of servicing the game regularly provoked issues to be dealt with, resulting in the additions of referees on to the List. As Class 4 changed into Class 2 and evolved into Categories 4A and 4B before transforming into the present Categories of 3 Development and 4, the overall numbers on the List naturally grew. The numbers at each of these categories does not have any real impact on the "true" List as the needs to service the game require to be met. Healthy numbers at Category 3

Development indicate the availability of likely future Class 3 officials.

The following table shows the List numbers from 1998 to 2020:

Table 8: Number of referees on the List of Referees 1998-99 to 2019-20

Season	Cat 1-3	Overall	Season	Cat 1-3	Overall
1998-00	147	187	2009-10	125	242
1999-01	145	188	2010-11	142	236
2000-01	150	187	2011-12	148	257
2001-02	143	185	2012-13	166	236
2002-03	147	197	2013-14	173	267
2003-04	148	199	2014-15	158	257
2004-05	149	200	2015-16	160	255
2005-06	149	243	2016-17	166	267
2006-07	145	230	2017-18	178	272
2007-08	143	230	2018-19	178	282
2008-09	147	225	2019-20	182	271

The increase in the number of referees in Categories 1-3 since 2012 is a result of the need to service the game combined with the influence of the removal of age limits.

Letter of Appointment/Notice of Classification
For season 2000-01, the Referee Committee introduced a Letter of Appointment which set out various relevant conditions which each referee on the List required to agree to when accepting their classification. The terms evolved over the years, to capture various changes within the game and refereeing.
In 2014, the letter was changed to a Notice of Classification which is no longer signed and returned to the SFA by each referee. After initially being issued to each category by email, the Notice is now made available through the SFA's Referee Extranet.

Conflict of Interest
The issue of referees having a potential conflict of interest with a club has been a constant theme down the years, usually in the minds of football supporters and, in some instances, clubs. Referees supporting a particular team, or coming from the same town or city as a team he is refereeing and being influenced by

that in his officiating, is something regularly raised by the ill-informed. Referees do support teams. A love of football is what gets them into refereeing and that generally comes through supporting a club. The question of bias in performance does not exist and, if it did, it would be quickly rooted out in the early stages of a referee's career, well before reaching the List. The potential for a conflict of interest operates at a much higher level than supporting a club. The Referee Committee addressed the issue in 2000 to ensure that a system was put in place for the List to deal appropriately with any such conflicts and to avoid any major issues emerging and causing difficulties. Referees have to declare when they perceive that they may have a conflict of interest, or potential conflict of interest, with a club. It was recognised at the outset that it is virtually impossible to properly define what constitutes a conflict or a potential conflict. These have included a business relationship through employment and a family relationship such as a brother playing for a club. The onus rests entirely with a referee to make a declaration to the SFA. Working on the basis that it is better to be safe than sorry, referees have acted extremely responsibly in regard to this requirement. Taking any such conflicts into account has become another strand in the drafting of referee appointments.

"Employment" Issues
In the modern age, the influence of the law has pervaded many areas of football, where previously there had been little or no activity. Football's business had very much been self-regulatory but that approach has had to adjust to take account of outside legal influences. Refereeing has not been immune to such developments.
In 2012 a Class 1 referee who had resigned from the List took the SFA to an Employment Tribunal on the causes of his resignation. He was not supported by the SSFRA in his action. The SFA vigorously defended its position but the Tribunal found in favour of referees being categorised as "Workers" (but not "Employees") which made them eligible for Workers' Rights. The SFA lost an appeal against that decision and a settlement was reached with the former referee.

Another Employment Tribunal case emerged in 2014, brought by another former Class 1 referee on the basis of "unfair dismissal" and "age discrimination". The case was abandoned by the former referee during the course of the Tribunal's proceedings.

The outcome of the original case had potential ramifications across the range of the SFA's operations which led to an impact assessment review being conducted. Over the years, the SFA had provided a number of benefits to referees (the provision of kit being a prime example) and choosing to remove them to demonstrate that referees were not workers was not an option to follow. It would not be a positive step for either the referees or the SFA.

For the Referee Committee, it means that it has to approach its decision making in a fair, consistent and robust manner at all times, particularly in respect of the Grading meeting. The system of referees' assessment was brought into focus by the second case and the SFA made adjustments in this regard.

A continual watching brief requires to be maintained by the SFA on such matters, given that the other British Associations have been faced with similar issues and the occurrence of comparable cases in other industries within the UK.

Assessment

The assessment of referees is the most important aspect of referee development, with significant attention given to it over the last 35 years. A major change to the ethos of assessment has occurred. Rather than listing right and wrong decisions, a previous common feature of reports, there was a move towards evaluating a referee's performance and giving advice for future performances. Assessment reports became more supportive of referees and had to offer constructive appraisal. The level of support now given to referees never existed to the same extent previously.

Refereeing has to operate with a sound assessment system, as it forms the foundation for very important decision making on referees' careers. Moreover, a sound system offers the basis of a stout defence against criticism of referees.

The media often liked to refer to Supervisors as the "spy in the stand", suggesting they were there to be critical of a referee, particularly when the perception amongst clubs and supporters was that a referee had had a "bad" game. This was anything but the case and on a number of occasions the Assessment Guidelines were issued to clubs to let them see what was involved in assessment.

Assessment System
Since the assessment system was revamped by George Cumming for season 1990-91, there have been eight versions used by the SFA. It has been a continual quest to find the optimum method, for the benefit of the referees and the Supervisors/Observers. The aim of identifying good referees has always been an inherent part of assessment and, to achieve this, the system has to function in the desired way.

It took a little coaxing of the Supervisors by Cumming to get to the stage of changing the system. Their traditional conservatism and reluctance to change had to be surmounted.

The new system introduced a mark for "Degree of Difficulty" for a match, to be combined with the actual assessment, but this caused some issues in the first season of operation. An imbalance in marking, depending on the degree of difficulty, was apparent. Carrying out assessments in "Easy" or Very Easy" matches caused concern.

Two important factors of assessment emerged during this period. Firstly, the contents of a report had to bear relation to the mark, and secondly, the report was intended to be of greater importance than the mark. Referees were, however, too interested in the mark rather than the report.

The assessment system was kept under constant review and changes to bring about improvements were introduced for season 1994-95. Five assessment categories were introduced – Very Good, Good, Moderate, Poor and Unsatisfactory, each with its own descriptive comment as a guide and operating on a scale of marks up to 80-90 for Very Good. The scale of marks for Degree of Difficulty was adjusted to Easy (1-2),

Straightforward (3-4), Fairly Difficult (5-6) Difficult (7-8) and Very Difficult (9-10).

The amendments proved to be beneficial, offering greater flexibility to Supervisors, with the changes to the Degree of Difficulty also helping. The first hint of the use of a "benchmark" emerged when assessment of SFL Reserve matches was discussed. It was decided that in matches categorised as "Easy" or "Straightforward" a referee should be able to receive a maximum mark of 79 (in the Good band of 65-79) and that he should be marked downwards from that mark to take account of matters affecting his performance.

Further adjustments to the system were made for season 1997-98. The banding marks were altered and the mark for Degree of Difficulty was dropped. It was now to be indicated by just selecting one of the five categories: Easy, Straightforward, Fairly Difficult, Difficult, Very Difficult. The new system settled down well but the quest for improvement continued, with revisions to the Guidelines being carried out for seasons 2001-02 and 2002-03.

The assessment system for assistant referees was also given appropriate focus. Guidelines for assessing assistant referees were developed and have been refined over time.

Modifications to the system were again made for season 2003-04. The term "major incident" was introduced and its categorisation was something that Supervisors had to do on the basis of their experience and knowledge of the game. To guide them, a "major incident" was defined as being factually clear cut and not involve an element of opinion.

When the new system was reviewed after its first season, the more experienced referees were considered to have received better marks than younger referees. A benchmark for assessment had now been introduced and this caused some issues, with variances in its use being evident despite reports from different Supervisors having essentially the same content.

Further change to the assessment system happened for season 2010-11 when the UEFA assessment model was adopted. Referees and assistant referees now received assessment marks between 5 and 10 to the nearest tenth. The concept of "one clear important mistake" was introduced into the marking system and brought with it a significant change to the assessment of referees in matches which were televised.

Over the next decade, a variety of amendments have been made on a regular basis as a means of continually refining the method of assessment. Often, the referees and the SSFRA have been involved in the process of review.

The "clear important mistake" issue was much debated for a few years. A referee could have had an excellent performance in a match but the occurrence of such a mistake would result in a mark of 7.9 regardless (7.9 being immediately below the Good – 8 grading). Once television evidence came into use, the top referees were regularly exposed to the dangers of receiving a mark of 7.9 as it became easier to prove that "one clear important mistake". By 2016, it was agreed than an alternative mark should be given – the mark the referee would have received but for the one "clear important mistake".

The changes in recent years have been made to the widening of the evaluation scales, to make it easier for the Referee Committee to better interpret the Referee Analysis. A lack of variance in assessments had given rise to referees having similar sets of marks, despite differing performance levels. The motive for the change was to better reward good performances.

Consistency of Assessment

Any system of assessment works only as well as the people who are making the assessments. Achieving consistency in marking is the "holy grail" of referee assessment and much work has been carried out since the 1990's to reach this goal. Adherence to the Assessment Guidelines and their correct use is crucial to successful assessing.

After the initial change to the assessment system, George Cumming quickly got the Supervisors on his side as they accepted that there were benefits to be gained by discussing supervisory methods and assessments. Seminars on assessment were introduced and became a regular and standing feature in each season. They have particular importance when changes are made to the assessment method and when reviewing its operation. Joint meetings with the Class 1 referees are also an important element of reviewing the assessment system. The first such joint meeting was held at the start of season 1998-99.

As an exercise to develop consistency in reporting, all the Supervisors carried out an assessment of the referee in the Scottish Cup Finals of 1991 and 1995. Attendances at matches came to be commonplace as Seminars were constructed around them to enable group assessment and discussion afterwards.

The Seminars have proved a very useful forum by which assessment can be discussed and reviewed. They helped shape the evolution of the system, as matters such as consistency of marking, the relevance of comments made in reports, the need to be concise and direction given and agreed on future application of the Guidelines, have been addressed.

Issuing of Reports

If George Cumming made headway in changing the assessment system and gained the Supervisors' support in discussing assessment on a regular basis, he had more difficulty in persuading them that all reports should be issued to referees. This was straightforwardly rejected in 1989. Due to their being too closely tied to the then reporting style, the Supervisors felt that it would be appropriate to only issue the report section "Any other Comments or Advice to Assist performance" which would enable the referee to know his mark. It took a year for them to be persuaded, although there was still some resistance expressed.

Within two years, the issuing of all reports had proved successful, with the Supervisors now in agreement with this happening. There were, however, diverging views as to whether marks should be issued to referees, given the focus the referees gave to them rather than the contents of the report. "Open" reporting won the day. The view that the committee's credibility would be diminished if marks were withheld prevailed. The arguments about issuing marks have surfaced periodically. In 1997, the issue even had to be put to a vote by the Supervisors – there was a small majority in favour of marks continuing to be issued. There have been brief periods when marks were not issued to newly promoted Class 1 referees in the first half of a season, the purpose of which was to allow them the maximum opportunity to benefit from the coaching advice contained in the reports and to reduce the perceived pressure to be successful quickly at their new category.

Up to season 2002-03, reports were posted by the SFA to the Supervisor of the referee. In turn, the Supervisor would pass the report on to the referee. That all changed for 2003-04 due to the advent of email. Reports were now issued to the referee and his Supervisor simultaneously, which was a huge step forward. This new arrangement brought with it other benefits. The report form was now "space limited" in its various sections – Supervisors had to become more concise in their reporting.

In 2014-15, the SFA's Referee Extranet superseded the use of email for the submission and issuing of Observers' reports. Once approved by the Referee Operations Department, reports are made available to the referee and his Manager.

Post-Match Contact

To a current referee, post-match contact with an Observer is taken as granted as an integral part of being assessed but, as with some other refereeing topics, it took some time from the idea first being floated to it becoming standard practice.

The move to have such contact emerged from a Class 1 referees' meeting in 1996. Indications were given that they would welcome the chance of occasionally being able to discuss a match performance with the Supervisor – but not immediately after the match. An informal arrangement of this nature had operated for a while and the Supervisors were happy to agree.

The methodology used then will appear very cumbersome to the modern referee – the referee was to ask his own Supervisor to contact the match Supervisor and request the chance to speak with him. The timing of the conversation was to be flexible and not be dependent upon the referee receiving the Supervisor's report.

The referee was to be the trigger for any contact. The match Supervisor had no role to play in that respect. At the end of season 1996-97, George Cumming encouraged the use of post-match contact given the value it held but the general consensus among the Supervisors was that it was not desirable. Dangers were perceived by them if there was to be such contact.

However, Supervisors were given the facility of making contact with the referee's Supervisor the day after the match to request the opportunity to speak directly with the referee. Such a move cut through the old fashioned way of a Supervisor seeking the written comments via the SFA from a referee on a match incident before submitting his report.

The next stage of evolution was reached in August 1999. Cumming successfully proposed the holding of an experiment through to the end of the year - Supervisors were given the option of speaking personally with the referee at the ground after a match, or telephoning them at some point in the days following, thus cutting out the need for the Supervisor to contact the referee's own Supervisor. Cumming, with good reason, wanted post-match contact to be automatic. It had been successfully introduced into the Referee Development Scheme and the Minor Grade Advisory Panel and, indeed, was happening throughout Europe. The mark to be given was not, under any circumstances, to be discussed during any post-match contact nor was the contact to be used as a means of negotiating an assessment mark.

By October, any fears held by the Supervisors had been dispelled. The experiment had proven to be of positive benefit to referees and the Supervisors. Post-match contact was adopted as normal practice. Some doubts persisted though. A variety of views were held by Supervisors on the worth of the contact, particularly in conducting it with experienced referees. In some cases, it was found difficult to find matters of real worth to discuss with referees. Issues had also been raised by referees regarding variances between points discussed during the contact and reports received by referees. Some firming up of the contact arrangements took place as a consequence. It was held that there should only be very few occasions when contact should be made in person directly after a match and that contact, in the main, should be made by telephone the day after the game and no later than two days after it. Importantly, the report was to be written before contact was made and was not to be altered as a result of the contact.

The system developed. From 2004, it became mandatory for the Supervisor to have to visit the referee in his dressing room after a match for a brief chat and make arrangements to have the telephone conversation. Gradually, much of the mystique surrounding the reporting system was taken away. The "them" and "us" scenario between Supervisors/Observers and referees was dismantled. Post-match contact provides the chance for an Observer to give advice to a referee which might not necessarily require to be contained in the assessment report. It has added to the Observer's role in trying to encourage and build confidence into referees.

Use of TV Evidence in Assessment

The use of TV evidence in assessment has mirrored in many ways its use in players' disciplinary cases. Its use was resisted for a long time but eventually the defences were reduced to the point where the sense of using it could no longer be ignored. Now, it is a fully accepted part of assessment.

Referees played a part in its introduction as the SSFRA suggested in 2006 that the use of television evidence should be considered. The nub of the matter was in the open right from the start of the debate on its use – that television evidence can work both ways – for and against a referee. The "against" factor was and is a crucial part: television highlights errors not identified by the Observer.

A pilot scheme was started in season 2006-07. Observers had the opportunity to make use of television footage as best evidence to review major incidents that had occurred in a game and had to state within their reports that reference had been made to television evidence.

It did not take long for the real issues to emerge. Refereeing errors were being picked up from the watching of matches on television but these were not always reflected in the Observer's report on the match. At the same time, it was accepted that Observers were not always in the best position to judge certain incidents. The arguments for the use of best evidence prevailed. The pilot scheme was deemed a success and a permanent system was introduced for season 2007-08 with the Assessment Guidelines being suitably amended.

Footage from accredited broadcasters covering the top league was the foundation of television evidence's use and over time the arguments for considering footage from other sources such as clubs built up and grew stronger. For a period, it was determined that such footage could be used for coaching purposes and not affect an assessment. However, it was difficult to ignore the compelling argument for using best evidence where available. Provided that the footage is clear and of a suitable quality, any available footage may now be utilised to review major decisions for all levels of football where observers are appointed.

Supervisors'/Observers' Appointments
Transparency was introduced into the weekly issuing of Supervisors' appointments from season 2002-03. A composite set was sent to them, to make them aware of all the appointments. That was soon extended to include the referees and the clubs. Full openness was achieved. Email facilitated that development and the Referee Extranet has taken the process further as appointments of match officials and Observers are now published through that platform.

Supervisors'/Observers' Coverage
The increase in the number of Supervisors in 1989 led to a natural rise in the number of assessments. The target of covering every SFL match was never actually achieved as the demands of assessing referees in lower categories was ever present. Information still had to be obtained on these referees for the purposes of the Grading meeting.

The volume of supervision steadily increased during the 1990's and reached a seasonal coverage of 1000 matches by 1995. Approximately 1200 matches per season came to be covered over the next decade and more, sustained by a supportive budget.

An equable balance of coverage of referees was always aimed for across Categories 1 and 2 and the coverage of referees in Categories 3 and 3 Development became an integral part of the system once the Development Plan was introduced.

The creation of the SPL required all its matches to be attended by a Supervisor and this skewed the number of assessments received by those referees officiating in the League. Their assessments increased considerably compared to their colleagues and for a short period there was a relaxation in the approach taken with not every match being covered. Blanket coverage of the SPL resumed on the SFA becoming a member of the UEFA Referee Convention, as that required all matches in a country's top league to be attended by an Observer.

In recent years, budgetary considerations have had an influence in the overall operation of the assessment system, with a more selective and targeted approach being taken to achieve the required outcome – to provide the Referee Committee with appropriate data to inform its deliberations on the List.

Supervisors'/Observers' Nominations

The culmination of the assessment system each season is the submission of the Supervisors'/Observers' Nominations for the Grading meeting. These provide the basis for the business to be conducted. The processes involved have been developed and refined over the last 30 years.

The first significant change was in 1994 when the Referee Analysis was no longer issued to the Supervisors at the end of the season prior to the submission of their nominations. It had become too easy for Supervisors to nominate referees at the bottom of the Analysis to be reclassified or "discussed". From this point on, nominations were to be based entirely on referees whom Supervisors had assessed during the season and derived from making genuine appraisals of referees' performances. This did create a little difficulty in some respects for some Supervisors. How could a Supervisor consider making a recommendation on a referee if he had been seen only once or twice? A little fat was trimmed out of the system as a consequence.

In 1996, Nomination Guidelines were produced, with all the various decisions taken in this connection over the years being consolidated into a document. The document is updated regularly to reflect changes.

One such change was the creation of the role of Association Manager. A Manager submits his nominations based on the Development Plan he is working to for his association.

Referee Analysis

George Cumming made good headway in making improvements to the assessment performance tables, which came to be known as the Referee Analysis. The historical format of combining Supervisors' marks with SFL Club marks was addressed. The SFL was persuaded to dispense with club marks and, as a result of this major change for season 1990-91, the performance tables were now based solely on Supervisors' marks. SFL clubs submitted a general grading on referees' performances: good, moderate, poor.

The nature of the data presented in the performance tables contributed to the changes made to the system of assessment at that point. Many referees, particularly Class 2, were grouped together on similar marks, which meant that it was hard to gain appropriate knowledge on how referees were performing.

Information on referees' ages and the number of assessments each had was introduced into the performance tables, to provide more appropriate information for the benefit of the Supervisors.

Over the years, the layout of the Analysis was continually developed to reflect changes in approach and to ensure that as much information is made available to the Referee Committee. Information on age was dropped once the retiral age was removed in 2012.

The advent of Specialist Assistant Referees in 1998-99 led to their assessment marks being included in the Analysis throughout a season. Prior to then, information on assistants' performances were only included at the end of each season. The introduction of Assistant Referee Observers has improved the level of information made available to the Referee Committee and has been beneficial.

Consideration of the Analysis is effectively the main business item at each Referee Committee. It forms the basis for in-depth discussion on the overall performances of referees, and informs decisions on which referees should be introduced to a higher level, or taken out from a higher level, and on assessment coverage of referees. It has also played a crucial part in the continual review of the assessment system. The Analysis is an invaluable tool for the Referee Committee. Its development over the last 30 years has kept pace with the progress in refereeing over that time.

Appeals-Review of Assessment

Developing a new Appeal Process

After a period of relative calm in the preceding seasons, there was an upsurge of appeals in 1989-90. 14 were dealt with. When the new assessment system was introduced for season 1990-91, there was hope that appeals would reduce, particularly as the Supervisors accepted a proposal from George Cumming that all reports should be monitored by the SFA before being issued.

It also became possible for a Supervisor to refer a report back to the SFA for further scrutiny before issuing it to his referee.

Five appeals were submitted during the season. Whilst the Executive Committee was reluctant to dispense with an appeal process, it held that the new reporting system needed time to settle down and that, as it did so, there was a likelihood that appeals would decrease. An adjustment to the basis of appealing was made - an appeal was only possible if it was considered that the assessment mark should be within a higher "banding". The degree of difficulty contained in the assessment was not open to alteration.

During the following season, the position of the Supervisors changed when they agreed that appeals should be abolished, with a caveat that, in highly exceptional circumstances, a request for a report to be reviewed could be made and that such a review would be conducted by the Chairman, Vice-Chairman and George Cumming.

The change proved successful. There was only a trickle of requests to have reports reviewed over the next few seasons, with the majority being unsuccessful.

Reviews of Assessments

Changes to the assessment system were always sensitive to variances in reports as Supervisors/Observers became accustomed to them. An upsurge in requests to review reports (all of which had been unsuccessful) resulted in the Referee Committee giving attention to the issue in 2006. This resulted in the RA Managers having to raise any potential review with their committee liaison member to assess the validity of any review before submission to the SFA. This was founded on the belief that that the assessment system had to be based on trusting the Observer's opinions and that aligning the assessment mark with the report's content was an important requirement. Moreover, the committee was mindful of the Referee Development Department's reviewing reports before issue.

Over the next three seasons, seven review requests were received. All were successful.

A further review and refinement of the process took place during season 2009-10. Reviews could only be considered for marks less than 8.0 and were to be dealt with by two members of the Referee Committee. Television footage relating to the review could be used if available. Little in the way of traffic was generated.

The Impact of Match Footage

In 2015, a system was put in place to cover the situation when footage from an approved broadcaster, depicting an important match incident that may lead to a mark of 7.9, or less, resulted in a difference of opinion between the Observer and the Referee Operations Department. When the opinions on the incident were sufficiently divergent, the clip of the incident was circulated to the specialist members of the Referee Committee for consideration.

The Current Style

Refereeing continually evolves in relation to new sets of circumstances. The use of television footage in assessment has created nuance.

Should the Referee Operations Department consider the mark (and alternative mark where applicable) submitted by an Observer to be clearly inappropriate, the Observer is informed of that opinion and asked to re-consider the proposed mark(s). If the Observer declines to do so, the Department has the discretion to refer the matter to a panel comprising three randomly chosen members of the Referee Committee. These members consider the matter without reference to each other. The Observer's mark will only be altered if all three agree on a change.

Examinations

Laying the Foundations
George Cumming quickly got to work on the referee training classes. A publicity campaign was undertaken to attract recruits prior to the start of the autumn diet of classes in season 1988-89. Various teaching aids were produced for the use of the training instructors.

A discussion on the December 1990 results heralded a change of outlook as to how the Entrance Examination was viewed. Rather than turn away those who failed the examination and lose them from the refereeing movement, Cumming's view was that the aim of the Entrance Examination should be to provide evidence that candidates had a basic knowledge of the Laws of the Game and that new referees could thereafter develop their knowledge and understanding of refereeing with practical experience. A paper prepared by him was used for the examinations in April 1990. There was a big reduction in the number of failures.

New papers for the Entrance and Refresher Examinations were prepared for the December 1991 diet. By this stage, a bank of questions had been prepared for the compiling of new papers as and when required.

Two major changes were introduced during season 1991-92. Firstly, as associations were given the option of holding shorter training classes, it was no longer the case that examinations had to be held in the first two weeks of April and December. Secondly, an association's own Supervisor could now be the invigilator at an examination, rather than an external Supervisor.

In a simple move to enable the SFA to gain a better understanding of those becoming referees and to coincide with the launch of the Registration Scheme that year, the ages of candidates sitting the examinations were obtained from 1992.

During 1992-93, a standard syllabus was prepared for the Entrance Examination Course.

The limit on the number of attempts a candidate could make to pass either Entrance or Refresher Examinations was removed in 1995.

Resources

The production of resources to be used in the training classes ran parallel with the progress in the revamping of the examination structure. A Laws of the Game Education Pack was produced during 1992 for use in the training classes. It was also used in schools and colleges.

Very innovatively, George Cumming managed to get Channel 4 to broadcast the video included in the Pack as a short series over six weeks. With FIFA's support, the Pack was made available on the international market. There was an excellent response to it.

A Referee Development Programme prepared by Cumming on behalf of FIFA became the new training class Pack from season 1999-00.

Training the Instructors

Standardising the instruction provided at the training classes was given attention. A Referee Coaching and Instructors' Course was held in 1992 to deal with basic instruction for Entrance Examination candidates. 40 attended, with all associations represented.

A Referee Instructors' Award was held in 1994, with 21 candidates gaining the award. In addition to acting as instructors at the training classes, the award qualified them to provide tuition on the Laws of the Game at SVQ courses and at the SFA's A and B Licence Coaching Courses.

With a roster of instructors now in place, re-certification courses were started to update them on new teaching methods and on changes to the Laws of the Game. New instructors needed to be trained too. Once the ball started rolling, momentum had to be maintained.

The Examinations are re-named

At the start of season 1999-00, the examination courses were re-named. The Entrance and Refresher Courses became the Introductory and Advanced Courses respectively.

There were to be two formats of the Introductory Courses to replace the standard 12 week course – an evening course over eight sessions and short courses over four Sundays. At the evening course, the aims were to cover the Laws of the Game, Refereeing Structure, Refereeing Techniques and Administration. The Short Course was to run for 20 hours in total and had three to four instructors to share the workload. Lanarkshire RA's success in holding some Short Courses had informed the basis for providing them on a wider scale.

The Supervisors were encouraged to influence their associations on the scheduling of the courses and to consider moving away from the traditional autumn and spring system. By offering greater flexibility in the holding of courses, the hope was that more people would be attracted to attend.

Examination Results

Despite the improved level of publicity given to the training classes during the 1990's, the number of attendees did not increase substantially from the years previously. There was an upsurge between 1993 and 1995 but the figures tailed off during the rest of the decade, as can be seen in the following table:

217

Table 9: Entrance and Refresher Examination Results 1988-89 to 2000-01

Season	Entrance	Passes	Refresher	Passes
1988-89	253	184	40	34
1989-90	262	195	40	24
1990-91	281	249	51	45
1991-92	227	207	89	80
1992-93	256	249	51	45
1993-94	295	262	52	45
1994-95	278	243	42	40
1995-96	251	237	54	54
1996-97	276	255	34	31
1997-98	207	183	49	49
1998-99	207	198	58	57
1999-00	225	198	41	7
2000-01	120	102	23	20
Average	241	212	49	44

As the results for season 2000-01 caused concern, a review of the examination system was undertaken.

A New Examination Structure
Donald McVicar formed a small group of Supervisors to assist him in the review. Glasgow RA acted as a pilot scheme for the new system during season 2001-02 prior to its adoption.
The new Introductory Examination comprised three Parts –
- Part 1 - the written examination
- Part 2 - an oral examination to determine the candidate's understanding of the Laws and their technical aspects
- Part 3 - a practical element whereby each candidate was required to referee two matches within a three month period and be monitored on each occasion by a senior member of his association, with the emphasis being on providing assistance to the new referee on the practicalities of refereeing and match-day situations.

After being raised periodically over the years but never progressed, an oral examination had finally come into operation. An induction course for the new system was attended by approximately 60 coaches and instructors. The Scottish Youth FA gave assistance in appointing the new referees in its football for the practical element of the examination.

A new style was introduced for the examination, with much less writing required. A candidate failing the written paper was not permitted to sit the oral examination.

A new examination paper for the Advanced Course came into use in 2003. The Course was now to be taken by referees in the season prior to progression to refereeing in Junior football, to ensure that they would have sufficient and up to date knowledge of the Laws at an important stage in their careers.

The new structure gave rise to the associations experiencing problems in arranging the coverage of referees' matches to enable completion of Part 3. These issues were included in a review of the new structure which was initiated in autumn 2004. The course content, delivery and the effectiveness of the current procedures and practices were also reviewed. A consultation exercise with the associations and Instructors was undertaken.

Four new examination papers and maintaining the requirement for a candidate to be assessed in two matches resulted from the review.

Achieving the coverage in two matches continued to be problematic for the associations with an amendment being made in 2007. The two match requirement was reduced to one, which became mandatory. It was still recommended that candidates complete two matches, if possible. To compensate for the reduction from two matches to one, it also became mandatory for prospective referees to attend a practical session on the essential aspects and requirements of refereeing.

Difficulties however continued to be experienced in arranging coverage of the new referees. Glasgow RA, for example, experienced a large intake of 68 candidates during season 2010-11. Co-ordinating the required match assessments proved problematic. Ensuring compliance with the one match requirement often took a bit of time to achieve and delayed the proper commencement of refereeing for a new candidate. In some associations, there was a lack of suitable games to use.

The Introductory Examination took on a new form altogether during season 2014-15 when it was trialled as an "on-line" examination before replacing the written examination paper.

Parts 1 and 2 of the Examination were merged into a web system that generated random questions from a bank of questions, with the final mark and feedback on incorrect answers being given immediately upon completion of the examination. As part of the change, the report writing element of the old examination became an assignment conducted during the Introductory Course, in order for specific feedback to be given to candidates and to better serve a purpose.

To reflect the growth in Scotland of the Futsal version of indoor football, a Futsal Conversion Course for all attendees is offered at the end of the Introductory Course.

An Online Introductory Course

A long held ambition to offer an online Introductory Course was realised in 2022 after a great deal of development work. Anyone who previously had been restricted in attending an Introductory Course through reasons of location or work can now undertake the Course, thus expanding the potential of attracting new recruits into refereeing.

In the development work, concerns were held regarding the loss of face to face contact between an Instructor and candidates. To surmount this issue, such sessions have been built in to the format of the course by the use of platforms such as Zoom. Modern technology has certainly brought its benefits and has totally transformed the landscape for conducting the Introductory Course. The modern course and examination would be unrecognisable to someone who became a referee 30 or 40 years ago.

Meetings of Referees

Organising meetings of referees was one of George Cumming's many initial aims when he commenced his job. The Supervisors supported the idea, although they recognised that too many meetings could put too many time demands on referees. Such a view point has always had some legitimacy and has been a constant consideration down the years.

One of the first meetings was one held jointly with the Class 1 referees and club representatives in August 1988, at which the SFA's Field Discipline Campaign was the main subject addressed.

October 1990 saw the first of what became a longstanding feature of the SFA's referee programme – Class 1 and Class 2 referees undertaking the Fitness Test in the morning before meeting in the afternoon. To signify the SFA's traditional support of referees, Jim Farry addressed the meeting. There was a discussion on the interpretation of serious foul play, following the issue of a recent mandatory instruction by FIFA. This simple occurrence - a discussion on a refereeing issue - was a major breakthrough in many ways. It would not have been possible previously. The Referees' Conference was the only avenue, on an annual basis, to raise such topics with referees in a group environment. The benefits to be gained from a discussion were much superior to reading about it in a circular. Being a Class 1 referee until taking up his appointment as Referee Training Officer provided George Cumming with instant credibility to be able to talk to the Class 1 group in a way that was not possible for the older group of Supervisors.

In 1993, the Supervisors gave backing to Cumming to hold Class 1 meetings on a regular basis throughout each season. The motivation for having these meetings existed in the desire to improve refereeing but was given particular impetus by FIFA starting to focus on improving refereeing standards. FIFA's drive to professionalise refereeing had arrived at a perfect time.

The series of Class 1 meetings during season 1994-95 set the template for the future. Other groups came to be involved in the meetings. Some referees in the Referee Development Scheme were invited to one in 1997, to give them a taste of what could lie ahead of them if they progressed in their careers. Joint meetings with Supervisors were also introduced. A pre-season Class 1 meeting was regularly followed by a joint meeting with club managers and coaches to address issues for the new season and other areas of mutual interest.

The meetings also gave a voice to the Class 1 referees. In February 2000, strong concern was expressed at the perceived lack of protection and support given to them by the Disciplinary

Committee in regard to the outcomes of recent cases. Jim Oliver, the then Chairman of the Referee Committee, was in attendance and reported these concerns to the committee. This ended in the two committees "falling out" for a period when the minutes of meetings went before the SFA Council. Also raised at that Class 1 meeting were concerns which the referees had conveyed to the SPL over the negative and critical publicity concerning referees which had occurred during the season. Such concerns did not subside as the years passed.

For a short period from 2004 to 2007, a mid-season Category 1 meeting was held in a hotel from a Saturday night to late on a Sunday afternoon, a format which worked extremely well and was a precursor to the introduction of the first Winter Training Camp in 2008.

Meetings extended to other categories of referees. Specialist Assistants and Category 3 officials met jointly in October after undertaking their fitness test as a consequence of the development of the fitness testing schedule during the 1990's.

By the mid-2000's, the meeting programme had been developed for all categories and was further extended following the introduction of the Development Categories in 2012. A Calendar of Events was introduced to set out the full programme for each season. Regular joint meetings of Category 1 referees and Specialist Assistant Referees are held, given the importance of teamwork and their operating together in the SPL and SPFL Premiership. Meetings of the FIFA Listed officials are held each season. Focus is given to meetings for female referees.

The programme of meetings for all the various categories each season is extremely extensive and is further confirmation of the huge progress made by the SFA in developing refereeing.

Fitness Test and Training

If one subject exemplifies the change in refereeing over the last 30 years or so, it is that of the fitness levels of referees. These have been dramatically transformed. Any follower of football over the age of 50 will recall how referees looked in the 1970's and 1980's – all generally in their 40's, reflecting the look and style of the time, in various shapes and sizes and usually moving about the pitch in a relaxed and unhurried manner. In the modern era, referees have become athletes. They have had to keep up with developments in football. The change happened gradually as the careers of the older generations of referees came to a close and as a younger breed of referees replaced them. As a consequence of referees starting at a younger age and coming through to the List quicker due to the strategies implemented over the years, the expected look of a modern referee is now almost taken for granted. The mindset of referees towards fitness has changed entirely. Whilst there was once a reluctant and relaxed approach towards training and fitness, nowadays it is an absolute pre-requisite for referees to take it seriously if they wish to make the most out of their careers.

The Fitness Test

How did this change come about? Quite simply, it stemmed from the desire of George Cumming to effect change. Having been a football player, he was well used to training regimes and appreciated that fitness provided the foundation for good performance. He brought this into refereeing.

He had firstly to win an argument with the Supervisors during 1988-89 that the new Fitness Test introduced by FIFA to replace the Cooper Test should be adopted for use domestically, with certain amendments. The natural conservatism of the Supervisors had once again to be overcome.

The new test came into operation for season 1989-90. The first real indication in a change of approach was the introduction of a Fitness Test to be conducted in October for the List, the purpose of which was to monitor fitness during the season to ensure that there was no slackening off in approach by referees. Referees had to focus on achieving and maintaining fitness, not just to be able to get through the Fitness Test held each spring for the annual application process for the List. Emphasis to this was given by the creation of conditions to the October test. The SFL was advised of any referee failing the Test and his name was excluded from the next set of appointments. In a further ramping up of approach, the Class 1 referees were to take the Test under Cumming on a national basis. All other Classes were to do the test at their own associations. As a consequence of the standard conditions for not having completed the Fitness Test by 31st December, four referees had their names removed from the List that season. The consequences of failing the Test were made known.

The expected response was forthcoming. Over the next few years, the standards of results in the Fitness test started to improve as higher levels of fitness were being reached. In 1993, the football broadcaster Chick Young took part in a Fitness test which gave television viewers the chance to see the demands which were being placed on referees.

The Fitness Test was revised by FIFA in 1994 and comprised two 50 metre sprints, two 200 metre runs and a 12 minute run which required a minimum of 2700 metres to be achieved. This was superseded by a new test in 2006, resulting from FIFA's continuous search to find a test related to the needs of refereeing. The test was a combination of short sprints and 150 metre sprints in an interval style for a defined number of laps. Specific times and number of laps were set for designated categories of officials.

Another new FIFA test was introduced in 2017. One aspect of the new test was brought in specifically for Specialist Assistant Referees – they need to complete a sprint test for Change of Direction of Ability (CODA) within a defined time limit.

The Development of a Fitness Test Schedule
The Fitness Test Schedule was expanded during season 1994-95, following a FIFA decision that international referees should do the Test four times per season. In addition to the spring and October tests, a pre-season test and one held between December and February were introduced. The latter test became optional within a year or so, largely due to the difficulties in arranging and holding tests in bad weather during the winter period.

A further change to the Test Schedule happened in 2004. The pre-season and October Tests were replaced by a Test in August. Tests on consecutive Sundays in August were held for the various classifications of referees as, by this time, the referees in Categories 1 to 3 were taking the test on a national basis.

In season 2009-10, a Test was held in November following UEFA confirming that, under the terms of its Referee Convention, the fitness test should be taken at least three times per year. A further change to the Test Schedule took place in 2010. The August test was moved to June in order to facilitate an earlier start of the football season and was held at the Summer Training Camp. The schedule was now spring, summer and autumn. The Category 4 referees undertake the Test at their own associations.

In a further streamlining of the schedule, the spring test was dropped from 2017 as its purpose had become redundant. It was a simple move to transfer the need to confirm fitness prior to the compilation of the List to have to prove it after the List was compiled.

Fitness Test Conditions

The conditions attached to the spring Fitness Test were added to very quickly as the test schedule expanded. The main conditions set out the impact of a referee failing the test, with these being developed and refined over the years. A failure or non-attendance meant that a referee was not allowed to officiate until such time as the test was passed. For a period, that applied just to senior football. Initially, it did not impact on Junior football as an adequate pool of referees had to be maintained to service the games but eventually the condition was extended to cover Junior football. Where once a third successive failure of the test would result in automatic deletion from the List, in recent years the conditions were amended to an automatic re-classification to the category lower than the official's category. This approach has an eye on the need to service the game.

One consistent element of the conditions has been that relating to removal from the List if the test has not been completed by 31st December each season. The Referee Committee took a hard line approach to this in its early years but, unless the circumstances are such that there is no option but to remove a referee, it now generally takes a more relaxed view and retains such officials on the List.

Medical Testing

The approach to fitness was developed further in 1993 when the Class 1 referees were required to undertake the same medical test as the referees nominated for inclusion in FIFA's International List. The Class 1 medical testing programme operated for more than a decade.

During season 1994-95, an analysis of fitness levels and of the demands placed upon referees during matches was undertaken. That same season, the FIFA referees undertook a fitness testing programme through Edinburgh's Moray House College of Education in respect of their fitness, health, diet and mental preparation. The eventual results and benefits were provided to all other referees to further their own knowledge on these subjects.

Fitness Clinic

In 2003, Donald McVicar organised a Fitness Clinic for Category 1 referees and the Referees' Associations' Physical Training Instructors which was taken by Dr. Werner Helsen, UEFA's Consultant in fitness and training programmes for referees. This led to improved training methods being used as Helsen provided training programme information to the Category 1 referees on a weekly basis.

Appointment of National Physical Fitness Co-ordinator

One significant consequence of Helsen's clinic was that it led to the appointment of John McQuade, a PE teacher and the Renfrewshire RA trainer, as the National Physical Fitness Co-ordinator to oversee a uniform approach to the Referees' Associations fitness programmes. He visited the associations to evaluate the training methods, assess equipment needs and to develop a national training policy.

It proved a worthwhile exercise. It gave McQuade an excellent overview as to the variances in approach which were taken and enabled the introduction of standardised programmes to suit the various levels of fitness of referees.

The creation of a National Fitness Co-ordinator was very timely given advances being made by UEFA in this field. McQuade has represented the SFA at UEFA Referee Fitness Coaches'

Courses. These courses are a regular feature of the UEFA programmes for National Associations.

Polar Watches
The drive to improve fitness levels moved up a notch in season 2006-07 when all the Category 1 referees were issued with a polar sports watch to record their training data. The data was sent to John McQuade on a weekly basis. At a stroke, the level of monitoring of training and fitness increased considerably. There was literally no hiding place for the referees. They responded well and the information received from them allowed individual fitness advice to be given.

The provision of polar watches was extended over the years to the Specialist Assistant Referees, Category 2 referees and to the women FIFA officials.

At the end of each season, the Referee Committee receives a report on the outcomes of the referees' training programmes.

Coaching

The Coaching Co-ordinator
Developing the coaching of referees at monthly meetings was one of George Cumming's early objectives.

A Seminar for training class instructors held in 1990 led to the creation of the position of Coaching Co-ordinator in each association, someone who would lead discussions at the meetings.

Although there were some initial variances in approach amongst associations, there was quick acceptance of the importance of the Coaching Co-ordinator's role. Work nonetheless had to be done to ensure that the Co-ordinator's slot at meetings was a prominent one. Every effort was made to develop coaching at each meeting and to use the video material provided.

To give further strength to the role, and to ensure the selection of an appropriate candidate, from 1991 the appointment of a Coaching Co-ordinator was made by an association in close consultation with its Supervisor.

To boost their standing within refereeing, the Coaching Co-ordinators acted as leaders of group discussions at the 1991 and 1992 Referees' Conferences.

The Coaching Co-ordinator's role has become an integral part of every association's organisation and has achieved all that it was set out to do – increase coaching at the meetings.

The Referee Coach

The idea of coaching a referee was a passion of Donald McVicar and he played a pivotal role in laying the foundations of the system now in operation. Although the Supervisors changed over the years, even the newer generations still maintained a trace of conservatism in its approach to new ideas. So it was in 2000 when McVicar raised the subject of a Referee Coach, something which had begun to emerge in other countries. The Supervisors' view was that coaching was carried out within the assessment system and that progressing the idea would require very careful consideration.

During season 2001-02, Regional Coaching Workshops were held for small groups of younger Class 1 and Class 2 referees at which Hugh Dallas and John Rowbotham gave the benefit of their experience. The programme of meetings was evaluated by the progress of the referees who were requested to develop self assessments of their performance.

A real step forward took place in season 2003-04. The Referee Committee members, Kenny Hope, George Smith and Bob Valentine, together with Donald McVicar, acted as coaches for small groups of Category 1 referees over three or four meetings during the season to aid their development. 20 referees were included in the groups. The scheme proved very successful with benefits quickly being realised. Positively, the Supervisors of the referees involved reacted very favourably.

Select Coaching Groups

The format was extended to Category 2 referees for the following season. Now called Select Coaching Groups, there were seven groups covering 43 referees. McVicar called upon George Cumming to oversee a group of the younger FIFA referees in a coaching capacity in view of his experience at international level. Unlike the other coaches, Cumming was not to observe a referee in a match.

The system proved very beneficial with the referees themselves making invaluable contributions. They were eager to participate and learn. A primary benefit of the groups was to enable the referees to share common ground at the same developmental stage. There was still a question mark being raised by the Supervisors and they had to be re-assured that the operation of the scheme did not impinge on their responsibilities.

The groups increased to nine in number for season 2005-06, covering 53 referees in Categories 1 and 2. The coaches were given the option of deciding whether to hold group meetings. Further refinement came along in the following season. The scheme was trimmed to six groups, covering just 23 Category 1 referees. Guidelines on the roles of the Coach and Referee in the operation of the scheme were brought in. All the coaches had a dual role as an Observer.

In the seasons since, the Select Coaching Groups have gone from strength to strength. For season 2019-20, there were 116 referees and 47 coaches involved. Coaches now include Category 1 referees, who coach referees in Category 2. Coaching was also extended to cover Specialist Assistant Referees and those seeking to reach that category. The passing of experience gained from one generation to another has been, and will continue to be, invaluable.

Referee Coaching Course

George Cumming set in motion the formation of a pool of coaches for the associations during the early 1990's. Donald McVicar expanded the coaching framework with the creation of Referee Coaches. That process began in season 2007-08 when he organised a course for prospective coaches. 19 candidates were chosen from 60 applicants. The candidates were assessed at monthly meetings and other seminars during the season prior to being confirmed as a coach.

Coaching Material

Where once the match incidents used for coaching purposes were drawn exclusively from televised matches in domestic football and were more applicable to referees in senior football, it became realised, especially during the review of the Referees' Associations, that more relevant clips were required for referees in grassroots football as these referees would readily identify with incidents from their own level. Allowing for the practicalities of filming such matches, progress was made in this regard and it has become a regular feature of the coaching material issued to the associations.

Educational Courses

Schools, College and Prison Officers Courses

The growing demand which arose in the 1980's from schools, colleges and other bodies continued into the next decade. George Cumming's teaching background provided the perfect foundation to respond. The resources he prepared for the training classes doubled up for use in the educational course offered by Scotvec, the forerunner to the Scottish Qualifications Authority (SQA). The course was part of a module for a certificate in Sports Officiating and for Standard Grade PE.

Courses were also held for Prison Officers. These courses were shorter in length than the typical Entrance Examination course and formed the template for the shorter courses which came to be offered by associations. A new type of examination paper was used for these courses.

Someone who successfully completed these courses was awarded a Laws of the Game Certificate, the equivalent of the Entrance Certificate with the holder automatically entitled to apply for membership of an association.

SQA Referee Professional Development Award

Glasgow RA played a pivotal role in the development of the current system of schools' courses. In 2009, one of its members, a teacher, held a course in his school which resulted in 20 registered referees being generated. Due to its success, the scheme was extended to seven schools in Glasgow. The results were very encouraging with around 25% of the pupils on the course becoming registered referees by joining Glasgow RA.

Completion of the "match under guidance" was undertaken with Glasgow RA.

Work started with the SQA on the development of a Laws of the Game training programme that complied with SQA guidelines. Following a successful pilot scheme, the SFA and the SQA entered into a partnership to deliver the "SQA Referee Professional Development Award" in schools. On completion of the course, any pupil wishing to join an association requires to fulfil Part 3 of the Introductory Course Examination – being assessed in a match.

Teachers are responsible for delivering the programme, with training courses held at Hampden Park for teachers to become recognised instructors. The SFA website is used to provide access to the course to teachers conducting the course.

The project was launched in the autumn of 2011 and it quickly made its mark. 16 schools registered for the Award. The course is now well established with over 40 schools offering the Award, with expressions of interest from other schools continually being received. An encouragingly good number of pupils have completed the Award and taken the next step and become a fully qualified referee.

From the outset of schools' courses being organised, a basic premise was to create an awareness of the Laws amongst the pupils, rather than to specifically increase the number of referees. It is always a bonus when new referees are gained through this route and it serves football well for refereeing to widen its net to recruit new referees.

Referee Development Scheme

Gaining Approval

Even after eight years in post, George Cumming still had to call on his powers of persuasion to convince the Supervisors of the merits of the Referee Development Scheme. The Scheme's purpose was to fill the gap between the Minor Grade Panel Advisory Panels and the Supervisors by identifying, and providing support to, referees who showed potential for eventual promotion within the List.

The aim was to appoint a group of Referee Development Advisers to assess the referees, primarily in Junior football. Given the normal demands placed on Supervisors to cover Class 1 and Class 2 referees, the opportunities to assess referees in Class 3 and below were much reduced and when they did occur, were often carried out towards the end of the season to ensure that the referees received the recommendations needed for promotion. The Advisers would enable coverage to take place throughout a season.

A whole host of points raised by the Executive Committee had to be clarified when Cumming set out the Scheme in May 1996. That he had to indicate that he would be responsible for the operation of the Scheme *"under the authority"* of the Chief Executive was a reflection of the approach he had to adopt to gain progress. The proposals were endorsed, with the Supervisors having to be reassured that their role would not be affected. It had to be emphasised to them that they were to retain full responsibility in respect of recommendations for the List and would still be able to recommend a referee not included in the Scheme.

Supervisors were to nominate referees for inclusion in the Scheme, which was to operate on a national basis with cross-association assessments of referees. It was also to be as flexible as possible, with a limited number of referees included within it, who could be withdrawn and re-entered at a later point. A crucial feature of the Scheme was that verbal contact between an Adviser and a referee was to happen after the match to discuss the referee's performance.

Given the increased focus to be given to their football, the Regional Junior Secretaries were supportive of the Scheme and agreed to submit their appointments to Cumming.

The Advisers were to be appointed after consultation with an association's Supervisor. They were to be carefully selected, as an important element of their role would be to pass on their experience to young referees. To begin the scheme, Cumming appointed four Advisers, three of whom were former Class 1 referees – Ray Morrison, Joe Timmons and Hugh Williamson. Eight referees were nominated by the Supervisors. Their quality was very good - three of the referees reached Class 1 and two became FIFA Assistant referees. The Scheme got underway in autumn 1996, with Cumming appointing the Advisers to their matches.

The Evolution of the Scheme

For season 1997-98, the number of Advisers and referees included in the Scheme was increased to nine and 15 respectively. It continued to flourish and the numbers of Advisors and referees increased further. By August 1999, 60 referees were included in the Scheme with 21 Advisers in place. As part of their development, the Advisors met at the start of the season to attend Junior matches in groups, with these meetings becoming an regular fixture each season. By April 2000, 400 Junior matches had been attended by the Advisers during that season. That year, the door was opened to the possibility of a female referee being included in the Scheme. Amateur football was to be used for assessment if that happened.

The Scheme went through some change and contraction in 2004. It was replaced by the Academy which had been introduced five years previously. The referees who were included in the Academy were now those to be covered by the Advisers. Supervisors were able to direct Advisers to assess referees when they did not receive an SFA appointment. For a few seasons, this became the normal way of operation as the increased number of Observers enabled appropriate coverage of the referees in the Academy.

RA Managers were enabled to nominate persons who were thought suitable candidates to be an Adviser.

The Scheme returned to operation with a little restructuring for season 2007-08. The appointment of Advisers to matches was made again by the SFA. The referees included in the Scheme were those who were not included in the Academy but were considered to benefit from coverage. They were covered four times during a season. Further change occurred three years later as responsibility for appointing Advisers to matches returned to the Association Managers.

In recent years, the Scheme's operation in Central Scotland has been co-ordinated by John Reid, a former Listed official, who is the epitome of the selfless volunteer in the refereeing movement. There is close liaison between the Referee Operations Department and Reid in regard to ensuring there is no clash of appointments between an Observer and Adviser.

The Referee Development Scheme has been an undoubted success. It has more than fulfilled the objective of being the intermediary level of assessing referees between the Minor Grade Advisory Panel and the Supervisors/Observers. Many referees have benefited from the advice received from the Advisers and made progress in their careers. The Scottish Junior FA benefited considerably too, given the level of focus its football received as a hugely important step in the referee pathway.

Development Plans

The creation of a Development Plan, to chart present and future promotion prospects, was a component element of the changes driven by Donald McVicar in 2002 relating to the introduction of Executive Supervisors. In their liaison roles with the associations, they were to assist the Association Supervisors in the preparation of a Development Plan for the association. Developing a greater knowledge of the referees for the future was an inherent aim. The plans for each association were combined into a national Development Plan.

It was a simple but very effective idea. Having to prepare a plan for his association focused the mind of the Supervisor and, when the position was created in 2005, that of the Manager. Where there was an informal way of working previously to gain an idea of the new referees coming through the system, the Supervisor/Manager now had to fully build up a very good working knowledge of such referees. Each Plan operates on a three year rolling basis.

Being on top of the Development Plan quickly became a priority of the Supervisor/Manager. In the early seasons of its use, the Plan was updated a couple of times per season but can now be updated at any point.

One fairly predictable outcome from combining all the Plans into a national one was the sizeable number of promotions to Class 1 which were envisioned by the Supervisors/Managers. Realism was required as an essential element of the planning. Whilst it is laudable for a referee wanting to reach Category 1, very few actually do. The potential numbers whittle down the higher up the referee tree an official goes. The Referee Committee wishes to identify those referees who show real potential to progress. Inclusion in the Plan at the current Categories 3 and 3 Development (and the equivalent previous categories) brings with it the opportunity of the referee being covered four times during a season. In that respect, the talent identification starts early enough to allow opinions to form and decisions to be made on a referee's future.

Another aspect of the Plans in the early years was the exact opposite effect of the many potential promotions – the lack, or even complete absence, of reclassification of referees down the way, something which had to be addressed with the Managers. Difficult though the task may be, the Managers have had to develop ways of managing the expectations of referees in regard to their desired career path. Once the retiral age limit was removed, a Manager had to have discussions with referees to determine their thoughts as to when they would choose to retire. The information gained feeds into the planning process.

Since the creation of Specialist Assistant Referees, that avenue has continually been put forward as potential path to follow, as an alternative option to that of the referee pathway. The proposition becomes attractive when the potential of becoming a FIFA Assistant Referee is factored in to a referee's thinking. In recent years, a good few referees in the early stages of their career have decided to pursue the Specialist Assistant pathway.

The national Plan is a very useful tool in providing an indication of the health of each of the associations in terms of future referees and likely progression to the List. The general overall situation has been very good at a national level in recent years but it also highlights those associations, normally the ones covering the more rural areas of the country, which struggle to attract new members.

The Referee Development Academy

If the SFA's historical focus had been on the List, George Cumming was able to broaden its horizons. He wanted to put in sound foundations below the List so that it would benefit from an improved quality of officials being admitted to it over time. The introduction of the Referee Development Scheme exemplified this approach and in 1999 Cumming took matters a stage further when he announced the formation of the Referee Development Academy at the Referees' Conference.

This was a major development programme for referees under 30 years of age. Training days were to be organised at centres throughout Scotland. Class 1 referees were to contribute by passing on the benefit of their experience on various refereeing topics.

The first course was held in Perth in August 1999, with 107 referees in attendance. Further meetings were held during the season at Glasgow, Edinburgh and Aberdeen. All were a resounding success and well attended. The meetings gave the chance to the SFA of identifying refereeing talent at an earlier stage than otherwise would have been the case and assisted in maximising the potential of the referees. The meetings also lent themselves to the retention of referees.

The Academy meetings continued over the next few seasons and were well attended and productive. The launch of the Academy had coincided with the inception of the Youth Development Initiative (YDI) operated by the SFL, a non-competitive form of football for age groups ranging from Under 13 to Under 17 intended to develop young players. The YDI provided an ideal development platform for referees included in the Academy and this continues through to the present day, with the YDI of the SFL and the SPL's own equivalent having been taken over by the SFA in 2002 and later rebranded Club Academy Scotland. Responsibility for making referee appointments was passed by the SFA to the Referees' Associations which are ideally placed to use young referees for the matches as part of their early stages in their careers. It also provides the opportunity for the referees to be covered in their matches by referees and Development Advisers. The support and guidance given stands the referees in good stead.

A repositioning of the Referee Development Academy was put into effect for season 2004-05. Now simply called the Academy, its future focus was to be on referees identified with the potential to progress. It also replaced the Referee Development Scheme with the referees included in the Academy to be assessed in four matches by Development Advisers during the season. 60 referees were included in the Academy during that season and several seminars were held at various venues around the country. Training sessions and fitness tests were part of the seminars' programmes, along with talks by experienced referees.

The number of referees in the Academy was trimmed to 30 from Categories 3 to 5 for season 2006-07 in order that greater concentration could be given to them. This concentrated focus grew further over the next few seasons and by 2009-10 the number was reduced to 22. By this time, referees identified as potential future Specialist Assistant Referees were being included in the Academy.

An onus was placed on the RA Managers to clearly identify those referees who they thought had significant potential to reach the top. By season 2011-12, the Academy had been refined further to limit it to those referees who are detailed in their Manager's Development Plan to progress to Category 2.

Complaints from Clubs

Throughout the 1990's, complaints on referees' performances continued to be submitted on a regular basis by clubs, with these being considered by the Disciplinary & Referee/Referee Committees and the Supervisors. The meeting schedule determined which of the committees had first sight of the complaints.

In the main, the complaints reflected the club's view that they had been hard done by the referee's decisions, either by one, by a few, or by his overall performance. Some were well constructed and made their points in cogent fashion, others less so. In the latter case, the reader was often left to wonder if the complaint had been reviewed before it had been sent, such was the poor standard, the gaping holes in the argument and a lack of knowledge on the Laws of the Game. Some complaints were lengthy, others brief and to the point which curtailed any chance the committee had to discern exactly what had upset the club in the first place.

All complaints received equal consideration by the committees. There were of course occasions when a club had been justified in what it had said, often confirmed by the assessment report of the Supervisor or Observer present at the match.

In 1992, the Supervisors, in considering comments from one club, debated whether or not referees were being overzealous in issuing cautions. Their view was that this appeared to be the case, particularly amongst Class 2 referees, who, they thought, seemed to over resort to the use of cautions as opposed to using their personalities to control situations. (That style of refereeing was relatively common amongst Class 2 referees on being promoted from Class 3 as they took time to settle into the higher category and reserve football.) Equally, it was recognised that referees were required to rigidly apply instructions issued by FIFA. It was also thought that some referees were cautioning in response to comments contained in previous Supervisors' reports. The importance for Supervisors to phrase advice in a thoughtful way and be constructive in their comments was referred to. Such a debate illustrated the worth of clubs being able to write to the SFA and the outcomes which could flow from that, not that the club would ever get wind of the debate it had generated with its letter.

On the other hand, a different outcome would be the result of committees discussing complaints which accused referees of bias. Phraseology used by the clubs would raise the hackles of the committees, even the Disciplinary & Referee/Referee Committee members who were "club" people. In a couple of instances in 1993, clubs made comments in a way as if they were trying to subvert the presence of the Supervisors and which exemplified the difficult nature of the referee's job and that of the Supervisors. As such complaints were held to be reflective of the apparent prevalent attitude within clubs, relevant information on Supervisors was issued to clubs to raise their awareness of their role.

Twice in the 1990's, the same club urged the use of television evidence to review the performances of match officials. This was rejected on both occasions and, following its second complaint, the club was issued with the assessment guidelines so that it had an understanding of the system which operated. The same club (and others from time to time) also requested sight of the Supervisor's report on the officials on one of its matches. The long standing policy of the reports being private and confidential to the SFA was easily maintained.

Another club in 1997 asked that it be provided with explanations from the referee of decisions he had taken in a match. This prompted the Referee Committee to instruct all clubs that officials should not approach referees at matches to seek explanations of decisions and that, if deemed appropriate, clubs should continue to submit their views on referees' performances to the SFA.

The serious charge of bias was raised by a club in a complaint against a referee in 2008. The Referee Committee acknowledged that the referee's decision making could have been better in respect of the incidents referred to, and was aware that this was accepted by the highly experienced referee. As the committee considered that referees set out in each game to officiate to the best of their ability, just as in the same way players take to field to perform to the best of their ability, it regarded the accusation of bias against the referee to be of the gravest concern. As there was nothing contained in the club's letter to support the charge, the committee invited the club to submit evidence to substantiate its claim within 14 days, failing which it would regard the matter to be closed. There was no further communication from the club.

In certain cases clubs, in the context of their complaint, seek to test the SFA in regard to what it does in refereeing and what happens in terms of the standards of officiating. A straightforward response is given: that the refereeing movement is constantly trying to improve standards. Often, in regard to points raised by clubs, there can only be very obvious and simple answers which can be given in response in terms of this or that decision made by a referee. Providing such answers do not go down well with clubs as they will still contest the point.

Over the last 20 years, the volume of club complaints has diminished to some extent following the establishment of an open communication channel between club managers and the Head of Referee Operations to enable match incidents to be talked though. This has had the effect of building relationships between clubs and referees. There have been wins and losses for both sides in these discussions.

Points of Play

The Supervisors' consideration of Points of Play became less formal during the 1990's, which reflected how things evolved following George Cumming's appointment. Any points which arose were generally addressed in a quicker fashion than before. The Referees' Conference continued to be used as a forum to consider Points of Play, but it became more a case of advising referees how a particular match incident should be dealt with, rather than inviting discussion with the referees to arrive at an outcome. The same principle applied to the various meetings of referees which grew in number during that decade.

The Supervisors continued to deliberate on Points of Play. Some dealt with potential gaps in the Laws of the Game (at the time of the Point arising). In 1990, the Supervisors determined that that a referee should caution a player for ungentlemanly conduct in the event of his refusing to comply with his request to leave the field of play to put shinguards in order that Law IV was complied with. Another point was determined by deciding that a goalkeeper was in control of the ball if he had it in the palm of his hand when an attacking player stoops and heads the ball from his hand and proceeds to kick the ball into the goal. The goal was not to be awarded.

Football has a fantastic capacity of throwing up incidents which demand consideration. One such incident arose in a SFL match in 1992. One of the teams wanted to make a double substitution, which although noticed and indicated by the standside linesman, was not noticed by the referee who gave an indication for a free-kick, in an attacking position, to be taken by the other team. The linesman, on noticing this, lowered his flag and took up a position at the corner flag. The two substitutes entered the field of play without the referee's permission, the free-kick was then taken and a goal was scored. When play resumed the linesman realised that the two substitutes were on the field of play and the two players who had been substituted were at their team's bench and he signalled to attract the referee's attention. After a lengthy discussion the two substitutes were cautioned and the game restarted with a place kick. The Supervisors agreed that the award of a goal should stand, that the two substitutes should be cautioned for entering the field of play without the referee's permission and that the two players who had been substituted should be cautioned at the end of the match for leaving the field of play without the referee's permission. In view of the complexity of the circumstances which had created this incident, the topic was a discussion point at the Referees' Conference as it emphasised the importance of diligence on the part of match officials towards the making of substitutions.

Another case arose in 1995 which was taken to the Conference for the purpose of advising referees how the matter should be dealt with. The Supervisors had decided that it was covered by the then IFAB Decision 11 of Law XII and that referees should be advised, of the following: i) that a player using undue force to kick the ball out of play (and striking a spectator) should be cautioned for ungentlemanly conduct, given that he had chosen not to exercise the option, open to him, of putting the ball out of play in a responsible manner, ii) the referee's interpretation of the exact circumstances of the player's actions and of the degree of force used is of paramount importance. It was recognised that also in addition to a player being guilty of ungentlemanly conduct, he could, in response to the individual action, alternatively be guilty of dissent, time wasting or violent conduct by such action. The following points were addressed at Conference: the punishment to be applied to a player for committing such an act; the example of a ball being kicked with force at an opponent or occupants of a technical area; the example of a goalkeeper throwing the ball with force at an opponent; the action of the match officials - the referee; the role of the linesman nearest to the incident; the role of the linesman furthest from the incident. In the case of the linesmen, it was incumbent upon them to draw the incident to the referee's attention if it has been witnessed by either or both of them.

This particular topic encapsulates perfectly the impact of a Point of Play – how it is initially addressed and how it is acted upon to give advice to referees to ensure that the point is consistently interpreted by them. This is more or less the standard process which has been followed for many years. The regular meetings of the various categories of referees enable a relatively quick means of disseminating advice and guidance to them to ensure the correct handling of incidents. If there is a special need to issue advice more quickly, use is made of the Referee Extranet to post video clips and written guidance to referees. Points of Play are also addressed in the coaching material issued to the Referees' Associations for their meetings, which ensures that the message is conveyed to as many referees as possible.

A Point of Play would occasionally emerge which led to it being addressed by IFAB and incorporated into the Laws of the Game. The following scenario was presented in 1997: "A defending player deliberately kicks the ball to his own goalkeeper. The goalkeeper misses the ball and as the ball is about to enter the goal another defender runs in and stops the ball with his hand deliberately. The referee stops the game and awards a penalty kick to the opposing team. What further action should be taken against the player?" The Supervisors acknowledged that a weakness existed in the then wording of the relevant section of Law 12 and they agreed that, in the circumstances set out, the spirit of Law 12 should be applied and the offending player should be sent off. IFAB subsequently made a change to the Law to cover the point.

Linesmen/Assistant Referees

There has been a continuous and increasing focus on linesmen, or assistant referees as the role was renamed in 1996, since the

1990's. This reflects the recognition of their vital importance to good match officiating. A referee benefits from having assistant referees of a high standard. The game benefits too.

Linesmanship Debated
The 1990's saw many instances of linesmanship issues being debated by the Supervisors. Tom Wharton commented on his seeing wrong signals being made by linesmen and blind acceptance of them by referees. The need for greater concentration by linesmen was deemed to be required and for referees to have the courage of their own call when in a better position to overrule the linesman's flag. Pre-match instructions given by referees to linesmen were much discussed during this period. Stories emerged at meetings of referees instructing linesmen that they did not wish any assistance from a linesman on incidents on the field of play and that a linesman had been told to signal when a player is in an offside position irrespective of whether or not he is interfering with play. The Supervisors told referees that such instructions should not be issued. Specifically on the point of offside, it was their view that linesmen were there to make a judgement on offside and that they should not raise their flags automatically if a player is in an offside position and so possibly obstruct the scoring of goals.

During season 1994-95, liaison between referees and linesmen was debated. Tom Wharton's view was that there had been an increasing number of instances where a match incident concerning players' misconduct had not been dealt with correctly. The Supervisors considered that the aim of such liaison was to ensure that the culprit of any misdemeanour was appropriately dealt with and, whilst undue interference from linesmen was not being sought, it was felt that on a number of occasions, linesmen had shown undue deference towards the referee. The discussion concluded with agreement that, when a major incident occurs involving misconduct and which was observed by both the referee and a linesman, it was the linesman's duty to signal to the referee and to advise him of his interpretation of the incident if the action taken by the referee in dealing with it differed from his own opinion e.g. if a caution had been administered rather than a sending-off, or if no action is being taken and a sanction should be administered. The referee had to act upon the advice he received in accordance with the Laws of the Game.

A Career Pathway

The status of assistant referees was raised greatly in 1998 with the creation of Specialist Assistant Referees. For the first time, a career path opened up for those referees who wished to become an assistant. This career path was given a further boost when Development Plans were introduced. Training programmes are specifically prepared for assistant referees in the same way as they are done for referees. If the physical appearance of referees has changed over the last 30 years, the same applies to assistant referees. The introduction of Assistant Referee Observers has been another very important strand in the focus given to assistant referees. Their guidance and advice to assistant referees in every category all helps to improve performance. The appointment of Tom Murphy, a former FIFA assistant referee, to the SFA staff in 2016 emphasised the commitment to develop assistant refereeing.

Mistakes will of course be made in matches, but these will be far fewer than many onlookers would say are being made. There is a high level of performances at the top level of the game in Scotland. Assistant referees are under great scrutiny and they strive to give of their best and to improve.

Scottish Football League

The SFL continued as the main "employer" of referees until the formation of the SPL in 1998. Dialogue between the SFA and the SFL was a necessary part of each body's operations.

Beyond the standing courtesy of inviting representatives of the SFL to be advised of the composition of the List for each season, there were a number of refereeing issues which became regular discussion points with the SFL from the early 1990's.

George Cumming's persuading of the SFL to drop the marking of referees in matches in 1990 was a key breakthrough moment in enabling the analysis of referees' performances to be based entirely on Supervisors' assessments.

Appointment of Fourth Officials to Premier Division matches

A recurring theme in the early to mid-1990's was the SFA's seeking the SFL to appoint Fourth Officials to Premier Division matches. The issue was raised a number of times with the SFL. Beyond covering the possibility of the Fourth Official having to replace an injured referee during a match, a Fourth Official would also assist in controlling any likely misconduct by the occupants of the technical areas, a problem which was increasing within the game. Such were the concerns in this period that there was a real fear within the SFA that the police would become involved in dealing with the misconduct of coaching staff.

The SFL rebuffed the requests. The increased costs to the SFL and availability of suitable officials were advanced for not introducing Fourth Officials. Equally, the SFL would have been also happy to rely on either a Class 1 or Class 2 referee, acting a senior linesman, being able to take over from a referee in case of injury.

Appointment System

Although there was enhanced liaison between the SFA and the SFL in this era, there were always underlying criticisms directed towards the SFL by the Supervisors in the realm of match appointments. The appointments, of course, were not in the control in any way of the SFA and the situation led to a feeling of frustration held by George Cumming, the Supervisors and the referees.

The feeling was that refereeing resources were not being used to best effect. In December 1994, Cumming cited that some FIFA referees would have only refereed four Premier Division matches by the turn of the year. Some issues were of a longstanding nature – the gap between appointments from the end of one appointment cycle and the start of another. From the SFL perspective, given the then number of Class 1 referees, it was aware of the need to have an equality of opportunity to allow the progression and development of referees.

The SFA's representations to the SFL on these matters never quite succeeded, although the SFL did agree to a proposal that a new Class 1 referee should not be appointed to a Premier Division match until his third season at Class 1, which was an extension of one season to the then system.

Reserve Football

Reserve football had long functioned as the testing ground of Class 2 referees and they were regularly supervised in these matches. By the late 1980's Premier Division Reserve League matches started to be increasingly scheduled during normal working hours and this caused problems to match officials in fulfilling appointments.

These problems intensified during the 1990's. Late changes of day, venue and kick-off became common and started having a real impact on achieving a balanced assessment of Class 2 referees.

Disciplinary Cases

The period from 1988 through to the mid-1990's was difficult for referees as they came under a great deal of scrutiny in regard to their performances.

Acting Upon Warnings

The Field Discipline campaign launched in 1983 had ramped up the requirements placed on referees to carry out the SFA's instructions. Strong hints were given at regular intervals to referees as to what could happen if they failed to do so, but without any real threat being carried out. Action was taken, however, in 1988.

In the Supervisors' reports on the matches Aberdeen v. Rangers in October and Rangers v. Aberdeen in November, it was indicated that referees Louis Thow and Kenny Hope, respectively, had failed to carry out the SFA's instructions. Thow had cautioned Neil Simpson of Aberdeen for a violent tackle on Rangers' Ian Durrant instead of sending him off, and Kenny Hope had been subjected to prolonged dissent from Aberdeen's Willie Miller as they walked off the pitch at the end of the match and had failed to caution him. Each case had generated huge publicity in the media.

Jack Mowat reckoned that the seriousness of these failures were such that they could not be overlooked. The warnings which had been given would be rendered meaningless otherwise. His view was that it was incumbent on the Supervisors to recommend that disciplinary action be taken against the referees and that this would have a salutary effect on the refereeing movement. He proposed that it should be recommended to the Disciplinary & Referee Committee that the two referees should not be appointed to matches in the SFL's next run of appointments and that they should not receive Scottish Cup appointments that season. Mowat's proposal won the day after some debate.

The two referees were interviewed by the Disciplinary & Referee Committee. Whilst agreeing that disciplinary action was justified, the committee only accepted part of the recommendation - that the referees should not be appointed to matches in the Scottish Cup. The referees were also severely censured, a time honoured SFA disciplinary decision.

Between the Supervisors' and the Disciplinary & Referee Committee meetings, football politics had kicked in with it becoming known that the SFL would not carry out any request not to appoint the referees. Somehow, this translated through to the Disciplinary & Referee Committee's deliberations. A "war" between the two bodies was therefore avoided.

In October 1990, Jack Mowat reported a linesman for not reporting to the referee a player assaulting an opponent when he was considered to have had a clear view of the incident. The linesman contended that he not seen the incident. He was duly interviewed and deleted from the List.

Difficult Times in the 1990's

From 1992 a number of investigations into the handling of match incidents involving Class 1 referees, and some linesmen, were conducted. It was a fraught time for referees as so much unwanted attention was brought upon them. The period coincided with Jim Farry's early years as the SFA Chief Executive. Having acted as the secretary to the Supervisors for a period in the 1970's prior to becoming SFL Secretary, he was well schooled in the importance of referees being the SFA's instruments of control of the game. He exercised very high level of expectations on referees when he returned as Chief Executive in 1990 and felt things very keenly as these various incidents unfolded. The Executive Committee came under pressure to deal with the cases. Interviews became the order of the day as investigations were carried out.

Jim Renton was censured in 1992 for not having a notebook when about to caution a player in a match. He had gone over to his senior linesman to borrow his notebook, only to find the linesman did not have one either. To compound matters, the linesman had turned up for the match without any kit and had to make hasty arrangements to borrow some. He was severely censured.

An infamous situation occurred in the Partick Thistle v. Dundee match in February 1993. Dundee United scored a goal which was not awarded – the ball had rebounded from the stanchion into the field of play when it was then handled by a defender with play being allowed to continue without any action taken by the referee Les Mottram or a signal for an offence being given by the standside linesman, Dougie Smith. Mottram was severely censured and Smith censured. The case had a lasting impact on football – as a consequence of the case, the SFA decided that its member clubs should adopt the style of support for goal nets as recommended by FIFA and UEFA.

At the end of season 1992-93, Jim Farry investigated allegations made by Partick Thistle against a linesman at an away match against Dundee United. He interviewed the three match officials and referred the case to the Executive Committee. The referee and the linesman were severely censured (the other linesman was censured), for failing to report an incident at the end of the match involving the linesman and the Partick Thistle Assistant Manager. There was little doubt that an incident had happened and that the Assistant Manager should have been reported for misconduct. The match officials had not helped themselves during the investigation.

Against the backcloth of the SFA affording full support to referees, Farry expressed his dissatisfaction on how the match officials had handled the affair. He made it clear that it was not the role of referees to act as censors and to decide what should or should not be reported.

A similar affair occurred during the following season when a linesman somehow did not report to the referee his intervention in an incident between personnel of the two clubs. The linesman was censured. Farry remained concerned at the inability or unwillingness of match officials to provide reports which the SFA could act upon. As it was obvious to the Executive Committee that the SFA's views on the reporting of incidents by referees had not had the expected response, a statement of specific instructions was issued to each Supervisor to read at their association's monthly meetings so that all referees could be advised in a uniform manner of the SFA's requirements.

A Class 2 referee was deleted from the List at the end of season 1993-94 for not having acted on the advice of a linesman to send a player off in a Junior Cup tie for violent conduct. Only a warning had been issued to the player. It was the referee's misfortune that a Supervisor was at the match and he had sought each official's comments on the incident before submitting his report. The linesman, to his credit, had also reported the referee to the SFA.

Jim Farry and Tom Wharton interviewed Kenny Clark on his failure to send off Duncan Ferguson in a Rangers v. Raith Rovers match in April 1994 for violently headbutting an opponent when apparently well positioned to witness the offence, which had been detailed in the Supervisor's report. The Executive Committee took the pragmatic view to defer consideration of the matter until Ferguson's disciplinary case was concluded. That took some considerable time due to a prolonged civil case which resulted in the player serving time in jail for his offence. When the case ended after a couple of years, another pragmatic view was taken: that there was little point in pursuing the matter due to the passage of time.

The lowest point in this lengthy saga of referees in bother was reached in December 1995 when three cases involving four match officials were dealt with by the Executive Committee. Each case was set in the same context – incidents of misconduct which had not been acted upon by match officials and which had jeopardised the SFA's disciplinary role within the game, all of which had followed the repeated warnings given to referees and the role they were required to perform. The SFA had taken action against the players on the basis of what had been reported by Supervisors, something which had caused concern amongst them. Farry set out that the role of the Supervisor was to report on the performance of the match officials and that it was for the SFA thereafter to deal with matters not acted upon by match officials as it saw fit utilising, if appropriate, the contents of reports in its possession.

George McGuire, a Class 2 referee and a FIFA linesman, was deleted from the List after being interviewed about an incident in a Rangers v. Heart of Midlothian match when the Supervisor considered that he was in a good position to see a player violently elbow an opponent in the face outwith the referee's vision and that he should have taken action.

Jim McCluskey was interviewed in regard to why he had not witnessed a player twice kicking an opponent in the stomach as he was on the ground during an Airdrieonians v. Dundee match. The Supervisor thought that it was inconceivable that the player's actions should have gone unpunished by the referee. McCluskey had been only five yards away from the incident but he gave his version as to why he had not seen the incident. He managed to answer the committee's questions to its satisfaction. No further action was taken.

In his report on a Rangers v. Aberdeen match, a Supervisor recorded that three or four players should have been sent off. The media coverage on the match was intense, with much criticism being directed towards the referee, John Rowbotham. A bad autumn for referees had just become a whole lot worse and heaped further pressure on to the SFA. Rowbotham and the standside linesman, Dougie McDonald, were interviewed. McDonald was questioned on his failure to advise Rowbotham to administer disciplinary sanctions to three players as a result of their misconduct in an incident when he had an uninterrupted view of it. Each official somehow escaped with a censure, each having accepted the serious criticism of their performances.

The period had been a tumultuous one for referees with the high profile nature of some of the cases dealt with causing real difficulties for the SFA. The cases seemed to spring up from nowhere and go on and on, but they eventually subsided, much to the relief of many in refereeing.

Any disciplinary cases which did emerge afterwards were extremely rare, the most notable one being when the Referee Committee fined Stuart Dougal £200 for having been caught on camera swearing at a player during a televised match in 2004.

Other Cases and the Judicial Panel Protocol

During the 2000's, cases involving referees for non-refereeing matters arose which were dealt with by other Standing Committees of the SFA. After the Judicial Panel was established in 2012, any refereeing issues which arise from football matches fall within the domain of the Referee Committee to deal with. Other cases which relate to breaches of the Protocol are handled by the Judicial Panel.

Taken to the Courts

The deletion of McGuire had dramatic consequences. In 1996, he sought a Judicial Review of the decision to remove him from the List. The case was heard in December 1996, with the outcome being in McGuire's favour. The SFA was required to consider a late application from him for inclusion in the List for season 1996-97 within 14 days of an application being received. The Supervisors found themselves in unchartered waters. With legal advice provided to the Executive Committee, it considered the various possibilities open to it. Each option was carefully considered and, deciding that his application should be accepted, it settled on placing McGuire at Class 4. It was a neat outcome as far as the committee was concerned. McGuire had been returned to the List, but not at a level which would enable him to officiate in SFL football. At the end of the season, McGuire did not submit a renewal application for the List. He had had his day in court and had won. His case caused the SFA to carry out a number of adjustments to the Referee Committee's Standing Orders, forcing the link between it and the Referee Supervisors' Committees to be formalised.

McGuire did not disappear altogether. He became a committee member of Civil Service Strollers and in 2000-01 was elected as the East of Scotland FA representative on the SFA Council. Staggeringly, he was appointed to the Referee Committee. Given all that that had happened following his deletion from the List, it was an astonishing appointment. In plain terms, here was a former referee who had been removed from the List now operating as a member of the Referee Committee, a level above the Supervisors. He served two seasons on the Referee Committee.

International Matters

Since the 1990's, there has been a considerable international perspective in Scottish refereeing, covering a number of areas. Relationships with FIFA and UEFA developed to an extent which never existed previously. Contact with other National Associations developed also.

Laws of the Game

Privileged to be a member of IFAB, the SFA has always played a key role in the development of the Laws of the Game. This role grew particularly in the 1990's due to George Cumming. As a refereeing specialist, he was the natural person to call upon to progress business items. The SFA, through Cumming, played a pivotal role in the introduction of the Fourth Official into the Laws of the Game and the adjustment of the scheduling of IFAB's AGM from the summer time to the spring, thus enabling the speedier dissemination of information on Law changes. Cumming had a major role in the redrafting of the Laws of the Game for season 1997-98.

All the refereeing specialists who have succeeded Cumming have continued to make a significant contribution to the continuing evolution of the Laws of the Game, through membership of IFAB's Technical Sub-Committee.

FIFA

During the 1990's, FIFA carried out a drive to professionalise refereeing. This was a backcloth to many of the programmes which were introduced during that decade. Given the connections Cumming had developed with FIFA, the SFA was able to keep pace with, if not be ahead of, FIFA's requirements. In 2008, FIFA launched its Refereeing Assistance programme (RAP), the basic objective which was to professionalise the environment in which referees develop and work. UEFA organises courses for referees, referee instructors and fitness coaches in partnership with FIFA. These RAP Courses, and the information which flow from them to the National Associations, play an extremely important part in the development of the uniform application of the Laws of the Game.

UEFA

As its wealth grew due to the sale of television rights to its major competitions, UEFA was able to devote appropriate resources to develop refereeing. Its reach to National Associations expanded greatly for the benefit of all parties and referees. UEFA's underlying aim was, and is, to improve the standard of performance of all the European FIFA referees and assistant referees for its competitions. The number of courses held by UEFA is extremely extensive. Its courses for the elite referees set the tone for its competitions and for national associations.

As part of its Referee Talents Programme, started in 2001, Bob Valentine was selected as a Mentor for two up and coming referees and acted in this role for four years. He was succeeded by Hugh Dallas. Craig Thomson and William Collum were selected as referees for the programme in 2004 and 2006 respectively.

UEFA changed tack on it Talents programme in 2010 when it turned its attention to match officials identified by their National Associations as potential candidates for future inclusion in the FIFA List. The Centre of Refereeing Excellence project (CORE) started. Nominated officials receive specialist advice on refereeing over two week-long courses and officiate at games in the lower Divisions of the French and

Swiss Championships. The course has proved to be an invaluable stepping stone for referees in their careers. The possibility of being selected for each CORE Course is a great motivation for referees. The officials selected have all progressed to the FIFA List. Scots have also been selected by UEFA to act as coaches and instructors for these courses.

International Referees' Instructors' Course
George Cumming organised this course at the University of Stirling over four days in April 1994. 33 participants from National Associations around the world attended. The course received support from FIFA and UEFA and, as part of its assistance programme for new member associations in Eastern Europe, UEFA arranged for representatives from Azerbaijan, Armenia, Georgia and Moldova to attend the course.

Attendance at National Associations' Referees' Courses
From 1991 to the mid-2000's a reciprocal exchange system operated of visits by representatives to various National Associations Referees' Courses in Europe. The SFA's representatives were drawn from the Executive Committee and senior SFA staff members. The information gleaned from attending such courses was invaluable and reassuring, in the sense that there was a commonality of problems being experienced amongst the various associations. It informed discussion, enabled best practice to develop and provided confirmation, where needed, of the correctness of the programmes being developed by the SFA.

Referee Exchange Programme
As a consequence of such developments being instigated between other neighbouring associations in Europe with the encouragement of UEFA, a Referee Exchange Scheme was introduced between the SFA, the FA of Wales, the Irish FA and the FA of Ireland in season 2004-05. The SFL agreed to co-operate with the scheme. The Scottish referees selected for the scheme were below FIFA level and the opportunities it provided further aided their development, operating in a

different environment to which they were used. The scheme operated for several seasons, culminating in season 2012-13. Cross-border referee appointments returned in 2016 when the SPFL invited clubs from England, Northern Ireland, Republic of Ireland and Wales to participate in the IRN-BRU Cup.

FIFA List of International Referees

Changes and Developing a Strategy
Throughout the 1990's, the SFA continued to use the Disciplinary & Referee Committee/Referee Committee to confirm the nominations to the FIFA List of International Referees. The Supervisors were not involved in the process. There was however liaison between George Cumming and Tom Wharton on the likely nominations as issues were teased out between them.

In 1992, FIFA announced major changes to match officials for international football. Firstly, the maximum age limit was dropped from 50 to 45. This change forced the hand of all National Associations to nominate younger referees for the List, a process which the SFA which was largely successful in achieving.

Secondly, linesmen were to be included in the International List. This provided the opportunity of an official acting as an international linesman and then progressing to be nominated as a FIFA referee. This change coincided with the SFA's restructuring of the List in 1991 which resulted in Class 1 and Class 2 referees acting as linesmen. A few Class 1 referees progressed from FIFA linesman to FIFA referee until a change of procedure was introduced by FIFA for its 1997 List. A minimum one year period was now required to be served between being nominated for each category. This led to the gradual removal of Class 1 referees as FIFA linesmen.

The creation of the Specialist Assistant Referee category in 1998 fed into the international sphere very quickly and a strong cadre of assistant referees soon emerged to represent the SFA on the FIFA List.

With the restructuring of the Referee Committee in 2003, this provided the opportunity, for the first time, for the former referees being able to decide on the nominations. An increased focus on the development and application of a strategy on the nominations resulted. To allow the referees to have an opportunity of developing a career at international level, a system of refreshing the nominees regularly by nominating younger referees to replace others whose international careers were not going to advance, was introduced. The same principle applies to the nomination of assistant referees.

Enacting this strategy was a sea change compared to what had gone before 20 years earlier, when the FIFA referees were deemed to be the best in the country, and regarded as such by the clubs. When a referee is admitted on to the FIFA List, it means he/she starts off at the lowest of UEFA's referees' categories. This equates to a referee being admitted to the SFA's List at Category 3 Development and having to be promoted a few times to reach Category 1. Thus, younger referees became FIFA referees before becoming fully established as referees in Scotland. This gave rise to some issues and for a brief period these referees were given permission not to wear their FIFA badge in domestic football to give them a bit of protection from criticism that might go their way at games.

The Referee Committee addresses the selection of the nominees extremely seriously, understanding full well the impact of removal from the FIFA List has on an official. There is an almost continual process of monitoring and evaluation of future prospective FIFA officials. The identification of future candidates starts early. The Referee Committee developed a protocol in 2017 which it follows in regard to the nomination decision making process.

Women Match Officials
The SFA has striven over the years to ensure that women referees have the opportunity to progress to the FIFA List. The first female to be included in the List, Morag Pirie, was nominated as a Woman Assistant Referee for the 2004 FIFA List. She was four years in the role before being nominated as a

FIFA Woman Referee in 2009. She served for nine years as a referee and had a superb career at international level.

Pirie was soon joined as a FIFA Referee by Lorraine Watson. Once women referees made it on to the FIFA List, it was essential to nominate women assistant referees and the SFA has been successful in this regard, with Kylie McMullan and Vikki Robertson being prominent in their achievements. In total, eight women Scottish officials have served on the FIFA List. Given the growth of women's football, particularly at international level, the opportunities for women officials in the modern era are boundless.

Futsal Referees
Futsal is a thriving worldwide version of indoor football and gaining popularity in Scotland. The SFA realised the importance of being able to give attention to this form of football and successfully nominated Gordon McCabe as a FIFA Futsal Referee in 2018.

Meetings of FIFA Officials
Meetings with the FIFA Officials are held each season. They cover many topics related to international football, with the referees who have attended courses organised by UEFA and FIFA giving updates on them to keep everyone abreast of the latest developments. The meetings can also serve as an induction to newly nominated FIFA officials so that they have a greater knowledge as to what lies ahead of them.

FIFA Dinner
To recognise their achievement of becoming a FIFA match official, a Dinner was instituted by the SFA in 2010 to present the officials with their badge. When an official retires from the FIFA List, a presentation is made to them by the SFA.

Scottish Premier League

The Formation of a New League
Given all that was happening in the world of refereeing, the emergence of the SPL at the end of season 1997-98 was very timely. It presented a huge opportunity for the SFA to exert influence and gain control of the League's refereeing appointments. All the background negotiations paid off. The SFA was invited to appoint the match officials for the proposed new League's competitions. The Referee Committee accepted the invitation, subject to such conditions as it determined. With the SFA having to give final approval to the formation of the SPL, things had fallen into place.

A New Appointment System
The SFA could now put into operation the appointment system which the SFL had declined to do a couple of years previously. Using the same cycle of appointment periods as the SFL, but rather than publishing all the appointments for the duration of that cycle, match officials were preselected for each round of fixtures with the actual match appointments published five days in advance of the fixtures. This provided a greater flexibility in making appointments and avoided referees being placed in unnecessarily difficult situations as had happened at times previously.
Increased levels of co-operation with the SFL was a natural by-product of the system as the SFL was effectively getting "second pick" of the match officials for its competitions.

Management Fee
The Referee Committee decided that a management fee should be charged to the SPL for the administrative functions to be carried out related to the appointment of match officials. If the prize which had been gained was the first team SPL League competition, the SPL also operated Reserve and Under 19 Leagues. The SFA was also to be dealing with the payments of fees and expenses of all the match officials on behalf of the SPL. The administrative workload was increased in the Finance

Department as well as in the Disciplinary & Referee Department.

The question of the management fee became a real political issue throughout season 1998-99, with negotiations taking place at the highest levels. As a fee could not be agreed by the summer of 1999, the SFA Executive Committee decided that the SFA would not provide the appointment service for the following season. The SPL, running a tight ship in terms of staff numbers, had little option but to get the SFL to do its appointments for season 1999-00. The hard fought for prize of appointing referees to the country's top league had slipped through the SFA's grasp.

Negotiations between the SFA and SPL continued during season 1999-00. All elements of the SFA's refereeing structure – the Referee Committee, the Supervisors and the referees – made it known that they wished the appointments to return to the SFA. The impasse was broken in the summer of 2000 when the SPL finally agreed to pay a management fee for season 1998-99 (part of the agreement struck when the formation of the SPL was approved) and for the following three seasons.

The management fee continued to be an issue for the term of the agreement. The fee was not renewed after the agreement expired. Perhaps even the football politicians had become weary of the issue. Charging a management fee had initially been attractive as a means of being recompensed for providing a service, and perhaps also to get something back from the SPL as a consequence of the political fallout following its formation, but using such a mechanism was not sustainable in the long term. As the SFA had an eye on gaining control of all senior and junior appointments, it would have been an impossibility to charge a fee to the various other Leagues and Associations for appointing referees.

Referee Panel

Once a management fee was established, the SPL wished to have an input to enable it to monitor, and have a say on, the operation of the appointment service. This resulted in the formation of the Referee Panel.

The Panel meetings, held periodically through each season, were based around the SFA conveying which referees were to be used in the SPL and reviewing referees' performances. The meetings also allowed other refereeing matters to be addressed. For a few seasons, the SPL paid a bonus to the referees appointed to the SPL matches. It wanted the bonus to be paid on a performance related basis but it was done on a per match basis. The referees who received the most appointments received the highest bonus at the end of the season.

Service Level Agreement
In 2009, the SFA and the SPL entered into a Service Level Agreement in regard to the provision of the referee appointment service.

UEFA Convention on Referee Education and Organisation

The UEFA Audit
UEFA's announcement in 2002 that it was to audit the organisation of refereeing within its member associations was the starting point of the Referee Convention. This had an immediate effect on refereeing in Scotland. The SFA decided to reconstitute the composition of the Referee Committee by effectively making the Supervisors' Executive Committee the committee from season 2003-04.

The UEFA Audit was carried out in May 2003. In addition to receiving a submission on refereeing, UEFA conducted interviews with the SFA Chief Executive, David Taylor, John Smith (Chairman, Referee Committee), relevant SFA staff, Michael McCurry (FIFA Referee) and Ian Blair (SPL Director of Administration). UEFA was more than satisfied with the outcome of the Audit.

The Convention
UEFA used the audits of its member association to formulate the Convention, which was launched at the UEFA Congress of March 2006. The Convention's aims were to:

- establish a refereeing organisation within each National Football Association which is not controlled or influenced by other bodies such as government, leagues or clubs;
- guarantee a unified level of education of match officials and refereeing specialists by delivering a comprehensive education programme from grassroots to professional football;
- continuously improve the status and quality of the above-mentioned match officials and refereeing specialists using appropriate tools and measures;
- define the legal and professional status of match officials in the different member associations

The Convention had two component elements – Education (encompassing the recruitment and retention of referees, the Referee Observer system, a talent and mentor programme and the education of referee at grassroots and elite level) and Organisation (covering the organisation and structure of refereeing matters, and the aims and main tasks of such a structure).

The Referee Committee straightforwardly confirmed that the SFA should apply to become a Convention member and to be considered for selection as a pilot association. As the SFA's refereeing structures largely complied with UEFA's requirements, it was felt that it would be better placed than many other National Associations to become a member. Being at the forefront of refereeing in Europe was held to be important.

The committee was also more than aware that certain areas of the refereeing structure needed attention to fully meet UEFA's requirements, prime amongst which was taking over the SFL's referee appointments. In this respect, and by good fortune, discussions had been held between the SFA and the SFL on the potential provision of services, including refereeing appointments, by the SFA. With the Convention now being on the scene, this provided added impetus to the SFA's case for assuming the SFL's appointments. After further talks, the SFL agreed to transfer its appointments to the SFA from season 2006-07.

The Referee Committee also appreciated that developing the existing referee development programmes to fully comply with the Convention would require an increase in the financial budget, in addition to the funding which UEFA was to provide to Convention members from season 2007-08. This funding was for new referee development projects only and was to be in addition to a National Association's annual refereeing budget.

The creation of the Convention was regarded by the Referee Committee as being "manna from heaven". It was very timely in the furtherance of refereeing in Scotland and referee development throughout Europe, given the common themes which had emerged in relation to recruitment, retention, education and training of referees. In the context of its application to Scotland, the committee considered that the Convention would greatly assist in reinforcing the status of referees within football and highlight their important contribution to the game. The connection to the playing side of the game was fully recognised too, given the SFA's plans to develop and grow the game. It was considered essential for resources to be directed to refereeing development to keep pace with the playing side of the game and to ensure that there were sufficient referees to meet the desired expansion of football in Scotland. Moreover, the education and training of referees would improve the quality of match officials at all levels.

UEFA selected the SFA as one of 11 pilot associations. As part of the application process, a major submission on specific criteria was provided to UEFA. Representatives attended a UEFA Workshop in December 2006, at which three objectives had to be set by each of the pilot associations. The SFA's objectives were:

- Immediate - To increase the number of meetings of elite and assistant referees.
- Medium Term - To provide Polar Heart Rate Monitors to Category 1 referees together with appropriate software for remote monitoring by a Fitness Specialist.
- Long Term - To ensure the certification of Referee Coaches.

A visit by members of UEFA's Certification Panel concluded the application process in May 2007. Similar to the Audit visit, a number of relevant personnel were interviewed, including Sandy Roy (Referee Observer/RA Manager), Craig Thomson (Elite Referee) and Euan Anderson (Talent Referee).

The SFA was admitted into the Convention, one of the first 10 member associations. Membership was subject to the following conditions being met:

- Separating the functions of the Disciplinary & Referee Department
- Regional referee committees or regional development officers to appoint the referees in the lower leagues, given that this is part of the referee's career development
- Senior referees' association to report only to the SFA and not have direct contacts/meetings with Leagues

All the conditions were met within the timescale set by UEFA. The Disciplinary & Referee Department split into the Referee Administration Department and the Disciplinary Department. The Referee Committee determined that, rather than set up regional committees or to create positions of regional development officers, the more appropriate way of dealing with the second condition was for the SFA to gain control of referee appointments in Scottish Junior FA football. This was achieved from season 2008-09. The third condition was surmounted by the SFA's facilitating meetings between the SSFRA and the SPL/SFL.

The SFA became a signatory of the Convention on 27th June 2007.

Panel Members

As part of the Convention, UEFA operates two panels to oversee its operation – the Refereeing Guidelines Panel and the Referee Certification Panel. Scotland's status in refereeing was recognised at the outset by UEFA when it appointed Donald McVicar and Hugh Dallas to the Guidelines Panel and the Certification Panel, respectively, when they were first formed. In his role, Donald McVicar gave assistance to a number of National Associations to support them in their application process to join of the Convention.

Evaluation Visits
To ensure continued compliance with the Convention, UEFA conducts Evaluation Visits every few years. Given the overall structures which are in place, the points which have emerged from these visits have generally been relatively minor and easy to address to meet UEFA's requirements.

UEFA Funding
The funding provided by UEFA has been of real worth to refereeing in Scotland, enabling a variety of projects to be undertaken, most notably the holding of Winter Training Camps and the purchase of Polar Watches for referees.

Convention Workshops
UEFA organises Workshops for the Convention members every few years. These enable UEFA to continue to work towards achieving a uniform approach across all the association. They also provide an excellent opportunity for best practice to develop in the operation of refereeing.

Referee Appointments

Although the SFA has controlled the List since it was created, it was effectively produced for the use of the various Leagues and Associations in senior football. The SFA was only directly responsible for appointing the match officials for its various Cup Competitions, home friendly matches of SFL clubs and a number of District FA Cups. This reflected the historical development of the game in Scotland and was accepted by all parties.

The SFL got "first pick" of referees. Once the SFL published its appointments for a six week cycle, the other Leagues and Associations which used referees on the List carried through their appointments on the basis of which referees were free on the days in question. Somehow, the game got by.

There had always been an element of occasional criticism within the refereeing movement towards the SFL's appointment system, whether in regard to particular individual match appointments or the frequency of their deployment, particularly the top referees. The feeling that things would be better if the SFA had more influence on the appointments, if not outright control, grew during the 1990's.

The opportunity of gaining some control was presented when the SPL was formed in 1998. Since then a complete and utter transformation has been achieved by the SFA as it now controls all the appointments in senior, Junior and women's football. First team competitions are the primary focus for many in football, but the SFA's responsibility extends to all subsidiary competitions (Reserve and Youth etc.) which are organised by Leagues and Associations. As a measure of how much has changed, the SFA was responsible for the appointing of officials to just under 300 matches per season in the 1980's. Now, that figure has exploded to just short of 10,000 matches per season. The change has been stunning.

The Factors behind the Changes
There were a number of factors which influenced this change. The restructuring of the List in 1991 and 1998 had unintended consequences due to the reduction of the number of officials, with regional senior Leagues and Associations experiencing difficulties in appointing referees due to these changes. The creation of the SPL and internal politics within the SFL played an important part at the top level. The designation of a class of referee for Junior football in 1998 had a contributory effect in that grade. The UEFA Referee Convention played a huge part gaining control of the appointments.

The Impact of the Restructuring of the List
The List's restructuring in 1991 had an influence on regional football appointments. Referees resident in the geographical areas of the Highland League, East of Scotland and South of Scotland Leagues were regularly appointed to matches in these competitions when free from an SFL appointment which meant that there was always a sufficient pool of referees available. The regular use of Class 1 and Class 2 referees as linesmen in the SFL reduced the pool for these leagues. The disappearance of Class 3B exacerbated the situation. That gave rise to the SFA

having to introduce schemes, with financial support, for each League to help service their appointments during that first season. These schemes subtly provided the SFA with an increased input into refereeing matters in each of these Leagues. Working relationships which never really existed previously began to be formed.

The changes to the List gave the SFA the chance to assume responsibility for appointing referees to all friendly matches played by its member clubs. Up to that point, the appointments for friendly matches played by clubs in the regional senior leagues were made by the respective League secretaries. The move brought about order in what had been an untidy area. Some form of control over appointments was beginning to take shape. The change increased the number of appointments made by the SFA. The number of friendly match appointments jumped from 85 in 1990-91 to an average of 150 per season over the next few seasons. That increase was to pale into insignificance given what was to come.

The 1998 restructuring of the List gave rise to immediate problems being experienced by football bodies both at national, regional and Junior levels in obtaining referees. The SFA itself experienced difficulties in appointing officials for its two Qualifying Cup competitions. The situation was particularly acute for the East of Scotland League. Very quickly, a number of Class 2 "Junior" Referees from Edinburgh & District RA had to be reclassified to Class 2 for the List so that they could referee in the League. During the autumn, 12 referees were promoted to the List at Class 1 Assistant Referee to provide a greater pool of referees to the SFL for appointment to its Youth League matches played on Sundays. The addition of these referees also increased the pool of officials for the regional Leagues.

These issues increased activity between the SFA and the regional Leagues, particularly the East of Scotland League, to a level which had not existed before. The League was in direct competition with Junior football in its geographical area and was probably seen by referees as being the "poor relation" of the two grades. It was in regular discussion with the SFA on appointment issues. Greater liaison between the League and the local Junior FA on fixture scheduling and the use of referees to best effect was mooted as an attempt to address the issues.

By 2000 the belief was growing within the Referee Committee that the problems might only be resolved in the long term by the SFA *"possibly having a greater input into referee appointments in several categories of football"*. That was merely a polite expression of what lay ahead – the SFA taking control of the appointments.

Setting the Objective

Servicing the game had become a recurring theme. The impact of the non-availability of referees due to injuries, work and holidays was starting to emerge. Regular assistance was given by the SFA administration and some Supervisors to Junior Secretaries on a weekly basis to help them appoint referees to matches. The Referee Committee took the matter seriously, given that it had worked to ensure that the size of the List was sufficient to service the game.

These circumstances, combined with the competing interests which existed in respect of referees' services between the various appointing bodies, were such that there was an increasingly obvious need for a co-ordinated approach to refereeing appointments to be adopted in senior and Junior football. The committee concluded that the SFA should fulfil this role. It just so happened that this discussion, in October 2003, took place at the same meeting when the committee had to address the setting of objectives as requested by the SFA Board. The timing of this coincidence could not have been better.

Thus, it was decided that one of the committee's objectives should be, in consultation with the relevant leagues and associations, to work towards the SFA becoming the central referee appointment body for senior football and, ultimately, for this function to extend to Junior football.

Achieving the objective was going to be an extremely tall undertaking, even allowing for the good sense underpinning it. Persuading the senior leagues to hand over responsibility for refereeing appointments to the SFA was not going to be easy. Quick gains were anticipated with the East of Scotland and

South of Scotland Leagues, but the SFL would present a huge task, given the status and history it held within the game in Scotland. The inclusion of Junior football in the objective was done almost as an afterthought, to make the objective more complete. It was a moment of a "nothing ventured, nothing gained" flight of fancy. The committee was entitled to dream. A timescale for achieving this dream, as well as for senior football, was not set. That was not necessary as the difficulties in doing so were realised. A long haul was expected. Astonishingly, the dream would be realised within five years.

Achieving the Objective
To progress the objective, all the relevant bodies were written to. Not unexpectedly, the East of Scotland and South of Scotland Leagues (and the related District FAs) agreed to transfer their appointments to the SFA from the start of the following season, 2004-05. Within a very short period of the start of that season, the benefits of the SFA carrying out these appointments proved very worthwhile, particularly for the East of Scotland League.

The Highland League, Aberdeenshire FA and North of Scotland FA intimated their agreement, in principle, to their appointments transferring to the SFA at a mutually suitable point in the future. On that basis, the SFA proposed that season 2006-07 should be the target season. Dialogue in the latter part of season 2005-06 was required to clinch the agreement of these bodies, the Highland League being the dominant player of the three. It agreed to transfer the referee appointments on a one season trial basis but wished to retain responsibility for assistant referees' appointments and the appointments for its Youth League competitions for the time being. Some fears were held by clubs about transferring the appointments to the SFA but these were allayed by the work carried out during season 2006-07. The operational benefits for referees and for the clubs which had emerged over the season were obvious. The Highland League was approached to transfer the appointments on a permanent basis, together with the assistants' appointments and its Youth competitions. The League agreed, with the sense of a single body carrying out the appointments being realised.

There was a very tentative and reluctant response from the SFL to the proposal that its appointments transfer to the SFA. Carrying out its own appointments was a longstanding cornerstone of its own activities and functions, similar to the field of player registrations. Removing such an important function would have a major impact on the SFL. Consideration of the transfer of the appointments continued into 2006 as part of discussions which the SFA was then having with the SFL on the provision of common services. These discussions coincided with major internal political issues affecting the SFL's organisation and operations. The advent of the UEFA Referee Convention played a significant part, giving added strength to the SFA's case. It was essential for the SFA's ambitions to take over the SFL's appointments if it was to stand a chance of becoming a member of the Convention.

The SFA won its case. The SFL accepted that its appointments should transfer to the SFA from the start of season 2006-07. It was a remarkable turn of events, given the historical strength of the SFL and its old rivalry with the SFA. To assist in the incorporation of the SFL's appointments into the SFA, the SFL staff member who had main responsibility for appointments transferred to the SFA.

The UEFA Referee Convention played an extremely influential part in gaining control of Junior appointments. Achieving one of the membership conditions became paramount. At this juncture, a wholly unexpected opportunity emerged when the East Region Junior FA invited the SFA to take over its appointments due to the difficulties it had experienced in the early part of season 2007-08. The invitation was gladly accepted. The Junior door was being prized open. The SFA's first appointments for the East Region Junior FA commenced from 27th October 2007.

Given the timescale of a year to implement all of UEFA's conditions, the Referee Committee quickly entered into a dialogue with the Scottish Junior FA in regard to all Junior appointments transferring to the SFA from the commencement of season 2008-09. The SFA Board gave its full support.

The dialogue was greatly assisted by the SFA demonstrating the benefits of carrying out the East Region Junior FA's appointments. It was a persuasive factor. The West Region Junior FA easily agreed but it took more time to persuade the North Region Junior FA. Eventually, after a bit of difficulty, agreement was reached. Gaining control of the appointments for the Scottish Junior Cup, the crown jewel of the Junior game and a hugely important competition for referees, was the icing on the cake for the SFA. The SFA succeeded in its aim of gaining control of all Junior appointments, which was a momentous outcome. A crucial person in the process was Tom Johnston, the Scottish Junior FA Secretary who was also a SFA Board member that season. He made an extremely important contribution in guiding his association and constituent regions through the discussions.

Women's Football
One part of Scottish football which was not covered by the Referee Committee's 2003 objective on appointments was women's football. The growth in women's football has been nothing short of spectacular since 2000, with the SFA directing a great deal of resources, both financial and administrative, towards developing the women's game. It did not take long before the issue of referee appointments arose.

Discussions during season 2005-06 with Scottish Women's Football resulted in the SFA taking over responsibility for the Scottish Women's Premier League (SWPL) for the second half of the season in January 2006.

Towards the end of the following season, the SFA Board, to overcome various difficulties which had emerged in the women's game, decided that the SFA would assume responsibility for the organisation and administration of the SWPL, and, from 2008-09, the Scottish Women's Football League Divisions and the Women's Scottish Cup. All these appointments had to be incorporated into the growing volume of appointments made by the SFA. To illustrate the growth in the women's game, the number of matches doubled from 700 in season 2008-09 to over 1500 in 2019.

A Co-ordinated Approach to Appointments

The SFA's gaining responsibility for the SPL appointments in 1998 enabled a fresh approach to be taken to appointing match officials. The SFL system to that point had been one of intended fairness to the referees in the distribution of appointments. The top referees were appointed to the major league matches but the SFL's well meaning approach to being equable was a restriction none the less. They were not being appointed to enough of these games.

For the SPL, the SFA used a core group of the top Class 1 referees to handle the majority of matches and appointed other referees deemed capable for the League. Aware of the need to maintain a flow of referees into the SPL, new referees were introduced on a selective basis depending on performance and potential. As the SFA now had "first pick" of the referees, the SFL then made its appointments from those who were free on the match days. This comparatively minor change had the consequential effect of forcing a change to how the SFL approached its appointments. For one thing, referees not selected for the SPL received an increased number of SFL match appointments. Refereeing more regularly was always a good thing in respect of performance. Excellent liaison and co-operation between the SFA and the SFL was essential to make the appointment system work and this was achieved.

Once the SFA took over the SFL appointments, it gained the ability to develop an integrated system of appointments as administrative processes became simplified. This integrated approach was taken further when the Junior appointments came under its control. The deployment of referees to match appointments could now be planned in a way which had never existed previously. As an example, referees could be pre-selected for the dates of the latter stages of the Scottish Junior Cup. In the days of the SFL doing its own appointments, it was not concerned with the needs of other competitions. Referees would regularly be denied the chance of refereeing a Junior Cup tie if they had an SFL appointment on that same day. The historical competing interests between appointing bodies had disappeared which benefited referees hugely. Whilst this ability to plan referees' appointments to best effect is a fantastic tool to have to help their progress and development, the clubs have also been beneficiaries of the new approach, although this would have largely gone unnoticed by them. In the Highland League, the referee appointments are made prior to the appointing of the majority of the area's officials to matches in the SFL/SPFL, thus achieving a wholly beneficial outcome to the clubs as the appointments are better planned than was ever possible before.

A fundamental of referee appointments is to appoint the referee most appropriate to the match. This principle is applied at every level of the game. With appointments issued on a weekly basis, the ability to have flexibility with appointments is a crucial aspect of the task. Changes can be effected to take circumstances into account. Referees can be switched between levels to resolve issues, either before or after appointments are published. Carrying out the task is similar to a giant jigsaw puzzle being put together each week. Issues regarding the servicing of the game are a constant factor in the world of referee appointments. It is so much better for everyone that a single body is responsible for overseeing the function, rather than the previous fractured means of appointing officials. Scottish football is in a much better place because of it.

Controlling the Game

The SFA's methods of controlling the game evolved through the 1990's once the Field Discipline Campaign drew to a close. The SFA had to act regularly in regard to external influences and deal with specific issues relating to misconduct which were being thrown up. The Laws of the Game also began to evolve to respond to unwanted trends in football.

George Cumming's appointment opened up the possibility of visiting clubs, at their request, to discuss matters relating to the Laws and field discipline with players and officials. There were not a huge number of requests but a channel of communication between the SFA and the clubs was created. He also attended meetings with the Players' Union and the Managers' and Coaches' Association.

Players' Goal Celebrations

This issue started to emerge slowly during the 1970's and, from the 1990's onwards, it blossomed into a real and recurring problem. Part of the issue has always been the clubs and players denying any responsibility for the problems created by goal celebrations. As ever, the referees had to apply the Laws and the SFA's guidance on such offences.

The Executive Committee took a relaxed view in February 1990, being of the opinion that it should be left to the referee's discretion to deal with players leaving the field of play to celebrate and gesticulate to spectators, given that the referee was able to issue a caution if he deemed that the circumstances merited it. Just a few months later, however, a tougher line had to be adopted following a player being fined in court for gesturing to spectators after a goal was scored. The player had been reported by spectators to the police. The SFA was rightly concerned about the case and notified clubs, the Players' Union, the Managers and Coaches' Association and referees of the part they were expected to play in keeping the police and the courts away from football. Referees had to become very alert to what players were doing when celebrating goals. Periodic reminders to be extra vigilant were issued to referees.

Even if players did not make any inflammatory gestures following a goal, their style of celebration began to create concern and the circumstances where a caution was warranted was addressed at the 1992 Referees' Conference.

A year later, the issue was given even greater focus following a meeting between the SFA and the Association of Chief Police Officers (Scotland). The Police expressed great concern at the failure of referees to caution players who deliberately left the field of play to celebrate a goal and whose actions provoked crowd reaction and crowd surges. Their issue was maintaining order within grounds and it was made extremely clear that they would not hesitate to arrest a player for leaving the field of play to celebrate a goal. Referees and clubs were advised that the immediate cautioning of players in these circumstances was essential if football was to be in control of its own affairs.

Goal celebrations, and the circumstances when cautions should be issued, were discussed at length by the Supervisors in 1995.

Bearing in mind the existing parameters, they were in little doubt that a caution should be issued when a player's gestures were inflammatory or when his celebrations were excessive. The Supervisors recognised that the use of discretion by referees in such matters was still important in judging situations as they arose, and that referees were intervening with players as a preventative measure to cut short their celebrations. Guidelines on dealing with the celebration of a goal were issued in 1996.

Players forever find new ways of celebrating a goal which take root in the game. In 1999, it was agreed that that a player should be cautioned for removing his jersey. Issuing a caution for this offence became part of the Laws of the Game some years later.

The issue evolved further during 2002-03. The likelihood of police intervention remained possible but there was also a realisation that influences from football in other countries were starting to make the SFA's approach look too severe. There was a wide variety of external opinion on what warranted a caution for celebrating a goal. Representatives of the police and the Football Safety Officers Association (Scotland) attended a Category 1 referees' meeting to review the situation. An understanding was reached and Leagues, clubs and referees were notified.

In 2016-17, Police Scotland indicated a shift in its position – the police were no longer going to intervene and take action against a player for excessive celebrations. The police were now content to leave matters entirely with match officials. The guidance given to referees was re-calibrated. A change that year to the Laws of the Game was hugely beneficial to the new guidance which set out that a caution should only be administered to a player celebrating a goal if their deliberate actions caused any safety issues with spectators.

Pre-match Dialogue between Referee, Managers and Captains

This initiative was introduced by the Disciplinary & Referee Committee in season 1992-93 following a suggestion by the Players' Union. It was intended to allow the referee to speak with club personnel on his application of the Laws of the Game which, in turn, would be relayed to the other players. It was hoped that the procedure, which was common in other countries, would have a beneficial effect in helping to improve communications and relationships between the participants and help to create a better pre-match environment than existed in some circumstances. The dialogue was effective for the opening period of the season when the referees carried out their part of the bargain. Soon though, there was a lack of interest shown by the club personnel who stopped attending and the worth of the dialogue petered out. It was tried again for the opening two months of the following season before falling into abeyance.

Occupants of the Technical Area
The Referee Committee issued guidance on how many persons could be in the Technical Area during season 1993-94. This followed a discussion within the game on the conduct of managers and coaches in the technical areas during matches in relation to unacceptable behaviour and the steps which could be taken to improve the situation.

Guidance and regular reminders have been given to referees to ensure that managers and coaches conduct themselves, as required by the Laws of the Game, in a responsible manner. It can be a thankless task at times. Misbehaviour by managers and coaches in Scottish football regularly stretches the boundaries and those who go too far can have no complaints when they find themselves removed from the Technical Area.

Police Involvement
In the early to mid-1990's, the police cast a big shadow over Scottish football which placed greater responsibility and pressure on referees to ensure that the Laws of the Game were complied with in matches.

By December 1995, when the SFA interviewed several match officials about their handling of match incidents, Jim Farry was compelled to advise the Supervisors that the SFA was under extreme pressure from outside agencies in terms of its control of the game and that these difficulties stemmed directly from the non-application of the Laws of the Game by top referees. He stressed that the SFA wished to retain its jurisdiction over sporting matters and that players adhering to the Laws and referees applying them were vital. A strong unambiguous signal was issued to all parties to this effect.

Within less than a year, the situation took a serious turn when, following the conclusion of the Duncan Ferguson case in the civil courts, the Lord Advocate issued Guidelines on incidents during sporting events, which set out the parameters for the potential involvement of the police and the courts in sporting matters. The SFA had been consulted by the Lord Advocate during the course of the preparation of the guidelines and its views were reflected in the Guidelines to a certain extent. The Guidelines placed an additional burden on referees to ensure that the Laws are adhered to and applied. Equally, that responsibility also lies with all other participants in the game - players, managers and coaches and spectators. Thankfully, and for the good of football, the Lord Advocate has kept his powder dry since the Guidelines were introduced.

Meetings of Club Personnel

Over the last 20 years, a system of meetings with club managers under the SFA's Club Licensing has been developed. It grew out of pre-season meetings, often joint ones with the Category 1 referees, to review changes to the Laws of the Game and the impact these would have on the refereeing of games. For a period, the club captain was required to attend such meetings. Under Club Licensing, attendance at the meetings became compulsory for managers. Guidance issued by UEFA on refereeing is disseminated at the meetings, with many video clips of match incidents used to demonstrate Law changes and how referees are expected to apply the Laws of the Game. Despite being kept well informed of how offences such as serious foul play are interpreted, managers continue to be totally mystified on far too many occasions when one of their players is sent off.

Setting the Tone

The SFA's role in setting the tone for controlling the game has altered over the years. Right from the birth of the SFA, there was an idealistic approach taken to ensure that the game was played in a sporting manner. That approach was maintained for many years through the operation of the committee system. The various Secretaries played a hugely important part in keeping the committees' hands on the tiller.

The approach has taken a different form in recent years, coinciding to some degree with the old committee system being abolished. The past focus on the manner by which the game is played has disappeared as other matters have come to pre-occupy the Boards at the SFA. Any gap which has been created in this regard has been filled by the Referee Operations Department having to ensure that the game's participants are properly advised of changes to the Laws of the Game. In the last 30 years there have been many key changes to the Laws to counteract developments in the playing of the game which reduced it as a spectacle. IFAB is now the world wide body trying to set the tone for how football is played, supported by FIFA and UEFA. Ultimately, it all comes down to referees applying the Laws of the Game.

Specsavers Sponsorship

Early in 2002, FIFA gave the go-ahead for match officials to carry advertising on their shirts. The SFA was quick off the mark to pursue this potential sponsorship avenue and, by June, had secured an agreement with Specsavers Opticians. A four year agreement worth £750,000 was reached and was launched in September. The SFA was the first National Association in the world to obtain such sponsorship.

With FIFA's regulations stipulating that all monies received by a National Association through such a contract must be invested in the development of refereeing, this was a huge boost to the SFA and greatly assisted in sustaining and expanding the referee development programmes.

With an opticians company sponsoring referees, this very predictably drew many wisecracks from the media and spectators in the beginning but things soon settled down.

The agreement between the SFA and Specsavers still continues and it has become the SFA's longest running deal in its history.

Specsavers has been delighted with the benefits it receives from its sponsorship. The SFA's relationship with Specsavers has gone from strength to strength with the company supporting a number of the referee development programmes over the years.

Referees' Conference

By the late 1980's, the Referees' Conference was firmly established as the high point of the refereeing calendar. It was the SFA's vehicle for bringing referees of all classes together for instruction, debate and discussion with a fine social aspect to it. Under the direction of George Cumming, the Conference was transformed into an even bigger event for the refereeing movement.

Format and content
With Cumming in place, it was an easy decision for the Supervisors to pass responsibility over to him to prepare the Conference programme. Having a full time staff member dealing with the programme meant that planning and preparation could be carried out in a way that was not possible under the Supervisors. This had a natural dramatic impact on the development of the Conference. So much more could be done.

Issues had firstly to be teased out between the Supervisors and Cumming in 1989. The Supervisors wanted to retain the Sports Competition held late on the Saturday afternoon, something which had been an integral part of Conference. The Sports continued for two more years before becoming a 5-a-side football competition for a while until the competiveness became too much (which was very typical of the way referees played, or tried to play, football). The quiz for the Peter Scott Trophy stopped in 1990. The Open Forum was limited to four panellists with questions being submitted in advance, thus getting round the awkward silences before a referee plucked up the courage to break the ice. A crucial element to the Conference was the ability to strike a balance between the serious and the lighter, more entertaining aspects. This was maintained over the years.

Practical sessions were introduced as a regular component of Conference. The use of video material on Laws of the Game issues for group discussions became a staple element. Within a couple years, the success of the changes led to the further evolution of the programme. A much higher degree of input on refereeing matters had been quickly achieved and more sessions for defined groups of referees became the norm. The Coaching Co-ordinators were used to conduct sessions and, in a sign of the progress being made, Cumming met with them on the Saturday morning before the Conference got underway to ensure that a uniform approach was taken at the coaching sessions.

New ground was broken as various themes, such as co-operation between referees and linesmen, dealing with touch-line confrontation, fitness, diet and warm-up, were addressed. Meetings of specialised groups such as Coaching Co-ordinators and Minor Grade Advisory Panel members were held. The needs of the different groupings of referees had to be balanced in each year's Programme.

In 1994, the four largest Referees' Associations conducted practical demonstrations. The use of match incidents from Scottish matches became a regular feature of discussion groups, with explanations being given by the match referees, supplemented by a Supervisor and, where appropriate, the linesmen. The Conference began to be given a theme each year and 1995's "Learning from Experience" captured perfectly the nature of such discussions.

The format continued to evolve with a greater use of specialised meetings of groups of referees alongside the standard plenary sessions. A major change was achieved in 1997 when the List was confirmed prior to the Conference rather than after it. This simple change of procedure enabled the group meetings of referees to be properly formed in the Classes which were to apply the following season. The Conference provided an excellent opportunity to issue guidance on the application of new Law changes.

Guest speakers continued to be invited to Conference. A major coup was achieved in 1993 when Sepp Blatter, then FIFA's General Secretary, addressed Conference. Other speakers included a return visit by Ken Ridden, a member of UEFA's Referee Committee and The Football Association's Director of Refereeing, a former Scottish international rugby referee, Jim Fleming, the athletics coach Tommy Boyle and the famous French referee Michel Vautrot.

Attendances

During the mid-1980's, attendances at the Conference were around the 250 mark. Attendance grew substantially throughout the next decade and into the 2000's to around 400, and sometimes more. The initial growth stemmed from a desire to have the all the referees on the List present. Whilst attendance previously had been on a voluntary basis, something of a "three line whip" was introduced. All Listed officials were encouraged to attend. With good reason, as the topics being addressed were very relevant to the performance of their duties. Absence, without advance intimation, was noticeable. It was a means to drive improvement in performance.

Another contributory factor to the increase in attendance was the move to attract younger and new referees to the Conference. In 1991, 25% of the attendance of 400 was first timers. Attending Conference became important for career progression. It also played a part in the retention of referees, with the hope that, by attending and being in the company of the country's top referees, the interest of the newcomers would be captured.

The success of the increased attendances was such that by 1998, a second lecture theatre had to be used for the opening and other plenary sessions. The age of technology enabled the sessions to be broadcast from the main theatre to the other.

Financial Support

The SFA continued to provide financial support to the referees attending the Conference. In 1991 a system was devised in an effort to attract greater numbers to attend.

Classes 1 and 2 paid the full cost, Classes 3A and 3B paid 75% and all other referees paid 50%.

The basis for the Class 1 and Class 2 referees paying the full charge was that they received the highest fees amongst referees. When the Registration Scheme for Referees was launched, referees who were not members of the Scheme paid the full charge.

Allowing for the alterations to the classification system which followed in later years, this fee structure remained in place. In 2003, the charge for Probationary and Youth referees attending the Conference for the first time was dropped to offer support to them and to provide the opportunity of discovering what the refereeing movement offered.

From 2006, the travelling expenses of referees attending the conference were no longer reimbursed, given the rising costs of the University charges and the level of subsidy provided by the SFA.

Financial Cost to the SFA

The net cost to the SFA of holding the Conference grew very quickly during the 1990's. From just over £10,000 in 1990, the cost more than doubled to £22,000 in 1992 and reached £36,000 in 1996. More resources had to be devoted to it to provide all the necessary materials, the cost of accommodation for committees and referees grew substantially as did the cost of the subsidies provided to the referees. During the 1990's, Rusacks Hotel in St. Andrews was taken over entirely by the SFA for Conference weekend. The SFA Office Bearers had maintained regular attendance at Conference and the demand for rooms at Rusacks Hotel led to their moving to the Old Course Hotel. From 1998, to save costs, the Supervisors and others were accommodated in New Hall at the University of St. Andrews.

International Guests

For the 1992 Conference, a number of refereeing guests from other European National Associations were invited to attend the Conference. This proved a great success and heralded the dawn of inter-Association exchange visits to referee courses. The guests gave lustre to Conference. The SFA's standing in the refereeing world was certainly boosted by their attendance. The Supervisors held a meeting with the international guests to start the weekend off. Common problems could be discussed and ideas picked up on how to deal with them. The guests were always staggered by the size of the attendance at Conference and its content given that referees from all categories were present. Their own courses were much smaller and focused on national groupings of referees.

A Dinner for the International Guests was held on Friday evenings, with the FIFA referees invited to attend.

All Good Things Come to an End

Following the 2002 Conference, the first indications of doubts about its future and continuing worth emerged when Donald McVicar flagged concerns at a Supervisors' meeting. The general thought was that the Conference had become too big with a view expressed that attendance should be restricted to only those who the SFA wished to be there.

A year later, the Referee Committee discussed the overall purpose and function of the Conference in the context of the various development programmes and meetings which were currently organised. The feeling was growing that these were detracting from the overall impact of Conference.

The committee reviewed the Conference again in 2005. The emphasis of Conference had increasingly shifted over the previous years from the educational to the social side given the advent of technology and the increased use of educational material at the associations' monthly meetings. The introduction of DVDs of coaching material had essentially superseded the need for Discussion Groups at the Conference, something that had been a traditional element of the programme. A crunch point was whether value for money was being achieved by Conference and if the financial resources could be put to better use for the benefit of refereeing. The annual net cost to the SFA by this time was approximately £40,000. The difficulties of compiling a fresh programme each year for over 400 referees, arranging Guest Speakers, and the problems caused every second year by major football championships being held at the time of the Conference were recognised. It was realised that the top referees were gaining little direct benefit from the Conference. This was still counterbalanced, however, by the beneficial effects of referees from all categories mixing at the Conference and the less experienced and younger referees being able to glean knowledge from senior referees.

After much deliberation, the committee decided that, despite the costs involved, there was still a purpose to be served by continuing with the Conference. An invitation-based system was introduced for the 2006 Conference to determine the attendees. The attendees were to be actively involved in refereeing and determined by attendance at five monthly meetings during the season, with the final decision being taken by the RA Managers. The non-payment of a fee by first time attendees continued to encourage their participation and involvement in the refereeing movement.

There was reluctance on the part of the committee to bring the Conference to an end given the understandable strong emotional ties the members had to it. It had been a constant throughout their time in refereeing. However, the realities of life had to be faced in 2007. Donald McVicar raised again the continuing place of the Conference within the overall Referee Development programme. The UEFA Referee Convention was now a major consideration in the equation, given that it required greater focus to be given to increasing the number of meetings of the top categories of referees and specialist groups. Consequently, it was accepted that the Conference had run its course. An announcement was made at that year's Conference to say that it was the last in its present format and that it would be replaced by specialist group meetings and workshops. It was a poignant day for many when the Conference ended given the special place it had held in the refereeing movement.

Summer Training Camp

The Summer Training Camp replaced the Referees' Conference for referees in Categories 1 to 3. The strong bonds with St. Andrews led to the first four Camps being held at the University in early June. The Camp quickly found its feet as a much leaner and fitter version of Conference. The Fitness Test was fitted into the schedule in response to the earlier start of the football season. Presentations were made and guidance given on the refereeing issues of the day.

The Camp was initially held over two days and was trimmed to one day after moving from St. Andrews.

To enable the SFA to conduct the Fitness test on a national basis for Category 1 through to 3 Development, two venues are arranged for the Test to be conducted in the morning with plenary and group sessions being held in the afternoon. The Camp has been held at the University of Stirling and Heriot-Watt University.

The Observers first attended the Camp in 2009 to participate in discussions on the new assessment system being introduced for the new season. Their attendance has become a standing element of the Training Camp, providing as it does the chance to have joint meetings with the referees.

Winter Training Camp

Donald McVicar had long wished to hold an overseas Winter Training Camp similar to those held by other European associations for their top referees. To have the ability to train referees as a group and to have in-depth discussions on refereeing was always an appealing thought. The possibilities were explored for a few years and the plan came to fruition in 2008.

Financial savings were generated by the ending of the Referees' Conference and other areas of refereeing operations and these, combined by the use of funding provided by UEFA for the Referee Convention, enabled the Training Camp to be introduced. Low cost flights helped considerably. Careful attention also had to given to selecting the Camp dates. The SPL and SFL co-operated to ensure that first team fixtures were not scheduled for the midweek in question. Avoiding dates for potential Scottish Cup replays was also part of the planning equation.

The Category 1 referees were taken to Marbella in Spain for four days in mid-February. A great deal of organisation took place in advance to determine the travelling party. The lure of the Camp paid off as the referees were able to arrange time off work to go.

The Camp was hugely successful. Under the supervision of John McQuade, the National Referee Fitness Coach, the referees went through intensive training schedules each day. The Camp was the first occasion that the Category 1 referees had trained as a group and that in itself was an important factor. Referees could compare themselves with the whole group, rather than just the colleagues they trained with at their own associations. Referees had to apply themselves, given the scrutiny they were under. The bonus of it all was that the training was done in warm weather, which was a complete contrast to the winter weather back home. For relatively little more expenditure, the Camp had provided much better value for four days than the weekend January courses which had been held at hotels in Scotland in the preceding years. The training and the level of coaching achieved would have been impossible to achieve at these meetings. The referees undoubtedly benefited from the Camp. Beyond the primary reasons for holding it, the event gave them the chance to be with their colleagues and to develop camaraderie.

The Camp became a fixture in the Referee Development Programme. After a couple of years in Marbella, the La Manga resort in Spain became the venue. The Specialist Assistant Referees were included in the party in 2015.

A high level of attendance of the referees is always achieved for the Camp, which is credit to them for using holiday entitlements. Conflicts of commitments arose with some FIFA referees as they were required to attend UEFA Courses around the same time, which took priority. Some Category 2 referees and some of the graduates of the SCORE Course attended the 2015 Camp.

The Camp has proved to be extremely beneficial to the SFA and to the referees since its inception. The referees approached it in exactly the correct manner and reaped the rewards. George Cumming set out to professionalise refereeing in the 1990's. The success of the Camp provides a great example of that aim being achieved.

Despite the Camp's success, it was not held in 2019 to allow the Online Introductory Course to be developed and financed. The intention was that the Camp should be held bi-annually but the

Covid pandemic unfortunately intervened and has interrupted plans for the Camp to return.

Regional Training Days

With the Summer Training Camp replacing the Referees' Conference for the Listed referees, Regional Training Days were introduced as the equivalent replacement for other referees.

They were aimed at referees below Category 3. The objective was to attract as many referees as possible to the Training Days and particularly those who would not usually attend the Conference. The Training Days are a mix of practical sessions and discussions. In their first year, 2008, events were held in Glasgow, Aberdeen and Tulliallan on Sundays in the spring. They got off to a very successful start and were well received by the referees.

The programme of meetings evolved to take account of logistical issues. A schedule was soon established along the following lines:

- West of Scotland - (Glasgow, Renfrewshire, Ayrshire, South of Scotland)
- North of Scotland - (Moray & Banff & North of Scotland)
- North East Scotland - (Aberdeen, Angus & Perthshire, Fife)
- Central Scotland - (Edinburgh, Lanarkshire, Stirlingshire)

The venues for the Camps can vary to balance out travelling times for the associations. In more recent years, the Oriam National Performance Centre at Heriot-Watt University has been used a central venue for all associations with the exception of Moray & Banff RA and North of Scotland RA which use the Highland Football Academy in Dingwall.

Referee Coaches, Category 1 referees and Category 3 Specialist Assistant Referees lead the practical sessions and discussions, which enable them to pass on the benefits of their experiences to the attendees.

Scheduling of the Training Days can be problematic given that they are held on Sundays, a day when many of the attendees are refereeing. Close liaison between the RA Managers and local football secretaries is required to enable the optimum date for a Training Day to be set.

As a consequence of the Review of the Referees' Associations, the SFA doubled the number of Regional Training Days held to enable an increase in practical coaching to balance off the reduction of meetings held by the associations.

The Regional Training Days have been a very welcome innovation into the Referee Development Programme. They are proof of the SFA's commitment to extend its involvement to referees of all categories. They are very successful and well regarded by those who attend. A great deal of preparatory work is required in advance to enable that to happen. The excellent contributions of the coaches and referees as the leaders demonstrate their commitment to the refereeing movement. It is not just the attending referees who benefit from their experienced input but the grassroots football clubs they referee each week. A better standard of referee is the desired end product.

SCORE

The success of UEFA's CORE Course prompted John Fleming to consider replicating a similar format for the benefit of Scottish refereeing, with the similar aim of identifying and developing young talented referees and assistant referees into future elite referees.

The Scottish Centre of Refereeing Excellence (SCORE) course was designed in conjunction with Heriot-Watt University during 2014. The course, to run over a season, consisted of a number of academic modules, such as sports science, psychology and management, together with advanced coaching on refereeing matters. The participants were offered individually tailored fitness sessions and assessments with designated fitness instructors throughout the year of the course. Nine referees were selected from 58 applicants, with three referees chosen from Categories 2 Development, 3 and 3 Development.

The course programme was intensive for the candidates. On the refereeing side, this involved specialist coaching, being filmed refereeing matches, the use of polar data for fitness and attendance at Category 1 and FIFA officials' meetings to aid their development.

The course was very successful and it was an easy decision to continue. SCORE has gone from strength to strength. In its second year, focus was given to selecting potential specialist assistant referees. In the succeeding years, a balance was struck in the selection of officials for the roles of referee and assistant referees to enable team appointments to be made to matches. The component elements of the course are continually refined and developed to maintain its quality.

The number of applications for each year's course is high, which reflects its success and how it is viewed by referees. Seven of the original nine selected referees progressed to Category 1. By 2021, an offshoot of SCORE came into being – SCORE Select, a course for SCORE graduates which aims to increase the performance standards of a small number of current Category 1 officials who are deemed potential candidates for FIFA status. These referees are provided with coaching and information on different aspects of football and refereeing at a more in-depth level than offered by the standard SCORE course.

Not long after the SFA started SCORE, similar courses came to be introduced by other European National Associations as they also copied the UEFA model. The creation of such courses is a clear indication of the continuing drive to develop refereeing. The SFA has been at the forefront of such progress.

Women Referees

The SFA has long been alert to the need to recruit and develop women referees. This focus has increased considerably since 2000 as women's football has grown rapidly over the period.

In 1999, there were 44 registered women referees. Attention was given to ensuring the inclusion of women in the Referee Development Academy launched that year. 10 females attended the first Academy meeting.

More encouragement had to be given to the development and promotion of women referees. It was always going to be helpful when a female referee emerged who wanted to progress and who could show the way for others to follow. That happened in 2001, when Aberdeen & District RA's Morag Pirie was admitted to the List at Class 2, the first female to progress to the List. She was promoted to Category 3 two seasons later, refereeing in the Highland League and running the line in SFL and SFA competitions.

In advance of her admission to the List, it was established that women had to meet the same Fitness Test conditions as males, an approach consistent with all other European associations. The FIFA List soon beckoned for Morag Pirie and she had a distinguished international career as both an assistant and as a referee. The SFA capitalised as much as possible to promote Pirie as a role model for other females. Local and regional press in her area did a similar job. She was followed on to the List by Lorraine Clark in 2005, who reached Category 1 status, and Kylie McMullan in 2012 who became a Specialist Assistant Referee.

The women who have progressed to the FIFA List have led the way for the development of female referees. They are the top of the pyramid but it is fully understood that a strong base has to be developed to provide for the future.

The recruitment of women referees was boosted in 2011 following the appointment of the Referee Recruitment and Education Managers. Meetings of women referees were introduced on a regular basis to assist with their development. Further impetus was given when the Referee Committee members assumed responsibility for various areas of refereeing – female referees being one such area.

Angus & Perthshire RA, with the support of the SFA East Region, held a successful female only refereeing course in 2014. Other associations were encouraged to follow suit. It was not always positive news though. The SFA North Region ran a female only Awareness Course but none of the 20 participants expressed an interest in completing the Introductory Course and becoming a registered referee.

Despite various campaigns over the years and much effort being expended, the recruitment of women referees has been problematic. In August 2023, the SFA had 99 registered women referees. It had taken 24 years to double their number.

A strategy for female refereeing has been implemented covering many strands of activity. Social media platforms such as Twitter and Facebook are heavily used to promote female refereeing. With the assistance of the SWPL and SWFL, information on refereeing has been regularly included within a regular newsletter issued to clubs. Women's football continues to grow and the potential for recruiting referees from players who stop playing at a young age exists. A recent development, in partnership with S1 Jobs, has been the provision of a female only online course.

Increasing the number of women referees is a constant goal of the SFA and it will continue to hold training and coaching meetings for them to help their development and progression. For those who demonstrate the commitment and ability, the opportunities which exist in women's football are growing all the time.

Radio Communication

Radio communication first appeared on the scene in the early 2000's. It had initially been tried in France with its success catching FIFA's and UEFA's attention. The equipment used quickly improved and, after a number of trials in SPL matches, it was clear that the match officials found using it to be very beneficial. The view was quickly reached the system had great potential to improve communication between a referee and his assistants. Liaison was instantly speeded up. The potential that the communication sets had as a coaching tool for young referees was recognised at the outset.

Four communication sets were purchased initially and more were bought as more funding became available. Funding received from the UEFA Referee Convention greatly assisted the expansion of the scheme. The systems were used initially in the SPL and extended to matches in other competitions as the number of sets increased.

FIFA referees were eventually provided with their own systems by UEFA. The use of the system extended in time to the Observers, who can listen in to the match officials' conversations to better understand their team work and decision making process. The option to connect in to the communications kit is now optional for Observers, with it being particularly helpful to use with lesser experienced referees for coaching purposes.

All Category 1 and Category 2 referees now use communication systems. It has become such an established part of refereeing that referees in lower categories have purchased their own equipment.

Scottish Senior Football Referees' Association

Formation

The Scottish Senior Football Referees' Association (SSFRA) was born out of a desire of Class 1 referees to have dialogue with the SFA on refereeing matters. In 2004, a Trades Union had written to all the Class 1 referees to encourage them to join it. The Referee Committee held the view that the more palatable option would be for a representative group of referees to meet with the SFA. It was hoped that such a development would stave off any perceived need on the part of referees to join a Union.

John Smith (Referee Committee Chairman) and George Peat (SFA Vice-President) met with representatives of the referees in August 2004 to discuss the various issues raised by them. That they were involved on behalf of the SFA was an indication as to the seriousness which the Board was taking the issue. The potential of referees becoming unionised was something which was to be resisted.

Agreement was reached on the formation of a Referees' Representative Group to enable dialogue with the SFA on refereeing issues beyond the existing available avenues.

When the referees submitted a draft Constitution and Rules for the SSFRA early in 2006, further dialogue ensued which concluded in the Board approving its formation. After past rejections of proposals relating to the formation of referees' bodies outside of the Referees' Associations, the SFA had finally agreed to the formation of such a group. In the modern era, it was hardly in a position to refuse given that its Articles of Association allowed for the formation of *"associations, leagues, or other combinations of clubs, officials, players or referees"*.

Business Issues

The Referee Committee is content for senior staff to conduct meetings with the SSFRA representatives and for reports to be made to it. The first meeting was held in the autumn of 2006 and, unsurprisingly, passed off well. The Referee Committee quickly came to recognise that these meetings provided a forum for improved communication and an opportunity for referees to raise a variety of issues. At that first meeting, the SSFRA put forward its views on the possibility of equalising the retiral ages of Category 1 referees and assistant referees, a matter in which it ultimately had success within a few years.

Meetings between the SSFRA and the SFA are generally held twice a season, and the same schedule operated for the SPL and SFL until these two bodies merged in 2013. The SSFRA has also had meetings with the Scottish Junior FA. To enable compliance with a membership condition of the UEFA Referee Convention, an SFA representative is always present at meetings between the SSFRA and other bodies. The main element of discussions between the SSFRA and the Leagues, the SPL and SPFL in particular, has been fees. These negotiations were often prolonged.

Numerous refereeing issues have been addressed between the SSFRA and the Referee Committee, with a positive working relationship being well established. The Referee Committee has supported the position of the SSFRA on several matters when submissions are made to the SFA Board, most notably on creation of a structure for friendly match fees and on the consideration every two years of the SFA's Referee Tariff. The SSFRA is consulted whenever any amendments are being considered for the Letter of Appointment/Notice of Classification. There has been a close relationship on the evolution of the assessment system.

Harmonious arrangements exist between the SSFRA and the football bodies but in 2015 there was a period of turbulence during negotiations with the SPFL on fees when relationships with the SPFL and the SFA deteriorated for a while. This led to the Referee Committee wishing the SFA to enter into a "Memorandum of Understanding" with the SSFRA to regularise the discussions on refereeing matters between each party. This was agreed to by the SSFRA.

The prospect of a Trades Union seeking to become involved with the SFA on behalf of the SSFRA emerged for a brief spell and, whilst there is still a possibility that this might crop up at some point, the SFA's view remains that football's interests, and those of the referees, will continue to be best served by the existing arrangements.

When the SFA replaced its Council with Congress in 2015, the SSFRA was invited to appoint a representative. Along with the standard representatives of Leagues and Associations, the Congress also comprises representative stakeholders in the game from managers, coaches, supporters, referees and the media. Due to the changes in the SFA's governance structures in recent years, referees now have a seat at a table in some form.

Child Wellbeing

Numerous societal changes over the years have had an impact on football. One has been that of child wellbeing, or child protection as it was initially termed. Football, along with other governing bodies of sports and many other organisations, had to respond to legislation in 2002 and has had to integrate child wellbeing procedures into its structures for the benefit of its participants. Whilst the main aim was to introduce procedures to protect young players in football, refereeing also had to be covered.

Initial steps had been taken in 2000 when a SFA-produced booklet on Child Protection was issued to all registered referees. As a consequence of the 2002 legislation, all persons entering the refereeing movement had to undertake a Scottish Criminal Record Office (SCRO) check with the SFA, as the responsible body, bearing the costs incurred for the SCRO checks conducted.

Each association adopted a Child Protection Policy and appointed a Child Protection Co-ordinator. A module on Child Protection was introduced into the Introductory Course training classes and courses were held for training class instructors on Child Protection.

Disclosure Checks (as the SCRO Checks were renamed) were introduced in 2004. These Checks were superseded in 2011 when the Protecting Vulnerable Groups (PVG) Scheme came into operation.

In 2015, the SFA appointed a Child Protection Officer to introduce a standardised approach across all elements of the game in Scotland. A new Child Wellbeing and Protection Policy was developed for football and adapted for the purposes of referees. A training workshop was held for the Child Protection Co-ordinators (now renamed Child Wellbeing and Protection Co-ordinator (CWPC)) to keep them alert to new developments. Trained tutors in Children's Wellbeing delivered a Module at Introductory Courses, thus removing the need for a Child Protection Co-ordinator to fulfil the task.

In 2016 the SFA Board issued major directives to all SFA members on Children's Wellbeing, given what had emerged on child abuse in Scottish football. The Referee Committee addressed how best to incorporate these directives into the refereeing movement. It decided that all referees who were registered prior to 2004 and who were still in membership should be required to go through a check. When Disclosure Checks were introduced, they were undertaken by those entering the refereeing movement. For cost reasons, registered referees at the time were excluded from the process. There were 780 referees in this category. A not inconsiderable financial cost was borne by the SFA in conducting these checks. By carrying this out, the committee considered that the SFA would be seen as having taken appropriate steps to mitigate any potential issues arising in future.

It was also decided that all registered referees should complete an online module on Child Wellbeing. It was a major undertaking to accomplish this task when it was launched during season 2018-19, but it was eventually completed. Close co-operation between the SFA and the associations was essential during the process. Predictably perhaps, some referees were lost as they did not wish to do the module. In the event of their choosing to return to refereeing in the future, these referees have to undertake a Disclosure Check and to complete the Module.

Another strand in the approach adopted is that referees are required to submit a self-declaration form to the SFA in the event of being found guilty in court of a relevant offence.

Consistent with the approach taken in club football, completion of the online module is certificated for three years. It is mandatory for a referee to complete the module to maintain registration. The Module is also completed by candidates taking the Introductory Course.

Any Child Wellbeing cases which arise in refereeing are referred to the SFA's Child Wellbeing and Safeguarding Officer for initial assessment and investigation. Once that is completed, the Safeguarding Officer can decide to act on the case or to refer it back to the referee's association. In the latter case, the expertise of the SFA is always available to the association.

Anti-Referee Culture

Regrettably, an anti-referee culture is deeply embedded in Scottish football. It manifests itself through various inter-connected strands – players, managers, clubs, supporters and the media – which feed off each other to the huge detriment of the game. As the years pass, it all seems to have got worse. Referees are blamed regularly by players and managers for defeats their team have suffered. Managers have no compunction about lambasting referees for all sorts of things, the media easily accept and report what they are told in interviews without any real thought of challenging what has been said. Pundits on television and the radio can spend more time berating referees' decisions in an ill-informed manner than they do giving any analysis on the game. Clubs feed off the furores which are created and form grievances against this or that referee. Supporters respond to all of this. The Scottish footballing public is subliminally conditioned by media reporting from an early age to have little respect for referees and to regard them as almost the root of all evil for decisions given against their club.

Preventative Measures

This backdrop forms a very difficult environment for referees to operate in. The issues created by this culture have increasingly impacted on referees and have led to measures being taken in an attempt to mitigate them.

In 1995 the Class 1 referees expressed their concern that their safety was becoming increasingly endangered when leaving grounds, primarily after SFL Premier Division matches. The fear of a referee being assaulted was real. The following season a referee was verbally abused by home supporters as he was leaving the stadium with his linesmen after a Premier Division match and was followed by a supporter, who continued to abuse him, on his way to the car park.

Clubs were reminded that it was their responsibility to ensure the safe arrival and departure of match officials to and from their grounds. Referees were given the option of either contacting clubs to seek assistance in travelling to and from an agreed location before and after matches, or to request the help of club stewards or officials to be escorted to their cars after matches.

When the SFA assumed responsibility for the SPL appointments in 1998, the referees for each match were collected and returned to a hotel to avoid these sorts of issues. It made their life easier and assisted also in the professionalising of refereeing.

Following media intrusion at a referee's house, the Referee Committee decided that a referee's place of residence should no longer be detailed in match appointments issued to clubs and the media, in match programmes and in team sheets. This approach was extended some years later when the SFA stopped providing referees' names and contact details in its handbook each season. Information could be passed on to others. Only the names of the referees are now provided.

These measures might seem to be somewhat slight in attempting to give some protection to referees, but when a referee received over 40 abusive and threatening calls following a match, as happened in 2000, something had to be done.

Disquiet at Disciplinary Case Outcomes

Over the years, a perception grew within the referee movement that there was a lack of support given towards them due to outcomes of SFA Disciplinary Committee cases. The feeling was that the sanctions issued were often too lenient and did little to discourage misconduct. As the 2000's progressed, these feelings grew, particularly when legal representation came to be allowed at disciplinary and appeal hearings. At times referees felt that they were under greater scrutiny than the person reported for misconduct.

Increasing Levels of Constant Criticism

By March 2008, the general climate had become so bad that the then Referee Committee Chairman, Alan McRae, expressed concern on the increasing trend of negative reports and comment on refereeing standards. The committee debated what could be done to help reverse the trend and improve attitudes but the intractable nature of the problems meant that it was virtually impossible to come up with proposals.

A classic situation of its kind hit the SFA that year when a club rebelled against the appointment of a replacement referee for a Scottish Cup tie. The club had somehow thought that, after a match a few seasons previously, the referee would never be appointed to one of its matches again. The club's stance was a clear indication of an anti-referee culture. It was disabused of its position and was dealt with by the General Purposes Committee for its troubles. The case generated media coverage and it was hard not to form the view that the club used the media to manipulate the situation to discredit the referee.

A tipping point was reached in the aftermath of a Dundee United v. Celtic match in October 2010 when an almighty furore broke out about the non-award of a penalty kick to Celtic. As the preceding weeks had seen an almost constant barrage of criticism against referees, their feelings boiled over. The impact of what flowed from this match and what had gone before led to the infamous "weekend of non-availability" in November when the majority of referees declared themselves to be unavailable for appointment. An extremely low point was reached in Scottish football. The referees tried to set out the reasons for their action through the media but any benefits gained were short-lived. Some involved in football had accepted that maybe the referees had a point but it did not take long for the normal service of referee criticism to be resumed.

When the SFA replaced its Council with Congress in 2015, a number of Advisory Groups from the Congress members were created to look into football issues. One group was set up to analyse the relationship between match officials, clubs, players, coaches and the media with a view to suggesting practical improvements for wider consideration and implementation. A survey was issued to clubs and referees as a starting point. The response from referees was excellent but, disappointingly, only nine clubs responded. That was a sad reflection of the attitudes held by clubs. The initiative floundered, unsurprisingly.

The introduction of VAR into Scottish football has added to the anti-referee culture. Some major clubs in the country have developed a tendency to "go after" referees in communications with the SFA, using the media to demonstrate to their supporters that they are taking the cudgels up on their behalf. The anti-referee culture is something which affects the recruitment and retention of referees. There is little doubt that the attitudes displayed by players and managers towards referees in senior football cascades its way down to grassroots football and causes problems at that level. Such problems are not unique to Scotland. They exist in every other country. Until football stops living in denial about them, resolving the issues will be an impossible task.

Referees and the Media

Referees giving explanations of decisions has been an issue spoken about for many years, driven by comment from club managers and the media for their own reasons of self interest rather than for the good of the game. It has become a standard part of the debate around football and life keeps getting breathed into it at regular intervals particularly after contentious decisions. The introduction of VAR into Scottish football brought a renewed focus to the whole issue.

The refereeing movement has not been entirely divorced from considering how the topic could be dealt with. There is some attractiveness in reaching the "Promised Land" where it would be possible to explain decisions which are accepted by the game's participants. That said, there is the ever present realisation which wins the day – that it would be nigh impossible to give explanations as the clubs and the media would never be satisfied and, rather than the issue being put to bed, arguments and discussion would rage on for days more. Attempts have, however, been made by the referee movement to move in a helpful direction.

The Development of Guidelines

The SFA's Articles of Association have historically prevented referees from speaking to the media to give explanations for decisions. The issue has never just been a modern one.

Slight adjustments to the relevant Article were introduced in 1996 as a consequence of a couple of radio interviews at matches. A referee had been coaxed into commenting on the match he was about to referee and at another game he had spoken on his decision to abandon it. Whilst the comments were in possible breach of the Articles, the Referee Committee took the view that adjusting the Article to allow referees to speak to the media on a match abandonment or postponement would be prudent.

A possible system of media briefings, based on a model adopted by UEFA for that year's European Championships, was considered in 2000. The idea was to hold briefings periodically throughout a season with a spokesman explaining referees' decisions on an educational basis. The Referee Committee supported the proposal, with the caveat that the scheduling and conducting of the briefings had to be carefully controlled and that the referee's authority should not be undermined. The Class 1 referees agreed with the proposal to some degree but it was never carried through. The referees were overwhelmingly opposed to their commenting to the media on match decisions.

The issue bubbled along. In 2002, Chris Robinson, the then Referee Committee Chairman, raised the possibility of the SFA working harder to develop a better understanding of the Laws of the Game amongst clubs and all other participants in the game, including the media, and to correct common misconceptions regarding the Laws and their interpretation. No doubt wearing his club hat as Heart of Midlothian Chief Executive, Robinson also referred to the possibility of referees speaking publicly on decisions, as another means to assist in this process. The Professional Football Committee remarkably suggested in 2003 that referees should meet with it to discuss issues relating to freedom of speech. This was flatly refused by the Referee Committee Chairman, John Smith.

"Whistleblower"

The desire for there to be more openness in relation to referees' decisions in matches continued to grow from elements within the game. This led to Donald McVicar proposing the use of the SFA's website as a platform for offering explanations on referees' decisions with the hope of raising awareness and understanding of the Laws and correcting ill-informed media comment.

Guidelines were approved in 2003 which set out the parameters on referees discussing points of play on the website. The rigid stance of not permitting referees to comment publicly on a point of play or a match incident at any time, was maintained. The SFA was to decide which incidents were referred to and the timescale for dealing with them. The referee was to be consulted on the comment to be given. To avoid being prejudicial to any disciplinary case arising from a match, statements were not to be provided until such time as the case was concluded. To try and present refereeing in a positive fashion, the Guidelines also allowed referees to participate in media interviews with the permission of the SFA (although being able to comment on specific match incidents was still ruled out).

The "Whistleblower" section on the SFA website became operational from the start of season 2005-06. The articles posted on it during the opening weeks of the season were well received and used by the media. As the season progressed, referees became reluctant to offer possible points for use. Potential, or real, refereeing errors became the external focus. The referees had no great desire to expose themselves to public scrutiny. The media also started to query why this or that incident was not being addressed. Comment was being demanded for too many match incidents, with the approach starting to come under siege and moved in a different direction to what was intended. It became too problematical to post explanations. Whilst it was meant as an educational tool to explain refereeing decisions, these issues resulted in "Whistleblower" withering on the vine.

The Guidelines have been subsequently revised on a few occasions. Each amendment resulted from gaps in the Guidelines being identified after refereeing personnel had been drawn into commenting to the media. The Guidelines now cover members of the Referee Committee, Referee Observers and RA Managers.

Dealing with the Media
The SFA has made constant efforts to engage with the media to further its knowledge and understanding of refereeing issues arising in football matches. Short Laws of the Games courses have been arranged for the media to inform them of Law changes being introduced for a new season, briefing days are regularly held, and dialogue has been had with producers, presenters and commentators of broadcasters to promote a better understanding of the application of the Laws. Such contact is worthwhile, but any beneficial effects wear off very

301

quickly as normal business of referee criticism resumes almost straightaway.

It is difficult to envisage a day when there is some form of harmony between referees and the media. As with other aspects of refereeing, the problem is not unique to Scotland. The refereeing movement fights an almost continuing losing battle to be able to get over its perspective in a fair and reasonable manner. The opportunities of promoting refereeing in a good light do present themselves on a regular basis – in advance of Cup Finals or with the launch of initiatives for example - when the media are very helpful. However, pursuing referees for explanations of decisions is the media's insatiable desire and that will never disappear. Referees will never really be the winners. There will never be any guarantees that any explanations which are provided will be straightforwardly accepted to put the matter to bed. They will only be the starting point for disagreement and further discussion. It is an unfortunate fact of life that the media always has the last word.

Recruitment and Retention

The words recruitment and retention have become joined at the hip in refereeing. The convergence of the two issues came about during the 1990's as proper focus began to be given to addressing them. To continue with the traditional way of operating, thinking that new referees would just naturally emerge as had happened over the years, was no longer an option. Work was required to be done, with recruitment being the dominant theme in the early period before retention was given the attention it warranted. The problems which are experienced in Scotland are no different to the other member associations of UEFA. The issues are universal, hence the focus on recruitment and retention as a module of the UEFA Referee Convention.

The 1990's Recruitment Drive
By the late 1980's awareness was emerging of a reduction in the number of new referees. This gave George Cumming a

strong basis to develop recruitment campaigns to attract more people into refereeing. Giving increased publicity to the referee training classes on a national basis was easily accomplished.

The context of football was changing during this period as grassroots football was growing. More clubs meant more matches and led to the need for more referees. A change in traditional thinking and existing practices was required if the demands of football were to be met. Two strands were developed in regard to recruitment.

The first related to the providing of flexibility in football's regulations to allow players or officials of teams to become referees, and vice versa, providing there was no conflict of interest. The second saw the minimum age to take the Entrance Examination lowered from 16 to 14 years of age. This resulted from a desire to widen the net to recruit new referees from the increasing number of Laws of the Game courses held by schools. The SFA's Articles of Association were amended to enable these changes in 1994. The Scottish Schools' FA issued promotional information on refereeing to schools to create interest amongst pupils.

The targeting of football clubs, at all levels of the game, as a potential source of new recruits was part of the campaigns of this era. Senior clubs co-operated by publishing adverts in match programmes for a few seasons. Information packs were issued to Junior clubs to target players. Discussions were held with the Scottish Women's FA as more required to be done to attract more women into refereeing.

Adverts on radio stations were used to publicise the classes with media releases on recruitment being issued to local newspapers throughout Scotland. A poster advertising the training classes was widely distributed. A recruitment video was produced for the Referees' Associations. The organising of shorter training class courses came into vogue, with there being a belief that a better retention rate of candidates was more likely compared to the standard courses.

Retention of Referees

The importance of the need to retain referees increased throughout the 1990's and became regularly discussed at committee meetings.

The introduction of the new classification system in 1998 was intended to allow new recruits to have an understanding, for the first time, of the refereeing structure. It was hoped that this would act as an incentive for an individual to progress and help to stem the losses of new entrants.

Support schemes for new members of the associations became increasingly used, with a senior member being designated to mentor new members and be a reference point for support in the early stages of a new referee's career. The changes to the Introductory Course and the requirement to complete a match under guidance strengthened this approach. Donald McVicar, in 2004, requested the referees on the List to cover three or four matches per season with new referees to provide encouragement and support to them.

Meetings of RA Managers and Secretaries from 2005 onwards provided an excellent forum to have detailed discussions on recruitment and retention. Such debates proved the worth of the creation of the role of RA Managers. The advent of the UEFA Referee Convention in 2007, with its focus on recruitment and retention, gave further impetus to these discussions and debates.

Discussions over a series of Managers-Secretaries meetings helped shape the direction taken. The new format of the Introductory Examination was successful in retaining new referees. Other points emerged which enabled best practice to evolve. Using different styles of recruitment campaigns, such as the targeting of schools, universities and colleges and the timing of such campaigns was regarded as being important. Attendance by candidates at training and meetings during the Introductory Course was encouraged and the holding of practical sessions for new referees was crucial. Strong support schemes with regular contact with new referees were essential. Fostering good relationships with local leagues in order to provide opportunities for new referees to be assessed at matches was a key aspect, together with emphasising the opportunities within refereeing to new members.

Despite the growth in grassroots football, difficulties are experienced by the associations in arranging the "match under guidance" for Part 3 of the Introductory Course. Being able to make that arrangement quickly is beneficial to keeping the interest of the prospective referee. The means of arranging these matches are continually being addressed, and the issue feeds into discussions as to when the best time is to schedule the Courses. Introducing new referees into Leagues and Associations can present issues, as secretaries can rely too much on referees who they know and are familiar with.

These discussions confirmed that retention of referees was a greater issue than recruitment. Despite all the efforts being made by the associations, members were still being lost to the movement. The first two seasons were long considered the most difficult for new members to come through. The main reasons for loss of referees are indiscipline and abuse by players, coaches and spectators in grassroots football. Assaults of referees, regrettably, have been a continuous issue, in spite of the Affiliated National Associations taking a very hard-line stance in dealing with offenders. Experienced referees are also lost due to these issues. There are other reasons beyond indiscipline in the game as to why referees leave the movement – a change of job, family reasons and sometimes a realisation that refereeing is not for them. The loss of any referee is always keenly felt. Losing even one referee from the List can have a significant impact on the servicing of the game depending where the referee stays.

The number of new recruits coming into refereeing each year is counterbalanced by more or less the same number of losses. Refereeing effectively runs to keep standing still, hence the need to focus on retention.

The Development of a Recruitment and Retention Strategy
Having served as Renfrewshire RA Manager, John Fleming had a solid grounding on these issues which stood him in good stead when he joined the SFA staff and became Head of Referee Operations. The development of a national recruitment and retention became a priority. This coincided with the SFA's development of a Strategic Plan for the period 2011-15. Given

that a major strategic aim was to increase participation in grassroots football it was essential that focus was also given to refereeing. Joined up thinking was taking place.

A UEFA Referee Convention Re-evaluation Visit had been held in April 2011 which generated a proposal that a Refereeing Development Officer should be appointed to take charge of recruitment and retention and grassroots education. This had been pre-empted by the appointment that summer of Craig Thomson and Steven McLean as Recruitment and Education Officers, on a job-sharing basis.

A number of initiatives were launched fairly quickly, most notably the SQA Referee Development Award Course. Recruitment efforts were made through the Players' Union. Referees' Courses were held for Heart of Midlothian and Hibernian youth players with the thought that refereeing might be attractive to a young player who might not progress in his football career for whatever reason. Scottish Women's Football assisted again with a campaign to contact its member clubs to encourage recruits.

To address the issues relative to grassroots football, an Awareness Award was introduced to allow coaches, parents and volunteers to referee small sided games. People passing the course become Category 8 Awareness referees, with this new category becoming part of the Referee Structure pathway which was revised to accommodate it.

With roles and responsibilities being created for the Referee Committee specialist members, it was natural that topics such Recruitment/Education and Grassroots would be captured in this approach. The roles encompass the identification of areas of concern, retention, devising initiatives for improvement in order to promote the sharing of best practice and new ideas. Visits have been made to the associations to establish a sound knowledge on recruitment and retention issues and these have helped to further develop best practice.

A Referee Recruitment and Marketing Strategy was prepared in 2017 for the period up to 2020. Support was given to the associations to assist in the strategy's implementation. A number of topics were covered by the strategy, including the use of a marketing toolkit by the associations to enable a consistent and standard approach to be taken to advertising and publicity, the use of the SFA website to garner interest from prospective candidates, the use of social and digital media in recruitment and specific recruitment initiatives for women.,

In 2018, a survey was undertaken with Introductory Course candidates to assist in the future direction of recruitment and retention. The survey was split into three parts – before the course started, once the course was completed and one year after the course was completed. Another survey was conducted with those referees who did not renew their membership, in order to ascertain the main reasons for the loss of referees from the movement.

The Covid pandemic disrupted much of the referee development programmes with the recruitment and retention of referees being seriously impacted. The introduction of the Online Introductory Course heralds a new way of being able to attract new recruits. The SFA and the Referees' Associations have done a terrific job in the last 20 years or so to attract new recruits, despite all the bad press dished out to referees. People still, thankfully, wish to take up refereeing. The overall level of intake has been very healthy over this period, especially amongst young people. The creation of a Referee Pathway sets out clearly the steps for progression. The associations do a sterling job in doing all they can to set referees on the Pathway, which provides an excellent framework to assist in their retention. With the SFA controlling significant appointments such as Club Academy Scotland and women's football, the ideal platform now exists to enable this to happen.

The issues will continue to exist and the work to improve retention will never halt. A Steering Group on Recruitment and Retention, comprising a cross section of the refereeing movement, has been created. A strategy has been developed for the short, medium and long term, encompassing the use of social media, advertising, the targeting of football clubs, the SQA, recruitment campaigns for women and ethnic minorities and colleges and universities. There is a deep rooted commitment within the refereeing movement to succeed. Whilst the associations are charged with the responsibility of recruiting and training referees, the issue should be of concern to everyone in football. It is just as much a football issue as it is a refereeing one.

Appendix

Referee Supervisors – 1945-2005

Over a period of 60 years, there were 92 Supervisors. 12 served for 20 years or more: Frank Crossley (34), Tom Wharton (32), Drew Fleming (31), Jack Mowat (30), Robbie Harold (28), George Mitchell (27), Jimmy Stewart (25), Archie Webster (24), David Turner (22), Bill Mullan (21), Donald Kyle (20) and Bill Quinn (20)

The full list of Referee Supervisors is:

Supervisor	Referees' Association (service)
Alexander, Douglas	Angus & Perthshire (1956-67)
Alexander, Hugh	Ayrshire (1988-00)
Anderson, Harold	Edinburgh and District (1953-61)
Baillie, John	Lanarkshire (1948-59)
Barbour, Ian	Glasgow (1976-79, 1990-92), Renfrewshire (1978-90)
Benzie, Bert	Ayrshire (1945-50)
Black, Tom	Angus & Perthshire (1966-81)
Brodie, Charles	Fifeshire (1945-49)
Bruce, Jim	Aberdeen and District (2002-05)
Byars, Ian	Renfrewshire (1989-2005)
Calder, Bobby	Glasgow, Dunbartonshire and Renfrewshire (1945-47)
Calder, James	East of Scotland (1948-51), Edinburgh and District (1951-53)
Campbell, Murray	North of Scotland (1984-87), Moray & Banff (1987-89)
Carruthers, Bob	Lanarkshire (1945-48), Glasgow, Dunbartonshire and Renfrewshire (1948-49), Glasgow & District (1949-50), Glasgow (1950-52)
Clark, Martin	Edinburgh & District (2002-05)
Craig, James	Glasgow, Dunbartonshire and Renfrewshire (1945-49), Glasgow & District (1949-50)
Craigmyle, Peter	Aberdeen & North of Scotland (1945-59)
Crighton, Bill	Aberdeen & District (1989-99)
Crossley, Frank	Lanarkshire (1962-96)
Delaney, Mike	Lanarkshire (1989-05)
Donaldson, Andrew	Angus & Perthshire (1945-56)
Downie, Douglas	Edinburgh & District (1986-99), Fife (1999-05)
Duff, Bert	South of Scotland (1957-76)
Easton, Willie	Glasgow & District (1949-50), Glasgow (1950-64)

Supervisor	Referees' Association (service)
Elliott, Willie	Renfrewshire (1969-76)
Evans, Gerry	Glasgow (1998-05)
Fleming, Drew	Glasgow (1975-88), Stirlingshire (1988-90),Renfrewshire (1990-99) Stirlingshire (1999-03)
Flockhart, George	Edinburgh & District (1959-65)
Foote, Ian	Ayrshire (1982-89), Glasgow (1989-90)
Gray, Tom	Glasgow (1982-99)
Harrold, Robbie	North of Scotland (1980-81, 1982-85), Moray & Banff (1981-83), Aberdeen & District (1984-05)
Hay, Ian	Edinburgh & District (1983-84)
Hope, Douglas	Glasgow (1994-99), Renfrewshire (1999-05)
Hope, Kenny	Glasgow (1991-03)
Horsburgh, James	East of Scotland (1948-51), Edinburgh and District (1951-60)
Johnston, Jim	North of Scotland (1987- 08)
Johnston, Robert	Edinburgh & District (2004-05)
Kilgallon, Barry	Glasgow (1999-05)
Kilgour, Nicol	East of Scotland (1945-48)
Kyle, Donald	Unattached (1962-65), Glasgow (1962-82)
Livingstone, Willie	Glasgow, Dunbartonshire and Renfrewshire (1945-49), Glasgow & District (1949-50), Glasgow (1958-71)
Logan, Gordon	Moray & Banff (1989-05)
Machray, Bill	North of Scotland (1995-05)
MacKay, Jim	Aberdeen & North of Scotland (1957-59), North of Scotland (1958-70)
MacKenzie, Alistair	Edinburgh & District (1976-78)
Marshall, Ian	Renfrewshire (1989-1990), Lanarkshire (1990-96)
McBurney, Jim	Angus & Perthshire (1990-05)
McCluskey, Jim	Ayrshire (2000-05)
McCulloch, David	Renfrewshire (1948-59)
MacIntosh, Campbell	Moray & Banff (1984-87)
McIntosh, John	Aberdeen & District (1959-67)
McMillan, Jim	North of Scotland (1970-83)
McVicar, Donald	Lanarkshire (1994-99)
Mitchell, George	Unattached (1962-67), Stirlingshire & Clackmannanshire (1967-82), Stirlingshire (1982-89)
Morrice, Bill	Aberdeen & District (1967-71)
Morrison, Ray	Lanarkshire (1999-05)
Mowat, Jack	Glasgow (1960-1990), Ayrshire (1970-82)
Mullan, Bill	Edinburgh & District (1978-99)
Oates, Joe	Fife (1965-71)
Orr, Bobby	Stirlingshire (2002-05)

Supervisor	Referees' Association (service)
Quinn, Bill	South of Scotland (1977-97)
Ramsay, Douglas	Edinburgh & District (1984-86)
Robertson, Bryan	Glasgow (1999-2005)
Ross, Colin	Edinburgh & District (1999-04)
Rowbotham, John	Stirlingshire (2005-06)
Rowe, Jim	Glasgow (1950-59)
Roy, Sandy	Aberdeen & District (1999-05)
Scott, Frank	Renfrewshire (1959-69)
Shirley, Tom	Ayrshire (1950-70)
Simpson, David	Moray & Banff (1982-84)
Sinclair, Colin	Angus & Perthshire (1989-00)
Small, Tom	Angus & Perthshire (1945-46)
Smillie, John	Glasgow (1952-58), Lanarkshire (1958--63)
Smith, George	Edinburgh & District (1992-03)
Stewart, Jimmy	Glasgow & District (1949-50), Glasgow (1950-75)
Sturgeon, Bert	Aberdeen & District (1971-85)
Symington, Jim	Edinburgh & District (1960-66)
Tait, Willie	Edinburgh & District (1966-76)
Taylor, Jimmy	Fifeshire (1949-57), Fife (1957-65)
Thomson, Eddie	Edinburgh & District (1989-90), Stirlingshire (1990-99)
Thomson, Sam	Glasgow (1959)
Thow, Louis	South of Scotland (1996-05)
Turner, David	Stirlingshire & Clackmannanshire (1945-67)
Valentine, Bob	Angus & Perthshire (1989-03)
Wallace, Johnny	South of Scotland (1954-58)
Watt, Andrew	East of Scotland (1945-50)
Webb, Willie	Glasgow, Dunbartonshire and Renfrewshire (1945-49), Glasgow & District (1949-50)
Webster, Archie	Fife (1975-99)
Wharton, Tom	Glasgow (1971-02), Renfrewshire (1976-79)
Wilkie, David	Angus & Perthshire (1980-89)
Wright, Andrew	Edinburgh & District (1965-83)
Young, Andrew	South of Scotland (1945-54)

Referee Supervisors' Sub-Committee/Executive Committee

35 Supervisors served on the Sub-Committee/Executive Committee. They were:

Supervisor	Service
Alexander, Douglas	1959-62
Anderson, Harold	1957-61
Baillie, John	1949-54
Barbour, Ian	1981-91
Carruthers, Bob	1946-52
Craig, James	1946-49
Craigmyle, Peter	1946-59
Crossley, Frank	1965-95
Donaldson, Andrew	1946-49, 1950-56
Easton, Willie	1954-59, 1962-63
Fleming, Drew	1990-03
Flockhart, George	1962-63
Hope, Kenny	1992-03
Horsburgh, James	1949-50, 1951-53, 1956-60
Kyle, Donald	1964-73, 1975-80
Livingstone, Willie	1948-49, 1963-64
MacKay, Jim	1963-70
McCulloch, David	1954-59
McVicar, Donald	1996-99
Mitchell, George	1963-65, 1967-88
Mowat, Jack	1961-90
Mullan, Bill	1980-95
Oates, Joe	1966-68
Rowe, Jim	1953-54
Smillie, John	1954-57, 1959-62
Smith, George	1992-03
Stewart, Jimmy	1959-66, 1971-75
Sturgeon, Bert	1974-80
Symington, Jim	1963-65
Tait, Willie	1969-74
Turner, David	1951-52, 1953-54, 1959-63
Valentine, Bob	1990-05
Watt, Andrew	1946-49
Webster, Archie	1980-99
Wharton, Tom	1975-03

Chairmen
6 Supervisors acted as Chairman of the committees over the 60 year period, once the initial rotation of the chairmanship ceased:

Craigmyle, Peter	1946-49, 1951-59
Carruthers, Bob	1950-51
Smillie, John	1959-62
Mowat, Jack	1962-90
Wharton, Tom	1990-03
Valentine, Bob	2003-05

Vice Chairmen
The following served as Vice Chairman of the committees:

Baillie, John	1950-53
Carruthers, Bob	1949-50
Craig, James	1946-47
Crossley, Frank	1966-75
Easton, Willie	1956-59, 1962-63
Mitchell, George	1963-65
Mowat, Jack	1961-62
Rowe, Jim	1953-54
Smillie, John	1954-56
Stewart, Jimmy	1959-61, 1965-66
Webster, Archie	1990-97
Wharton, Tom	1976-90

Executive Supervisors
The following operated as Executive Supervisors:

Fleming, Drew	2002-05
Hope, Kenny	2002-05
Smith, George	2002-05
Valentine, Bob	2002-05
Wharton, Tom	2002-03

Match Assessors

The position of Match Assessor operated between 1999 and 2002.

Bruce, Jim	2000-02
Clark, Martin	2000-02
Crighton, Bill	1999-00
Mullan, Bill	1999-00
Thomson, Eddie	1999-00
Timmons, Joe	1999-02
Webster, Archie	1999-00

Referees' Association Managers

The following have held positions as Managers or Assistant Managers since 2005:

RA Manager	Association (service)
Alison, Graeme	South of Scotland (2005-)
Brown, John*	Renfrewshire (2015-)
Clark, Martin	Edinburgh & District (2010-)
Corrie, Gerry*	Glasgow (2018-)
Cunningham, Alan**	Glasgow (2011-)
Downie, Douglas	Fife (2005-2007)
Doyle, Mark*	Edinburgh & District (2015-)
Drummond, George***	Lanarkshire (2014-)
Fleming, John	Renfrewshire (2005-09)
Johnston, Robert	Edinburgh & District (2005-10)
Laird, Jim*	Ayrshire (2015-)
Logan, Gordon	Moray & Banff (2005-06)
Lowe, Derek*	Fife (2016-)
Macaulay, Stuart	Fife (2015-)
Machray, Bill	Moray & Banff (2005-), North of Scotland (2008-17)
Mackay, Craig	Aberdeen & District (2022-)
McBurney, Jim	Angus & Perthshire (2005-16)
McDowall, Joe	Renfrewshire (2009-)
McDuffie, Brian	Fife (2006-11)
McGarry, Brian****	Stirlingshire (2015-)
Mitchell, Stephen*	Lanarkshire (2018-)
Mooney, Ricky*****	Stirlingshire (2005-20)
Morrison, Ray	Lanarkshire (2005-14)
Murray, Billy	North of Scotland (2015-)
Pocock, Mike*	Aberdeen & District (2015-21)

RA Manager	Association (service)
Pullar, Steve*	Angus & Perthshire (2016-20)
Robertson, Bryan******	Glasgow (2005-18)
Roy, Sandy	Aberdeen & District (2005-)
Smith, Ricky	Fife (2011-16)
Watters, Neil	Angus & Perthshire (2015-20)
Winter, Brian	Lanarkshire (2014-18)

Having been appointed as a Supervisor for North of Scotland RA in 1995, Bill Machray completed his 29th year of service to the SFA in season 2022-23 as the Moray & Banff Manager.

* Assistant Manager
** Assistant Manager 2011-18
*** Assistant Manager 2014-17, Manager since 2017
**** Assistant Manager 2015-16, Manager since 2017
***** Manager 2005-17, Assistant Manager 2017 –
****** Manager 2015-17, Assistant Manager 2017-18

Referee Observers
There have been 74 Referee Observers/Assistant Referee Observers since the introduction of the positions in 2005 and 2014 respectively.

Observer	Service
Alison, Graeme	2006-
Allan, Crawford	2017-20
Brines, Iain	2014-19, 2021-
Bruce, Jim	2005-
Cassidy, Brian	2005-
Charleston, Craig	2019-20
Clark, Kenny	2016-
Clark, Martin	2005-
Clyde, George	2005-
Corrie, Gerry	2018-
Dallas, Hugh	2005-06
Delaney, Mike	2005-09
Doig, David	2005-10
Downie, Douglas	2005-08
Evans, Gerry	2005-21
Finnie, Stephen	2018-
Fleming, Drew	2005-10
Fleming, John	2005-09

Observer	Service
Freeland, Alan	2008-21
Fyfe, Ian	2007-
Harrold, Robbie	2005-09
Hope, Douglas	2005-
Hope, Kenny	2005-11
Johnston, Jim	2005-10
Johnston, Robert	2005-10
Kilgallon, Barry	2005-10
Logan, Gordon	2005-06
Machray, Bill	2005-
Mackay, Craig	2011-
McBurney, Jim	2005-15
McCluskey, Jim	2005-13
McDowall, Joe	2005-14
McDuffie, Brian	2008-11
McElhinney, John	2005-14
McVicar, Donald	2009-16
Miller, Bill	2005-07
Morrison, Ray	2005-14
Murray, Billy	2019-
Murray, Calum	2015-
Norris, Euan	2015-
Norris, Les	2005-18
Pocock, Mike	2010-
Robertson, Bryan	2005-20
Rowbotham, John	2005-06
Roy, Sandy	2005-
Shearer, Stewart	2012-14
Smith, Dougie	2006-
Smith, Eddie	2011-17
Smith, George	2005-2018
Thomson, Craig	2019-
Thow, Louis	2005-21
Toner, Kevin	2013-
Valentine, Bob	2005-11
Watson, Paul	2005-
Watters, Neil	2016-22
Winter, Brian	2012-
Yeats, Douglas	2008-22
Young, John	2005-

Assistant Referee Observer	Service
Conquer, Willie	2018-
Cryans, Martin	2015-
Cunningham, Alan	2016-
Doyle, Mark	2019-
Drummond, George	2015-
Harris, Gavin	2018-
Macaulay, Stuart	2015-
McDowall, Joe	2014-
McElhinney, John	2014-
McGarry, Brian	2015-
Mitchell, Stephen	2018-
Murphy, Tom	2015-16
Rose, Derek	2015-17
Shearer, Stewart	2014-
Sorbie, Keith	2015-18

Milton Keynes UK
Ingram Content Group UK Ltd.
UKHW030015010324
438562UK00014B/445

9 781916 981546